C-3589 CAREER EXAMINATION SERIES

This is your
PASSBOOK for...

Senior Motor Vehicle License Examiner

Test Preparation Study Guide
Questions & Answers

COPYRIGHT NOTICE

This book is SOLELY intended for, is sold ONLY to, and its use is RESTRICTED to individual, bona fide applicants or candidates who qualify by virtue of having seriously filed applications for appropriate license, certificate, professional and/or promotional advancement, higher school matriculation, scholarship, or other legitimate requirements of education and/or governmental authorities.

This book is NOT intended for use, class instruction, tutoring, training, duplication, copying, reprinting, excerption, or adaptation, etc., by:

1) Other publishers
2) Proprietors and/or Instructors of "Coaching" and/or Preparatory Courses
3) Personnel and/or Training Divisions of commercial, industrial, and governmental organizations
4) Schools, colleges, or universities and/or their departments and staffs, including teachers and other personnel
5) Testing Agencies or Bureaus
6) Study groups which seek by the purchase of a single volume to copy and/or duplicate and/or adapt this material for use by the group as a whole without having purchased individual volumes for each of the members of the group
7) Et al.

Such persons would be in violation of appropriate Federal and State statutes.

PROVISION OF LICENSING AGREEMENTS – Recognized educational, commercial, industrial, and governmental institutions and organizations, and others legitimately engaged in educational pursuits, including training, testing, and measurement activities, may address request for a licensing agreement to the copyright owners, who will determine whether, and under what conditions, including fees and charges, the materials in this book may be used them. In other words, a licensing facility exists for the legitimate use of the material in this book on other than an individual basis. However, it is asseverated and affirmed here that the material in this book CANNOT be used without the receipt of the express permission of such a licensing agreement from the Publishers. Inquiries re licensing should be addressed to the company, attention rights and permissions department.

All rights reserved, including the right of reproduction in whole or in part, in any form or by any means, electronic or mechanical, including photocopying, recording, or by any information storage and retrieval system, without permission in writing from the Publisher.

Copyright © 2024 by
National Learning Corporation

212 Michael Drive, Syosset, NY 11791
(516) 921-8888 • www.passbooks.com
E-mail: info@passbooks.com

PASSBOOK® SERIES

THE *PASSBOOK® SERIES* has been created to prepare applicants and candidates for the ultimate academic battlefield – the examination room.

At some time in our lives, each and every one of us may be required to take an examination – for validation, matriculation, admission, qualification, registration, certification, or licensure.

Based on the assumption that every applicant or candidate has met the basic formal educational standards, has taken the required number of courses, and read the necessary texts, the *PASSBOOK® SERIES* furnishes the one special preparation which may assure passing with confidence, instead of failing with insecurity. Examination questions – together with answers – are furnished as the basic vehicle for study so that the mysteries of the examination and its compounding difficulties may be eliminated or diminished by a sure method.

This book is meant to help you pass your examination provided that you qualify and are serious in your objective.

The entire field is reviewed through the huge store of content information which is succinctly presented through a provocative and challenging approach – the question-and-answer method.

A climate of success is established by furnishing the correct answers at the end of each test.

You soon learn to recognize types of questions, forms of questions, and patterns of questioning. You may even begin to anticipate expected outcomes.

You perceive that many questions are repeated or adapted so that you can gain acute insights, which may enable you to score many sure points.

You learn how to confront new questions, or types of questions, and to attack them confidently and work out the correct answers.

You note objectives and emphases, and recognize pitfalls and dangers, so that you may make positive educational adjustments.

Moreover, you are kept fully informed in relation to new concepts, methods, practices, and directions in the field.

You discover that you are actually taking the examination all the time: you are preparing for the examination by "taking" an examination, not by reading extraneous and/or supererogatory textbooks.

In short, this PASSBOOK®, used directedly, should be an important factor in helping you to pass your test.

SENIOR MOTOR VEHICLE LICENSE EXAMINER

DUTIES:
As a Senior Motor Vehicle License Examiner, you would supervise Motor Vehicle License Examiners; provide guidance and technical assistance to staff; evaluate performance; arrange for and provide training; and assign staff to inspect driving schools and public carriers. You would supervise multiple road test lines, assign specific duties for Motor Vehicle License Examiners on a daily basis, coordinate road test assignments and activities at multiple test sites, prepare daily road test schedules, assign staff, and ensure that road test conditions meet Department standards. You would investigate and resolve complaints about procedures and staff behavior. You would regularly review and audit testing and investigate activities for fraud and malfeasance. You would also perform related duties as required, including performing the duties of a Motor Vehicle License Examiner if there was not enough coverage for a road test post. You must be able to use and maintain a computerized tablet (electronic scoring device).

SUBJECT OF EXAMINATION:
The written test is designed to test for knowledge, skills, and/or abilities in such areas as:
1. **Public contact principles and practices** - These questions test for knowledge of techniques used to interact with other people, to gather and present information, and to provide assistance, advice, and effective customer service in a courteous and professional manner. Questions will cover such topics as understanding and responding to people with diverse needs, perspectives, personalities, and levels of familiarity with agency operations, as well as acting in a way that both serves the public and reflects well on your agency.
2. **Preparing written material** - These questions test for the ability to present information clearly and accurately, and to organize paragraphs logically and comprehensibly. For some questions, you will be given information in two or three sentences followed by four restatements of the information. You must then choose the best version. For other questions, you will be given paragraphs with their sentences out of order. You must then choose, from four suggestions, the best order for the sentences.
3. **Work Planning and Scheduling** - These questions test for knowledge of the principles used in developing and implementing work plans and for the ability to within scheduling criteria. This may include setting up vacation or work schedules, arrange work assignments in a manner that will achieve work goals while staying taking into consideration such factors as seniority, work skills, duty hours, and shift coverage.
4. **Vehicle and Traffic Law, Department of Motor Vehicles Commissioner's Rules and Regulations, and Department policies and procedures** - These questions test for knowledge of the Vehicle and Traffic Law, Department of Motor Vehicles Commissioner's Rules and Regulations, and Department policies and procedures covering such areas as licensing of drivers, safe driving practices, commercial driving schools, and special requirements for bus drivers.
5. **Supervision** - These questions test for knowledge of the principles and practices employed in planning, organizing, and controlling the activities of a work unit toward predetermined objectives. The concepts covered, usually in a situational question format, include such topics as assigning and reviewing work; evaluating performance; maintaining work standards; motivating and developing subordinates; implementing procedural change; increasing efficiency; and dealing with problems of absenteeism, morale, and discipline.

HOW TO TAKE A TEST

I. YOU MUST PASS AN EXAMINATION

A. *WHAT EVERY CANDIDATE SHOULD KNOW*

Examination applicants often ask us for help in preparing for the written test. What can I study in advance? What kinds of questions will be asked? How will the test be given? How will the papers be graded?

As an applicant for a civil service examination, you may be wondering about some of these things. Our purpose here is to suggest effective methods of advance study and to describe civil service examinations.

Your chances for success on this examination can be increased if you know how to prepare. Those "pre-examination jitters" can be reduced if you know what to expect. You can even experience an adventure in good citizenship if you know why civil service exams are given.

B. *WHY ARE CIVIL SERVICE EXAMINATIONS GIVEN?*

Civil service examinations are important to you in two ways. As a citizen, you want public jobs filled by employees who know how to do their work. As a job seeker, you want a fair chance to compete for that job on an equal footing with other candidates. The best-known means of accomplishing this two-fold goal is the competitive examination.

Exams are widely publicized throughout the nation. They may be administered for jobs in federal, state, city, municipal, town or village governments or agencies.

Any citizen may apply, with some limitations, such as the age or residence of applicants. Your experience and education may be reviewed to see whether you meet the requirements for the particular examination. When these requirements exist, they are reasonable and applied consistently to all applicants. Thus, a competitive examination may cause you some uneasiness now, but it is your privilege and safeguard.

C. *HOW ARE CIVIL SERVICE EXAMS DEVELOPED?*

Examinations are carefully written by trained technicians who are specialists in the field known as "psychological measurement," in consultation with recognized authorities in the field of work that the test will cover. These experts recommend the subject matter areas or skills to be tested; only those knowledges or skills important to your success on the job are included. The most reliable books and source materials available are used as references. Together, the experts and technicians judge the difficulty level of the questions.

Test technicians know how to phrase questions so that the problem is clearly stated. Their ethics do not permit "trick" or "catch" questions. Questions may have been tried out on sample groups, or subjected to statistical analysis, to determine their usefulness.

Written tests are often used in combination with performance tests, ratings of training and experience, and oral interviews. All of these measures combine to form the best-known means of finding the right person for the right job.

II. HOW TO PASS THE WRITTEN TEST

A. NATURE OF THE EXAMINATION

To prepare intelligently for civil service examinations, you should know how they differ from school examinations you have taken. In school you were assigned certain definite pages to read or subjects to cover. The examination questions were quite detailed and usually emphasized memory. Civil service exams, on the other hand, try to discover your present ability to perform the duties of a position, plus your potentiality to learn these duties. In other words, a civil service exam attempts to predict how successful you will be. Questions cover such a broad area that they cannot be as minute and detailed as school exam questions.

In the public service similar kinds of work, or positions, are grouped together in one "class." This process is known as *position-classification*. All the positions in a class are paid according to the salary range for that class. One class title covers all of these positions, and they are all tested by the same examination.

B. FOUR BASIC STEPS

1) Study the announcement

How, then, can you know what subjects to study? Our best answer is: "Learn as much as possible about the class of positions for which you've applied." The exam will test the knowledge, skills and abilities needed to do the work.

Your most valuable source of information about the position you want is the official exam announcement. This announcement lists the training and experience qualifications. Check these standards and apply only if you come reasonably close to meeting them.

The brief description of the position in the examination announcement offers some clues to the subjects which will be tested. Think about the job itself. Review the duties in your mind. Can you perform them, or are there some in which you are rusty? Fill in the blank spots in your preparation.

Many jurisdictions preview the written test in the exam announcement by including a section called "Knowledge and Abilities Required," "Scope of the Examination," or some similar heading. Here you will find out specifically what fields will be tested.

2) Review your own background

Once you learn in general what the position is all about, and what you need to know to do the work, ask yourself which subjects you already know fairly well and which need improvement. You may wonder whether to concentrate on improving your strong areas or on building some background in your fields of weakness. When the announcement has specified "some knowledge" or "considerable knowledge," or has used adjectives like "beginning principles of…" or "advanced … methods," you can get a clue as to the number and difficulty of questions to be asked in any given field. More questions, and hence broader coverage, would be included for those subjects which are more important in the work. Now weigh your strengths and weaknesses against the job requirements and prepare accordingly.

3) Determine the level of the position

Another way to tell how intensively you should prepare is to understand the level of the job for which you are applying. Is it the entering level? In other words, is this the position in which beginners in a field of work are hired? Or is it an intermediate or advanced level? Sometimes this is indicated by such words as "Junior" or "Senior" in the class title. Other jurisdictions use Roman numerals to designate the level – Clerk I, Clerk II, for example. The word "Supervisor" sometimes appears in the title. If the level is not indicated by the title, check the description of duties. Will you be working under very close supervision, or will you have responsibility for independent decisions in this work?

4) Choose appropriate study materials

Now that you know the subjects to be examined and the relative amount of each subject to be covered, you can choose suitable study materials. For beginning level jobs, or even advanced ones, if you have a pronounced weakness in some aspect of your training, read a modern, standard textbook in that field. Be sure it is up to date and has general coverage. Such books are normally available at your library, and the librarian will be glad to help you locate one. For entry-level positions, questions of appropriate difficulty are chosen – neither highly advanced questions, nor those too simple. Such questions require careful thought but not advanced training.

If the position for which you are applying is technical or advanced, you will read more advanced, specialized material. If you are already familiar with the basic principles of your field, elementary textbooks would waste your time. Concentrate on advanced textbooks and technical periodicals. Think through the concepts and review difficult problems in your field.

These are all general sources. You can get more ideas on your own initiative, following these leads. For example, training manuals and publications of the government agency which employs workers in your field can be useful, particularly for technical and professional positions. A letter or visit to the government department involved may result in more specific study suggestions, and certainly will provide you with a more definite idea of the exact nature of the position you are seeking.

III. KINDS OF TESTS

Tests are used for purposes other than measuring knowledge and ability to perform specified duties. For some positions, it is equally important to test ability to make adjustments to new situations or to profit from training. In others, basic mental abilities not dependent on information are essential. Questions which test these things may not appear as pertinent to the duties of the position as those which test for knowledge and information. Yet they are often highly important parts of a fair examination. For very general questions, it is almost impossible to help you direct your study efforts. What we can do is to point out some of the more common of these general abilities needed in public service positions and describe some typical questions.

1) General information

Broad, general information has been found useful for predicting job success in some kinds of work. This is tested in a variety of ways, from vocabulary lists to questions about current events. Basic background in some field of work, such as sociology or economics, may be sampled in a group of questions. Often these are principles which have become familiar to most persons through exposure rather than through formal training. It is difficult to advise you how to study for these questions; being alert to the world around you is our best suggestion.

2) Verbal ability

An example of an ability needed in many positions is verbal or language ability. Verbal ability is, in brief, the ability to use and understand words. Vocabulary and grammar tests are typical measures of this ability. Reading comprehension or paragraph interpretation questions are common in many kinds of civil service tests. You are given a paragraph of written material and asked to find its central meaning.

3) Numerical ability

Number skills can be tested by the familiar arithmetic problem, by checking paired lists of numbers to see which are alike and which are different, or by interpreting charts and graphs. In the latter test, a graph may be printed in the test booklet which you are asked to use as the basis for answering questions.

4) Observation

A popular test for law-enforcement positions is the observation test. A picture is shown to you for several minutes, then taken away. Questions about the picture test your ability to observe both details and larger elements.

5) Following directions

In many positions in the public service, the employee must be able to carry out written instructions dependably and accurately. You may be given a chart with several columns, each column listing a variety of information. The questions require you to carry out directions involving the information given in the chart.

6) Skills and aptitudes

Performance tests effectively measure some manual skills and aptitudes. When the skill is one in which you are trained, such as typing or shorthand, you can practice. These tests are often very much like those given in business school or high school courses. For many of the other skills and aptitudes, however, no short-time preparation can be made. Skills and abilities natural to you or that you have developed throughout your lifetime are being tested.

Many of the general questions just described provide all the data needed to answer the questions and ask you to use your reasoning ability to find the answers. Your best preparation for these tests, as well as for tests of facts and ideas, is to be at your physical and mental best. You, no doubt, have your own methods of getting into an exam-taking mood and keeping "in shape." The next section lists some ideas on this subject.

IV. KINDS OF QUESTIONS

Only rarely is the "essay" question, which you answer in narrative form, used in civil service tests. Civil service tests are usually of the short-answer type. Full instructions for answering these questions will be given to you at the examination. But in case this is your first experience with short-answer questions and separate answer sheets, here is what you need to know:

1) Multiple-choice Questions

Most popular of the short-answer questions is the "multiple choice" or "best answer" question. It can be used, for example, to test for factual knowledge, ability to solve problems or judgment in meeting situations found at work.

A multiple-choice question is normally one of three types—
- It can begin with an incomplete statement followed by several possible endings. You are to find the one ending which *best* completes the statement, although some of the others may not be entirely wrong.
- It can also be a complete statement in the form of a question which is answered by choosing one of the statements listed.

- It can be in the form of a problem – again you select the best answer.

Here is an example of a multiple-choice question with a discussion which should give you some clues as to the method for choosing the right answer:

When an employee has a complaint about his assignment, the action which will *best* help him overcome his difficulty is to
- A. discuss his difficulty with his coworkers
- B. take the problem to the head of the organization
- C. take the problem to the person who gave him the assignment
- D. say nothing to anyone about his complaint

In answering this question, you should study each of the choices to find which is best. Consider choice "A" – Certainly an employee may discuss his complaint with fellow employees, but no change or improvement can result, and the complaint remains unresolved. Choice "B" is a poor choice since the head of the organization probably does not know what assignment you have been given, and taking your problem to him is known as "going over the head" of the supervisor. The supervisor, or person who made the assignment, is the person who can clarify it or correct any injustice. Choice "C" is, therefore, correct. To say nothing, as in choice "D," is unwise. Supervisors have and interest in knowing the problems employees are facing, and the employee is seeking a solution to his problem.

2) True/False Questions

The "true/false" or "right/wrong" form of question is sometimes used. Here a complete statement is given. Your job is to decide whether the statement is right or wrong.

SAMPLE: A roaming cell-phone call to a nearby city costs less than a non-roaming call to a distant city.

This statement is wrong, or false, since roaming calls are more expensive.

This is not a complete list of all possible question forms, although most of the others are variations of these common types. You will always get complete directions for answering questions. Be sure you understand *how* to mark your answers – ask questions until you do.

V. RECORDING YOUR ANSWERS

Computer terminals are used more and more today for many different kinds of exams.

For an examination with very few applicants, you may be told to record your answers in the test booklet itself. Separate answer sheets are much more common. If this separate answer sheet is to be scored by machine – and this is often the case – it is highly important that you mark your answers correctly in order to get credit.

An electronic scoring machine is often used in civil service offices because of the speed with which papers can be scored. Machine-scored answer sheets must be marked with a pencil, which will be given to you. This pencil has a high graphite content which responds to the electronic scoring machine. As a matter of fact, stray dots may register as answers, so do not let your pencil rest on the answer sheet while you are pondering the correct answer. Also, if your pencil lead breaks or is otherwise defective, ask for another.

Since the answer sheet will be dropped in a slot in the scoring machine, be careful not to bend the corners or get the paper crumpled.

The answer sheet normally has five vertical columns of numbers, with 30 numbers to a column. These numbers correspond to the question numbers in your test booklet. After each number, going across the page are four or five pairs of dotted lines. These short dotted lines have small letters or numbers above them. The first two pairs may also have a "T" or "F" above the letters. This indicates that the first two pairs only are to be used if the questions are of the true-false type. If the questions are multiple choice, disregard the "T" and "F" and pay attention only to the small letters or numbers.

Answer your questions in the manner of the sample that follows:

32. The largest city in the United States is
    A. Washington, D.C.
    B. New York City
    C. Chicago
    D. Detroit
    E. San Francisco

1) Choose the answer you think is best. (New York City is the largest, so "B" is correct.)
2) Find the row of dotted lines numbered the same as the question you are answering. (Find row number 32)
3) Find the pair of dotted lines corresponding to the answer. (Find the pair of lines under the mark "B.")
4) Make a solid black mark between the dotted lines.

VI. BEFORE THE TEST

Common sense will help you find procedures to follow to get ready for an examination. Too many of us, however, overlook these sensible measures. Indeed, nervousness and fatigue have been found to be the most serious reasons why applicants fail to do their best on civil service tests. Here is a list of reminders:

- Begin your preparation early – Don't wait until the last minute to go scurrying around for books and materials or to find out what the position is all about.
- Prepare continuously – An hour a night for a week is better than an all-night cram session. This has been definitely established. What is more, a night a week for a month will return better dividends than crowding your study into a shorter period of time.
- Locate the place of the exam – You have been sent a notice telling you when and where to report for the examination. If the location is in a different town or otherwise unfamiliar to you, it would be well to inquire the best route and learn something about the building.
- Relax the night before the test – Allow your mind to rest. Do not study at all that night. Plan some mild recreation or diversion; then go to bed early and get a good night's sleep.
- Get up early enough to make a leisurely trip to the place for the test – This way unforeseen events, traffic snarls, unfamiliar buildings, etc. will not upset you.
- Dress comfortably – A written test is not a fashion show. You will be known by number and not by name, so wear something comfortable.

- Leave excess paraphernalia at home – Shopping bags and odd bundles will get in your way. You need bring only the items mentioned in the official notice you received; usually everything you need is provided. Do not bring reference books to the exam. They will only confuse those last minutes and be taken away from you when in the test room.
- Arrive somewhat ahead of time – If because of transportation schedules you must get there very early, bring a newspaper or magazine to take your mind off yourself while waiting.
- Locate the examination room – When you have found the proper room, you will be directed to the seat or part of the room where you will sit. Sometimes you are given a sheet of instructions to read while you are waiting. Do not fill out any forms until you are told to do so; just read them and be prepared.
- Relax and prepare to listen to the instructions
- If you have any physical problem that may keep you from doing your best, be sure to tell the test administrator. If you are sick or in poor health, you really cannot do your best on the exam. You can come back and take the test some other time.

VII. AT THE TEST

The day of the test is here and you have the test booklet in your hand. The temptation to get going is very strong. Caution! There is more to success than knowing the right answers. You must know how to identify your papers and understand variations in the type of short-answer question used in this particular examination. Follow these suggestions for maximum results from your efforts:

1) Cooperate with the monitor

The test administrator has a duty to create a situation in which you can be as much at ease as possible. He will give instructions, tell you when to begin, check to see that you are marking your answer sheet correctly, and so on. He is not there to guard you, although he will see that your competitors do not take unfair advantage. He wants to help you do your best.

2) Listen to all instructions

Don't jump the gun! Wait until you understand all directions. In most civil service tests you get more time than you need to answer the questions. So don't be in a hurry. Read each word of instructions until you clearly understand the meaning. Study the examples, listen to all announcements and follow directions. Ask questions if you do not understand what to do.

3) Identify your papers

Civil service exams are usually identified by number only. You will be assigned a number; you must not put your name on your test papers. Be sure to copy your number correctly. Since more than one exam may be given, copy your exact examination title.

4) Plan your time

Unless you are told that a test is a "speed" or "rate of work" test, speed itself is usually not important. Time enough to answer all the questions will be provided, but this does not mean that you have all day. An overall time limit has been set. Divide the total time (in minutes) by the number of questions to determine the approximate time you have for each question.

5) Do not linger over difficult questions

If you come across a difficult question, mark it with a paper clip (useful to have along) and come back to it when you have been through the booklet. One caution if you do this – be sure to skip a number on your answer sheet as well. Check often to be sure that you have not lost your place and that you are marking in the row numbered the same as the question you are answering.

6) Read the questions

Be sure you know what the question asks! Many capable people are unsuccessful because they failed to *read* the questions correctly.

7) Answer all questions

Unless you have been instructed that a penalty will be deducted for incorrect answers, it is better to guess than to omit a question.

8) Speed tests

It is often better NOT to guess on speed tests. It has been found that on timed tests people are tempted to spend the last few seconds before time is called in marking answers at random – without even reading them – in the hope of picking up a few extra points. To discourage this practice, the instructions may warn you that your score will be "corrected" for guessing. That is, a penalty will be applied. The incorrect answers will be deducted from the correct ones, or some other penalty formula will be used.

9) Review your answers

If you finish before time is called, go back to the questions you guessed or omitted to give them further thought. Review other answers if you have time.

10) Return your test materials

If you are ready to leave before others have finished or time is called, take ALL your materials to the monitor and leave quietly. Never take any test material with you. The monitor can discover whose papers are not complete, and taking a test booklet may be grounds for disqualification.

VIII. EXAMINATION TECHNIQUES

1) Read the general instructions carefully. These are usually printed on the first page of the exam booklet. As a rule, these instructions refer to the timing of the examination; the fact that you should not start work until the signal and must stop work at a signal, etc. If there are any *special* instructions, such as a choice of questions to be answered, make sure that you note this instruction carefully.

2) When you are ready to start work on the examination, that is as soon as the signal has been given, read the instructions to each question booklet, underline any key words or phrases, such as *least, best, outline, describe* and the like. In this way you will tend to answer as requested rather than discover on reviewing your paper that you *listed without describing*, that you selected the *worst* choice rather than the *best* choice, etc.

3) If the examination is of the objective or multiple-choice type – that is, each question will also give a series of possible answers: A, B, C or D, and you are called upon to select the best answer and write the letter next to that answer on your answer paper – it is advisable to start answering each question in turn. There may be anywhere from 50 to 100 such questions in the three or four hours allotted and you can see how much time would be taken if you read through all the questions before beginning to answer any. Furthermore, if you come across a question or group of questions which you know would be difficult to answer, it would undoubtedly affect your handling of all the other questions.

4) If the examination is of the essay type and contains but a few questions, it is a moot point as to whether you should read all the questions before starting to answer any one. Of course, if you are given a choice – say five out of seven and the like – then it is essential to read all the questions so you can eliminate the two that are most difficult. If, however, you are asked to answer all the questions, there may be danger in trying to answer the easiest one first because you may find that you will spend too much time on it. The best technique is to answer the first question, then proceed to the second, etc.

5) Time your answers. Before the exam begins, write down the time it started, then add the time allowed for the examination and write down the time it must be completed, then divide the time available somewhat as follows:
   - If 3-1/2 hours are allowed, that would be 210 minutes. If you have 80 objective-type questions, that would be an average of 2-1/2 minutes per question. Allow yourself no more than 2 minutes per question, or a total of 160 minutes, which will permit about 50 minutes to review.
   - If for the time allotment of 210 minutes there are 7 essay questions to answer, that would average about 30 minutes a question. Give yourself only 25 minutes per question so that you have about 35 minutes to review.

6) The most important instruction is to *read each question* and make sure you know what is wanted. The second most important instruction is to *time yourself properly* so that you answer every question. The third most important instruction is to *answer every question*. Guess if you have to but include something for each question. Remember that you will receive no credit for a blank and will probably receive some credit if you write something in answer to an essay question. If you guess a letter – say "B" for a multiple-choice question – you may have guessed right. If you leave a blank as an answer to a multiple-choice question, the examiners may respect your feelings but it will not add a point to your score. Some exams may penalize you for wrong answers, so in such cases *only*, you may not want to guess unless you have some basis for your answer.

7) Suggestions
   a. Objective-type questions
      1. Examine the question booklet for proper sequence of pages and questions
      2. Read all instructions carefully
      3. Skip any question which seems too difficult; return to it after all other questions have been answered
      4. Apportion your time properly; do not spend too much time on any single question or group of questions

5. Note and underline key words – *all, most, fewest, least, best, worst, same, opposite,* etc.
6. Pay particular attention to negatives
7. Note unusual option, e.g., unduly long, short, complex, different or similar in content to the body of the question
8. Observe the use of "hedging" words – *probably, may, most likely,* etc.
9. Make sure that your answer is put next to the same number as the question
10. Do not second-guess unless you have good reason to believe the second answer is definitely more correct
11. Cross out original answer if you decide another answer is more accurate; do not erase until you are ready to hand your paper in
12. Answer all questions; guess unless instructed otherwise
13. Leave time for review

  b. Essay questions
1. Read each question carefully
2. Determine exactly what is wanted. Underline key words or phrases.
3. Decide on outline or paragraph answer
4. Include many different points and elements unless asked to develop any one or two points or elements
5. Show impartiality by giving pros and cons unless directed to select one side only
6. Make and write down any assumptions you find necessary to answer the questions
7. Watch your English, grammar, punctuation and choice of words
8. Time your answers; don't crowd material

8) Answering the essay question

Most essay questions can be answered by framing the specific response around several key words or ideas. Here are a few such key words or ideas:

M's: manpower, materials, methods, money, management
P's: purpose, program, policy, plan, procedure, practice, problems, pitfalls, personnel, public relations

  a. Six basic steps in handling problems:
1. Preliminary plan and background development
2. Collect information, data and facts
3. Analyze and interpret information, data and facts
4. Analyze and develop solutions as well as make recommendations
5. Prepare report and sell recommendations
6. Install recommendations and follow up effectiveness

  b. Pitfalls to avoid
1. *Taking things for granted* – A statement of the situation does not necessarily imply that each of the elements is necessarily true; for example, a complaint may be invalid and biased so that all that can be taken for granted is that a complaint has been registered

2. *Considering only one side of a situation* – Wherever possible, indicate several alternatives and then point out the reasons you selected the best one
3. *Failing to indicate follow up* – Whenever your answer indicates action on your part, make certain that you will take proper follow-up action to see how successful your recommendations, procedures or actions turn out to be
4. *Taking too long in answering any single question* – Remember to time your answers properly

IX. AFTER THE TEST

Scoring procedures differ in detail among civil service jurisdictions although the general principles are the same. Whether the papers are hand-scored or graded by machine we have described, they are nearly always graded by number. That is, the person who marks the paper knows only the number – never the name – of the applicant. Not until all the papers have been graded will they be matched with names. If other tests, such as training and experience or oral interview ratings have been given, scores will be combined. Different parts of the examination usually have different weights. For example, the written test might count 60 percent of the final grade, and a rating of training and experience 40 percent. In many jurisdictions, veterans will have a certain number of points added to their grades.

After the final grade has been determined, the names are placed in grade order and an eligible list is established. There are various methods for resolving ties between those who get the same final grade – probably the most common is to place first the name of the person whose application was received first. Job offers are made from the eligible list in the order the names appear on it. You will be notified of your grade and your rank as soon as all these computations have been made. This will be done as rapidly as possible.

People who are found to meet the requirements in the announcement are called "eligibles." Their names are put on a list of eligible candidates. An eligible's chances of getting a job depend on how high he stands on this list and how fast agencies are filling jobs from the list.

When a job is to be filled from a list of eligibles, the agency asks for the names of people on the list of eligibles for that job. When the civil service commission receives this request, it sends to the agency the names of the three people highest on this list. Or, if the job to be filled has specialized requirements, the office sends the agency the names of the top three persons who meet these requirements from the general list.

The appointing officer makes a choice from among the three people whose names were sent to him. If the selected person accepts the appointment, the names of the others are put back on the list to be considered for future openings.

That is the rule in hiring from all kinds of eligible lists, whether they are for typist, carpenter, chemist, or something else. For every vacancy, the appointing officer has his choice of any one of the top three eligibles on the list. This explains why the person whose name is on top of the list sometimes does not get an appointment when some of the persons lower on the list do. If the appointing officer chooses the second or third eligible, the No. 1 eligible does not get a job at once, but stays on the list until he is appointed or the list is terminated.

X. HOW TO PASS THE INTERVIEW TEST

The examination for which you applied requires an oral interview test. You have already taken the written test and you are now being called for the interview test – the final part of the formal examination.

You may think that it is not possible to prepare for an interview test and that there are no procedures to follow during an interview. Our purpose is to point out some things you can do in advance that will help you and some good rules to follow and pitfalls to avoid while you are being interviewed.

What is an interview supposed to test?

The written examination is designed to test the technical knowledge and competence of the candidate; the oral is designed to evaluate intangible qualities, not readily measured otherwise, and to establish a list showing the relative fitness of each candidate – as measured against his competitors – for the position sought. Scoring is not on the basis of "right" and "wrong," but on a sliding scale of values ranging from "not passable" to "outstanding." As a matter of fact, it is possible to achieve a relatively low score without a single "incorrect" answer because of evident weakness in the qualities being measured.

Occasionally, an examination may consist entirely of an oral test – either an individual or a group oral. In such cases, information is sought concerning the technical knowledges and abilities of the candidate, since there has been no written examination for this purpose. More commonly, however, an oral test is used to supplement a written examination.

Who conducts interviews?

The composition of oral boards varies among different jurisdictions. In nearly all, a representative of the personnel department serves as chairman. One of the members of the board may be a representative of the department in which the candidate would work. In some cases, "outside experts" are used, and, frequently, a businessman or some other representative of the general public is asked to serve. Labor and management or other special groups may be represented. The aim is to secure the services of experts in the appropriate field.

However the board is composed, it is a good idea (and not at all improper or unethical) to ascertain in advance of the interview who the members are and what groups they represent. When you are introduced to them, you will have some idea of their backgrounds and interests, and at least you will not stutter and stammer over their names.

What should be done before the interview?

While knowledge about the board members is useful and takes some of the surprise element out of the interview, there is other preparation which is more substantive. It *is* possible to prepare for an oral interview – in several ways:

1) Keep a copy of your application and review it carefully before the interview

This may be the only document before the oral board, and the starting point of the interview. Know what education and experience you have listed there, and the sequence and dates of all of it. Sometimes the board will ask you to review the highlights of your experience for them; you should not have to hem and haw doing it.

2) Study the class specification and the examination announcement

Usually, the oral board has one or both of these to guide them. The qualities, characteristics or knowledges required by the position sought are stated in these documents. They offer valuable clues as to the nature of the oral interview. For example, if the job involves supervisory responsibilities, the announcement will usually indicate that knowledge of modern supervisory methods and the qualifications of the candidate as a supervisor will be tested. If so, you can expect such questions, frequently in the form of a hypothetical situation which you are expected to solve. NEVER go into an oral without knowledge of the duties and responsibilities of the job you seek.

3) Think through each qualification required

Try to visualize the kind of questions you would ask if you were a board member. How well could you answer them? Try especially to appraise your own knowledge and background in each area, *measured against the job sought*, and identify any areas in which you are weak. Be critical and realistic – do not flatter yourself.

4) Do some general reading in areas in which you feel you may be weak

For example, if the job involves supervision and your past experience has NOT, some general reading in supervisory methods and practices, particularly in the field of human relations, might be useful. Do NOT study agency procedures or detailed manuals. The oral board will be testing your understanding and capacity, not your memory.

5) Get a good night's sleep and watch your general health and mental attitude

You will want a clear head at the interview. Take care of a cold or any other minor ailment, and of course, no hangovers.

What should be done on the day of the interview?

Now comes the day of the interview itself. Give yourself plenty of time to get there. Plan to arrive somewhat ahead of the scheduled time, particularly if your appointment is in the fore part of the day. If a previous candidate fails to appear, the board might be ready for you a bit early. By early afternoon an oral board is almost invariably behind schedule if there are many candidates, and you may have to wait. Take along a book or magazine to read, or your application to review, but leave any extraneous material in the waiting room when you go in for your interview. In any event, relax and compose yourself.

The matter of dress is important. The board is forming impressions about you – from your experience, your manners, your attitude, and your appearance. Give your personal appearance careful attention. Dress your best, but not your flashiest. Choose conservative, appropriate clothing, and be sure it is immaculate. This is a business interview, and your appearance should indicate that you regard it as such. Besides, being well groomed and properly dressed will help boost your confidence.

Sooner or later, someone will call your name and escort you into the interview room. *This is it.* From here on you are on your own. It is too late for any more preparation. But remember, you asked for this opportunity to prove your fitness, and you are here because your request was granted.

What happens when you go in?

The usual sequence of events will be as follows: The clerk (who is often the board stenographer) will introduce you to the chairman of the oral board, who will introduce you to the other members of the board. Acknowledge the introductions before you sit down. Do not be surprised if you find a microphone facing you or a stenotypist sitting by. Oral interviews are usually recorded in the event of an appeal or other review.

Usually the chairman of the board will open the interview by reviewing the highlights of your education and work experience from your application – primarily for the benefit of the other members of the board, as well as to get the material into the record. Do not interrupt or comment unless there is an error or significant misinterpretation; if that is the case, do not hesitate. But do not quibble about insignificant matters. Also, he will usually ask you some question about your education, experience or your present job – partly to get you to start talking and to establish the interviewing "rapport." He may start the actual questioning, or turn it over to one of the other members. Frequently, each member undertakes the questioning on a particular area, one in which he is perhaps most competent, so you can expect each member to participate in the examination. Because time is limited, you may also expect some rather abrupt switches in the direction the questioning takes, so do not be upset by it. Normally, a board member will not pursue a single line of questioning unless he discovers a particular strength or weakness.

After each member has participated, the chairman will usually ask whether any member has any further questions, then will ask you if you have anything you wish to add. Unless you are expecting this question, it may floor you. Worse, it may start you off on an extended, extemporaneous speech. The board is not usually seeking more information. The question is principally to offer you a last opportunity to present further qualifications or to indicate that you have nothing to add. So, if you feel that a significant qualification or characteristic has been overlooked, it is proper to point it out in a sentence or so. Do not compliment the board on the thoroughness of their examination – they have been sketchy, and you know it. If you wish, merely say, "No thank you, I have nothing further to add." This is a point where you can "talk yourself out" of a good impression or fail to present an important bit of information. Remember, *you close the interview yourself*.

The chairman will then say, "That is all, Mr. _____, thank you." Do not be startled; the interview is over, and quicker than you think. Thank him, gather your belongings and take your leave. Save your sigh of relief for the other side of the door.

How to put your best foot forward

Throughout this entire process, you may feel that the board individually and collectively is trying to pierce your defenses, seek out your hidden weaknesses and embarrass and confuse you. Actually, this is not true. They are obliged to make an appraisal of your qualifications for the job you are seeking, and they want to see you in your best light. Remember, they must interview all candidates and a non-cooperative candidate may become a failure in spite of their best efforts to bring out his qualifications. Here are 15 suggestions that will help you:

1) Be natural – Keep your attitude confident, not cocky

If you are not confident that you can do the job, do not expect the board to be. Do not apologize for your weaknesses, try to bring out your strong points. The board is interested in a positive, not negative, presentation. Cockiness will antagonize any board member and make him wonder if you are covering up a weakness by a false show of strength.

2) Get comfortable, but don't lounge or sprawl

Sit erectly but not stiffly. A careless posture may lead the board to conclude that you are careless in other things, or at least that you are not impressed by the importance of the occasion. Either conclusion is natural, even if incorrect. Do not fuss with your clothing, a pencil or an ashtray. Your hands may occasionally be useful to emphasize a point; do not let them become a point of distraction.

3) Do not wisecrack or make small talk

This is a serious situation, and your attitude should show that you consider it as such. Further, the time of the board is limited – they do not want to waste it, and neither should you.

4) Do not exaggerate your experience or abilities

In the first place, from information in the application or other interviews and sources, the board may know more about you than you think. Secondly, you probably will not get away with it. An experienced board is rather adept at spotting such a situation, so do not take the chance.

5) If you know a board member, do not make a point of it, yet do not hide it

Certainly you are not fooling him, and probably not the other members of the board. Do not try to take advantage of your acquaintanceship – it will probably do you little good.

6) Do not dominate the interview

Let the board do that. They will give you the clues – do not assume that you have to do all the talking. Realize that the board has a number of questions to ask you, and do not try to take up all the interview time by showing off your extensive knowledge of the answer to the first one.

7) Be attentive

You only have 20 minutes or so, and you should keep your attention at its sharpest throughout. When a member is addressing a problem or question to you, give him your undivided attention. Address your reply principally to him, but do not exclude the other board members.

8) Do not interrupt

A board member may be stating a problem for you to analyze. He will ask you a question when the time comes. Let him state the problem, and wait for the question.

9) Make sure you understand the question

Do not try to answer until you are sure what the question is. If it is not clear, restate it in your own words or ask the board member to clarify it for you. However, do not haggle about minor elements.

10) Reply promptly but not hastily

A common entry on oral board rating sheets is "candidate responded readily," or "candidate hesitated in replies." Respond as promptly and quickly as you can, but do not jump to a hasty, ill-considered answer.

11) Do not be peremptory in your answers

A brief answer is proper – but do not fire your answer back. That is a losing game from your point of view. The board member can probably ask questions much faster than you can answer them.

12) Do not try to create the answer you think the board member wants

He is interested in what kind of mind you have and how it works – not in playing games. Furthermore, he can usually spot this practice and will actually grade you down on it.

13) Do not switch sides in your reply merely to agree with a board member

Frequently, a member will take a contrary position merely to draw you out and to see if you are willing and able to defend your point of view. Do not start a debate, yet do not surrender a good position. If a position is worth taking, it is worth defending.

14) Do not be afraid to admit an error in judgment if you are shown to be wrong
   The board knows that you are forced to reply without any opportunity for careful consideration. Your answer may be demonstrably wrong. If so, admit it and get on with the interview.

15) Do not dwell at length on your present job
   The opening question may relate to your present assignment. Answer the question but do not go into an extended discussion. You are being examined for a *new* job, not your present one. As a matter of fact, try to phrase ALL your answers in terms of the job for which you are being examined.

Basis of Rating
   Probably you will forget most of these "do's" and "don'ts" when you walk into the oral interview room. Even remembering them all will not ensure you a passing grade. Perhaps you did not have the qualifications in the first place. But remembering them will help you to put your best foot forward, without treading on the toes of the board members.
   Rumor and popular opinion to the contrary notwithstanding, an oral board wants you to make the best appearance possible. They know you are under pressure – but they also want to see how you respond to it as a guide to what your reaction would be under the pressures of the job you seek. They will be influenced by the degree of poise you display, the personal traits you show and the manner in which you respond.

ABOUT THIS BOOK

   This book contains tests divided into Examination Sections. Go through each test, answering every question in the margin. We have also attached a sample answer sheet at the back of the book that can be removed and used. At the end of each test look at the answer key and check your answers. On the ones you got wrong, look at the right answer choice and learn. Do not fill in the answers first. Do not memorize the questions and answers, but understand the answer and principles involved. On your test, the questions will likely be different from the samples. Questions are changed and new ones added. If you understand these past questions you should have success with any changes that arise. Tests may consist of several types of questions. We have additional books on each subject should more study be advisable or necessary for you. Finally, the more you study, the better prepared you will be. This book is intended to be the last thing you study before you walk into the examination room. Prior study of relevant texts is also recommended. NLC publishes some of these in our Fundamental Series. Knowledge and good sense are important factors in passing your exam. Good luck also helps. So now study this Passbook, absorb the material contained within and take that knowledge into the examination. Then do your best to pass that exam.

EXAMINATION SECTION

EXAMINATION SECTION
TEST 1

DIRECTIONS: Each question or incomplete statement is followed by several suggested answers or completions. Select the one that BEST answers the question or completes the statement. *PRINT THE LETTER OF THE CORRECT ANSWER IN THE SPACE AT THE RIGHT.*

1. Which of the following is LEAST correct according to Article 375 V.T.L.? 1.____

    A. No vehicle shall be towed by a rope or other non-rigid connection which is longer than 16 feet.
    B. A motor vehicle being towed by a non-rigid connection must have a licensed driver in such motor vehicle who shall steer it when it is being towed.
    C. This rule (as in "B") does not apply in the counties of Nassau or Suffolk when a tractor is towing two trailers.
    D. The general rule is that a motor vehicle shall not be used to tow more than one other vehicle.

2. During daylight hours, when visibility for a distance of _____ feet ahead is not clear, a motor vehicle driven upon a public highway shall display its lights. 2.____

    A. 350   B. 500   C. 1,000   D. 100

3. Motor vehicles manufactured after 1/1/52 are required to display two rear red lamps during certain periods. These red lamps shall be visible from the rear for a distance of _____ feet. 3.____

    A. 500   B. 1,000   C. 350   D. 100

4. When a vehicle is required to display a number plate on the rear, a white light must be available to illuminate the number plate to make the numerals legible for at least _____ feet from the rear. 4.____

    A. 50   B. 75   C. 100   D. 350

5. Which of the following is LEAST correct concerning the use of colored and flashing lights? 5.____

    A. Green lights may be affixed to any motor vehicle owned by a volunteer ambulance worker.
    B. Blue lights may be affixed to motor vehicles owned by a member of a volunteer fire department.
    C. Amber lights may be used by hazard vehicles.
    D. Red lights or oscillating white lights may be used by either authorized emergency vehicles or by hazard vehicles.

6. Which of the following statements is LEAST correct concerning accident reports under Section 605 V.T.L.? 6.____

    A. An accident report is required whenever any person is killed or injured.
    B. An accident report is required whenever property damage to any one person exceeds $1000.

C. If the operator of the involved vehicle cannot make the report, then the owner should make it within 10 days after he learns the facts.
D. The report required shall be made in duplicate.

7. Every police or judicial officer to whom an accident resulting in injury to a person shall reported to the V.T.L., shall IMMEDIATELY investigate the facts, or cause the same to be investigated provided, however, that the report of the accident is made to the police officer or judicial officer within _____ days after such accident.

  A. 5   B. 10   C. 15   D. 20

7.____

8. Which of the following is LEAST correct concerning the requirement of stopping before passing or overtaking a stopped school bus in this state?

  A. The rule in a city is the same as the rule in the remainder of the state.
  B. If the stopped school bus does not have its red visual signal in operation, it may be passed or overtaken.
  C. If the school bus is stopped for the purpose of receiving or discharging any school children, and a red visual signal is in operation on said bus, then an overtaking or passing vehicle approaching from EITHER direction must be stopped before reaching the school bus.
  D. The driver of a vehicle stopped as per choice C above may not proceed until the school bus resumes motion.

8.____

9. Reckless driving means driving or using any motor vehicle, motorcycle, or any other vehicle propelled by any power other than muscular power or any appliance or accessory thereof in a manner which unreasonably interferes with the free and proper use of the public highway.
The above statement defines a

  A. traffic infraction
  B. misdemeanor
  C. violation
  D. petty offense
  E. felony if there has been a prior conviction within 18 months

9.____

10. Which of the following is MOST accurate according to 1195 of the V.T.L.?

  A. No person shall operate a motor vehicle while he has .10 of one percentum or more by weight of alcohol in his blood.
  B. Any person who operates a motor vehicle or motorcycle in this state shall be deemed to have given his consent to a chemical test of his breath, blood, urine, or saliva for the purpose of determining the alcoholic or drug content of his blood.
  C. Only a physician or a registered professional nurse, acting at the request of a police officer, shall be entitled to withdraw blood, urine, or saliva for the purpose of determining alcoholic or drug content.
  D. The person tested shall be permitted to have a physician of his own choosing administer a chemical test in addition to the one administered at the direction of the police officer.

10.____

11. Which of the following is LEAST accurate according to 1192 of the V.T.L.? 11.____

    A. Driving with .08% or more alcohol in the blood is a misdemeanor.
    B. A person who now stands convicted of A or B above and who has a prior conviction of either within ten years is guilty of a felony.
    C. Driving while ability to operate is impaired by drugs is a misdemeanor.
    D. A person who now stands convicted of D above and who has a prior conviction of A, B, or D above within 10 years is guilty of a felony.

12. Which of the following is LEAST accurate according to the V.T.L.? 12.____

    A. Driving while intoxicated is a misdemeanor.
    B. Driving with more than .08% alcohol in the blood is a misdemeanor.
    C. Driving while ability is impaired by the consumption of alcohol is a traffic infraction
    D. Driving while ability is impaired by drugs is a traffic infraction.

13. According to Section 116 of the V.T.L., a FLAMMABLE LIQUID is defined as a liquid which has a flash point of less than _____ degrees Fahrenheit. 13.____

    A. 70   B. 80   C. 60   D. 90

14. According to Section 125 of the V.T.L., which of the following would be considered to be a motor vehicle? A(n) 14.____

    A. motorcycle
    B. snow-mobile
    C. vehicle which runs only upon rails or track
    D. electrically driven invalid chair operated or driven by an invalid

15. Which of the following is LEAST correct according to the V.T.L.? 15.____

    A. The defined term "police officer" includes every duly designated peace officer acting pursuant to his special duties.
    B. The defined term "person" includes a corporation.
    C. A "pedestrian" is any person who is afoot.
    D. An "omnibus" is any vehicle used in the business of transporting people for hire which has a carrying capacity of more than 10 persons.

16. Which of the following would NOT be considered a "vehicle" as that term is defined in Section 159 of the V.T.L.? A(n) 16.____

    A. device used exclusively upon stationary rails or tracks
    B. motor-driven bicycle
    C. air-powered four-wheeled wagon
    D. horse being ridden

17. According to the V.T.L., the "parking area of a shopping center" is sometimes subject to the traffic control regulations of the V.T.L. Which of the following is MOST correct concerning the size of such parking area? It must be 17.____

    A. at least one acre
    B. at least 100 feet of business frontage
    C. at least 500 feet along a highway
    D. any size if the public has access and more than one business is serviced thereby

18. A "vanpool vehicle" is said to have a seating capacity, in addition to the driver, of

    A. not less than 6 nor more than 15 passengers
    B. not more than 10 passengers
    C. nine passengers
    D. ten passengers or less

19. P.O. Collins observes Sam drive through a red light and he "pulls him over." When Collins asks Sam for his license and registration, Collins sees actions which makes him think Sam was drinking. Collins asks Sam to submit to a breath test to determine if Sam has consumed alcohol. Sam submits and the test indicates that Sam has consumed alcohol, amount unknown. Collins' NEXT action should be to

    A. arrest Sam for violation of 1192 V.T.L.
    B. direct Sam to engage in coordination tests such as "finger to nose," "walking a straight line," etc.
    C. require Sam to submit to a chemical test as per 1194 of the V.T.L.
    D. release Sam if the amount of alcohol consumed, as indicated in the field breath test, is .05% or less

20. Which of the following statements concerning the court order to compel a chemical test is MOST accurate?

    A. Application may be made to the judge of any criminal court.
    B. Application must be made in person and in writing.
    C. When the order is issued, the chemical test may be administered even if the two hour time limit in Section 1194 has expired.
    D. If the defendant is unable to give his consent to a chemical test (unconscious), a court order may be obtained.

21. Which of the following substances is NOT listed in Section 1194 of the V.T.L. as a substance which may be tested to determine blood alcohol content?

    A. Breath   B. Blood
    C. Urine   D. Perspiration

22. The chemical test authorized under Section 1194 of the V.T.L. must be administered at the direction of

    A. a police officer
    B. the judge of a criminal court
    C. a physician
    D. the desk officer

23. Persons who may be authorized to withdraw blood for the purpose of determining alcoholic content include
    I. a physician
    II. a registered professional nurse
    III. any laboratory technician
    IV. a registered physician's assistant

    The CORRECT answer is:

    A. I, II   B. I, II, III
    C. I, II, IV   D. II, III, IV

24. Any person operating a motor vehicle that is involved in an accident resulting in death, injury, or property damage exceeding $1000 must report the accident to the Department of Motor Vehicles within _____ days.

   A. 7 B. 10 C. 20 D. 30

25. Article 140 of the C.P.L. contains the rules which govern "arrests without a warrant." These, however, are NOT the only arrest laws. The V.T.L. contains a "law of arrest" in Section 1193 that governs arrests without a warrant for violations of Section 1192 of the V.T.L. Consider the following statements regarding this "law of arrest" which may or may not be CORRECT:
   I. The police officer needs R.C.T.B. that the person to be arrested violated Section 1192.
   II. The violation of Section 1192 must in fact have been committed.
   III. The violation of Section 1192 need not have been committed in the arresting officer's presence if such violation is coupled with an accident or collision in which such person is involved.

   The choice below which most accurately describes which of the above statements is/are consistent with the provisions of Section 1193 V.T.L. is:

   A. I, II, III B. II, III
   C. I, III   D. I, II

KEY (CORRECT ANSWERS)

1. C		11. D	
2. C		12. D	
3. A		13. B	
4. A		14. A	
5. D		15. D	
6. D		16. A	
7. A		17. A	
8. D		18. A	
9. B		19. C	
10. D		20. D	

21. D
22. A
23. C
24. B
25. A

TEST 2

DIRECTIONS: Each question or incomplete statement is followed by several suggested answers or completions. Select the one that BEST answers the question or completes the statement. *PRINT THE LETTER OF THE CORRECT ANSWER IN THE SPACE AT THE RIGHT.*

1. Which of the following are considered to be "Authorized Emergency Vehicles" under the V.T.L.?

    A. Ambulance, police and fire vehicles only
    B. Civil Defense emergency, police, fire and ambulance vehicles only
    C. All of the above plus utility company repair trucks
    D. All of C plus emergency ambulance service vehicles and ordinance disposal vehicles of U.S. Armed Forces

    1.____

2. Which of the following defined terms is LEAST correct according to the V.T.L.?

    A. A "driver" means every person who operates or drives or is in actual physical control of a vehicle.
    B. The term "drug" as used in the V.T.L. includes depressant, stimulant, hallucinogenic and narcotic drugs.
    C. A "motorcycle" is a motor vehicle having a seat or saddle for the rider and designed to travel on not more than three wheels, any two of which are more than twenty inches in diameter.
    D. An "owner" of a vehicle does NOT include a lien holder.

    2.____

3. According to Article 1 of the V.T.L., which of the following is LEAST correct?

    A. A bus includes every motor vehicle used for transporting persons and designed to carry more than seven passengers.
    B. An omnibus is any motor vehicle used in the business of transporting passengers for hire, except those used to transport agricultural workers to and from their employment.
    C. A snow-mobile is specifically excluded from the definition of a motor vehicle.
    D. Parking means the standing of a vehicle, whether occupied or not, except when done temporarily for the purpose of and while actually engaged in loading or unloading merchandise or passengers.

    3.____

4. According to the V.T.L., a "business district" is defined as the territory contiguous to and including a highway when within 600 feet along such highway there are buildings in use for business or industrial purposes which occupy a certain amount of frontage along the highway.
   Which of the following is MOST correct concerning the frontage along the highway? It must be

    A. at least 300 feet on both sides of the highway
    B. at least 600 feet collectively on both sides of the highway
    C. at least 300 feet on one side or 300 feet collectively on both sides
    D. a minimum of at least 150 feet on each side of the highway

    4.____

5. Which of the following is LEAST correct according to the V.T.L.?

   A. A "traffic infraction" is a violation of any law regulating traffic which is NOT declared to be a felony or a misdemeanor.
   B. Punishment for a traffic infraction shall NOT be deemed a penal or criminal punishment.
   C. For purposes of arrest without a warrant, a traffic infraction shall be deemed an offense.
   D. Any fine imposed by an administrative tribunal for a traffic infraction shall NOT be a civil penalty.

6. According to Section 251 of the V.T.L., a member of the Armed Forces who has been issued an Operator's License by the Armed Forces may operate a motor vehicle upon the highways of the state WITHOUT being licensed under the V.T.L. for a period of _____ days after he has entered the state.

   A. 45   B. 30   C. 20   D. 60

7. According to Section 252 of the V.T.L., a temporary in-transit or transportation registration or permit issued by another state to the purchaser of a motor vehicle shall be valid only for a period of _____ days after the holder thereof has entered this state for the purpose of transporting the vehicle to the jurisdiction in which it will be regularly registered.

   A. 3   B. 5   C. 7   D. 10

8. Which of the following is LEAST accurate concerning required lights on motor vehicles?

   A. Two front lamps, one on each side, having light sources of equal power, shall be displayed from 1/2 hour after sunset to 1/2 hour before sunrise.
   B. The lamps referred to in A shall also be displayed at such other times when visibility for a distance of 1000 feet ahead of such motor vehicle is not clear.
   C. At least one lighted red lamp on the rear of such motor vehicle if manufactured before 1/1/52 visible for a distance of at least 500 feet shall be displayed during the times referred to in A and B.
   D. All motor vehicles shall be equipped with a white rear light which shall be lighted when, the ignition is energized and reverse gear is engaged.

9. According to Section 304b V.T.L., if a vehicle is inspected and found to be in need of repairs or adjustment, a period of _____ is allowed for the making of the repairs.

   A. 10 days   B. one week
   C. 15 days   D. one month

10. According to Section 306 of the V.T.L., which is LEAST accurate? A

    A. motor vehicle parked without a proper inspection certificate constitutes a parking violation
    B. person who unlawfully removes an inspection certificate from a vehicle is guilty of a traffic infraction
    C. person who makes a false inspection certificate is guilty of a misdemeanor
    D. person who displays on a motor vehicle an inspection certificate without an inspection having been made commits a misdemeanor

11. Which of the following is LEAST correct concerning items subject to inspection according to Article 301 V.T.L. dealing with periodic inspection of motor vehicles?

    A. Wheel alignment is included.
    B. The vehicle identification number is included.
    C. The odometer is not included.
    D. Lights, brakes, and steering are included.

12. If one is arrested and charged with "operating a motor vehicle while under the influence of alcohol or drugs" and evidence of the amount of alcohol in the defendant's blood is admitted, it would be MOST INACCURATE to state that

    A. .02 of one percent or less is prima facie evidence that defendant was neither impaired nor intoxicated
    B. more than .02 but not more than .04 of one percent is prima facie that defendant was not intoxicated but is not prima facie that he was impaired
    C. more than .04 but less than .08 of one percent is prima facie that defendant was not intoxicated but is prima facie that he was impaired
    D. .08 of one percent or less precludes a finding that defendant was guilty of driving while intoxicated

13. If one is arrested and charged under Section 1192 of the V.T.L., and convicted of same, the conviction may be for a felony if certain conditions are present. It would NOT result in such felony conviction if he is now charged with driving

    A. while intoxicated with a prior conviction for same within the preceding 10 years
    B. with .08 percent, or more, of alcohol in the blood with a prior conviction for same within the preceding 10 years
    C. with .08 percent, or more, of alcohol in the blood with a prior conviction for driving while intoxicated within the preceding 10 years
    D. while impaired by the use of a drug with a previous conviction of driving with .10 percent, or more, of alcohol in the blood within the preceding 10 years

14. Under the V.T.L., various tests may be administered to determine blood-alcohol content. Of the following, it would be MOST INACCURATE to state that

    A. every person operating a motor vehicle and who violates a provision of the V.T.L. may be requested to submit to a breath test
    B. one, properly arrested for violation of Section 1192 V.T.L., is deemed to have consented to a chemical test to determine his blood alcohol or drug content
    C. such test in C above must be administered at the direction of a police officer
    D. only a physician, or other specifically qualified person, may obtain blood, urine, or saliva samples for such test

15. According to the provisions of the V.T.L., in which of the following offenses would a second (or third) offense committed within 10 years amount to a felony?

    A. Reckless driving
    B. Third speed coupled with accident involving serious physical injury
    C. Leaving the scene of a physical injury accident
    D. Sale of a false certificate or registration

16. Under the provisions of the V.T.L., the percentage of blood alcohol which is to be given prima facie effect in determining that a person is neither intoxicated nor impaired is

    A. .02% or less
    B. .06% or .07%
    C. .08% or .09%
    D. less than .10%

17. A blood alcohol reading of .08% or .09% shall be given which of the following weights of evidence?

    A. Prima facie not intoxicated, but relevant regarding driving impaired
    B. Relevant regarding intoxication, but prima facie regarding driving impaired
    C. Prima facie not intoxicated, but prima facie impaired
    D. Relevant regarding both intoxication and driving impaired

18. The current charge and prior conviction within ten years, respectively, which will result in a felony charge according to the V.T.L. is:
    I. Driving impaired alcohol, driving impaired drugs
    II. Driving intoxicated, driving impaired alcohol
    III. Driving .10% or more blood alcohol, driving intoxicated
    IV. Driving impaired drugs, driving impaired drugs
    V. Driving intoxicated, driving impaired drugs
    VI. Driving intoxicated, driving .10% or more blood alcohol

    The CORRECT answer is:

    A. I, III, IV, VI
    B. III, IV, VI
    C. IV *only*
    D. all of the above

19. When a person refuses to submit to a chemical test after arrest for D.W.I., the report of said refusal shall be

    A. sent to the Commissioner of Motor Vehicles within 72 hours
    B. presented to the court upon arraignment of the defendant
    C. disclosed only if convicted of the offense
    D. sent to the Department of Motor Vehicles by the police agency involved so that a hearing may be scheduled

20. Following an arrest for D.W.I, and a refusal to submit to a chemical test, a court order may be issued directing the defendant to submit to the test when

    A. an accident involving property damage in excess of $1000 or personal injury has occurred
    B. the arrested person was the operator of the vehicle which was involved in an accident resulting in death or in serious injury to the operator or another person
    C. the arrested person was the operator of a vehicle which was involved in an accident resulting in death or serious injury to other than the operator
    D. an accident involving either death or physical injury has occurred

21. Boating accidents in which someone is killed or injured, or in which property damage exceeds $100.00, must be reported by the operator on a Boating Accident Report to the Office of Parks and Recreation within _____ days.

    A. 7
    B. 10
    C. 20
    D. 30

22. In the event of a snowmobile accident resulting in death, personal injury, or property damage in excess of $1000.00, a report must be prepared by the operator.
The CORRECT statement(s) regarding this report is(are):
    I. It must be filed within 7 days of the accident.
    II. It must be filed with the Office of Parks & Recreation.
    III. A copy of the report must be prepared for the sheriff of the county where the accident occurred.
The CORRECT answer is:

    A. I, II   B. I, II, III
    C. I, III   D. II, III

23. When you consider the sections of the V.T.L. that contain the blood alcohol percentages required for various D.W.I. offenses, which of the following would NOT be prima facie evidence that the person was impaired?

    A. .07%   B. .05%
    C. .02%   D. less than .10%

24. The definition which is INCONSISTENT with Article 10 of the R L. is that a

    A. "traffic infraction" means any offense defined as a "traffic infraction" by Section 155 of the V.T.L.
    B. "violation" means an offense for which a sentence to a term of imprisonment in excess of 15 days cannot be imposed
    C. "misdemeanor" means an offense for which a sentence to a term of imprisonment in excess of 15 days may be imposed, but for which a sentence to a term of imprisonment in excess of one year cannot be imposed
    D. "felony" means an offense for which a sentence to a term of imprisonment in excess of one year must be imposed

Questions 25 to 30.

DIRECTIONS: Each question consists of a statement. You are to indicate whether the statement is TRUE (T) or FALSE (F). *PRINT THE LETTER OF THE CORRECT ANSWER IN THE SPACE AT THE RIGHT*

25. According to the V.T.L., any police officer or peace officer acting pursuant to his official duties, can seize any motor vehicle or trailer when any original identification number or special identification number is destroyed, removed, altered, defaced, or covered.

26. Between ten and fifteen percent of reported auto thefts are fraudulent.

27. When vehicles are stolen in one state and recovered in another, the F.B.1, should be immediately notified because the interstate transportation of vehicles or aircraft known to be stolen is a federal felony.

28. Recovered stolen vehicles must be considered evidence and should be tagged, examined, and secured.

29. Upon satisfactory proof of ownership and payment of the reasonable and necessary expenses incurred in its preservation, the court in which the criminal action (if any) is pending MUST order the recovered vehicle to be delivered to the owner.   29.____

30. It is a Class E felony under the V.T.L. for any person to sell or offer for sale a motor vehicle, trailer or part thereof which has a destroyed, removed, altered, defaced, or covered VIN or special identification number.   30.____

KEY (CORRECT ANSWERS)

1.	D	16.	A
2.	C	17.	C
3.	A	18.	B
4.	C	19.	B
5.	D	20.	C
6.	D	21.	A
7.	D	22.	B
8.	D	23.	C
9.	A	24.	D
10.	B	25.	T
11.	C	26.	T
12.	D	27.	T
13.	D	28.	T
14.	D	29.	F
15.	D	30.	T

EXAMINATION SECTION

TEST 1

DIRECTIONS: Each question or incomplete statement is followed by several suggested answers or completions. Select the one that BEST answers the question or completes the statement. *PRINT THE LETTER OF THE CORRECT ANSWER IN THE SPACE AT THE RIGHT.*

1. When a driver with a learner's permit is practicing driving, he must be accompanied by a
    A. New York State licensed driver at least 18 years of age
    B. licensed driver at least 18 years of age
    C. duly licensed instructor in New York State
    D. police officer from your precinct

    1._____

2. The violations which charge one point against a driver's record are
    A. speeding or reckless driving
    B. failure to keep right
    C. failure to signal properly, dim headlights, or illegal turn
    D. passing stopped school bus, failing to obey traffic controls or yield right of way

    2._____

3. A junior driver's license is NOT valid in the county of
    A. Westchester   B. Nassau   C. Suffolk   D. Sullivan

    3._____

4. The serious traffic offense for which more than one conviction is required for your license to be revoked is
    A. parking too far from the curb
    B. parking too near fire hydrants
    C. speeding
    D. having more than 3 people in the front seat

    4._____

5. With only an operator's license, rather than a chauffeur's license, a driver can LEGALLY operate
    A. tractor-trailers
    B. buses
    C. regular passenger cars and motorcycles
    D. regular passenger cars

    5._____

6. New York State will honor a driver's license of another state is the
    A. other state honor's a New York State license
    B. test requirements are the same
    C. age requirements are the same
    D. driver is licensed for at least 2 years

    6._____

13

7. The road test for a classified chauffeur's license is different from that of an operator's license in that it
   A. is much longer
   B. is much more difficult
   C. is more practical
   D. must be taken in the type of vehicle for which you wish to qualify

8. New York State has set up controls and tests with regard to driver's licenses to
   A. make it more difficult to get a license
   B. give jobs to more people
   C. charge fees that better roads may be built
   D. protect the public from dangerous drivers

9. To obtain a junior operator's license, a driver must be at least
   A. 18   B. 21   C. 16   D. 17

10. If there is no district office of the Department of Motor Vehicles in his county, a driver should apply for a driver's license at the
    A. police station
    B. tax collector's office
    C. county clerk's office
    D. firehouse

11. When a driver changes his name or address, the law requires that he must
    A. notify the Department of Motor Vehicles in writing
    B. take new tests
    C. pay for a new license
    D. notify the Police Department in your community

12. New York State demands that every driver be licensed
    A. because the law requires it
    B. because it needs money to build roads
    C. for the protection of the public
    D. to see if everybody who drives can read

13. A junior license holder may operate a motor vehicle ONLY
    A. if he's in New York City or Nassau County limits
    B. when driving for compensation
    C. between the hours of sunrise and sunset
    D. when going to and from school

14. In order to apply for a license before 18 years of age, a drive must obtain the permission of
    A. the Commissioner of Motor Vehicles
    B. a parent or guardian
    C. the school principal
    D. the president of the school council

15. A road test may be taken _____ time(s) on one application.
    A. four   B. one   C. three   D. two

16. A junior operator may drive at night
    A. when accompanied by a licensed driver over 18 years of age
    B. if he is a member of the National Guard
    C. never
    D. for credit-bearing classes or activities at school

17. A person under 18 years of age may obtain a regular operator's license by
    A. writing a special letter to the Commissioner of Motor Vehicles
    B. showing that he has above-average skill
    C. passing an approved driver training course in a junior or senior high school which he is attending
    D. passing the driving test the first time

18. When driving, the identification or documents that the driver must have with him is(are)
    A. the license stub
    B. the "Record of Conviction" stub
    C. stubs to both your license and car registration
    D. proof of age

19. A driving license may be used by a person other than the one to whom it was issued
    A. only if he has the same name   B. never
    C. only if he has paid half the fee   D. only on weekends

20. The Department of Motor Vehicles may require a re-examination of a driver
    A. for not paying the proper fee
    B. because the testing examiner who administered the test was fired
    C. because the person's car is too old
    D. if the driver is involved in 3 reportable accidents within 18 months

21. When applying for a license, proof of date of birth must be shown by
    A. people of all ages
    B. only those people under 21 years of age
    C. only those people over 21 years of age
    D. only those people applying for junior operator's license

22. It is recommended that a driver should have _____ total hours of practice driving.
    A. 4   B. 10   C. 20   D. 12

23. When a driver appears for the road test for a driver's license, he must be accompanied by a
    A. parent or guardian
    B. high school teacher
    C. New York State licensed driver at least 18 years of age
    D. licensed driver, from any state, at least 18 years of age

24. After passing an approved training course while in high school, a driver must take which of the following Department of Motor Vehicle examinations? 24.____
   A. The vision and road tests   B. The written and road sign tests
   C. A test in simple mathematics   D. A test in geographical location

25. What visual acuity is required to pass the vision test for a driver's license? 25.____
   A. 20-20   B. 20-30   C. 20-40   D. 20-10

KEY (CORRECT ANSWERS)

1.	A	11.	A
2.	C	12.	C
3.	B	13.	C
4.	C	14.	B
5.	C	15.	B
6.	A	16.	D
7.	D	17.	C
8.	D	18.	C
9.	C	19.	B
10.	C	20.	D

21. A
22. C
23. C
24. A
25. C

TEST 2

DIRECTIONS: Each question or incomplete statement is followed by several suggested answers or completions. Select the one that BEST answers the question or completes the statement. *PRINT THE LETTER OF THE CORRECT ANSWER IN THE SPACE AT THE RIGHT.*

1. The MAXIMUM gross weight of a truck that can be legally driven with an operator's license is _____ lbs.
   A. 24,000 B. 18,000 C. 36,000 D. 10,000

   1._____

2. After failing a road test, a driver can apply for a new learner's permit WITHOUT taking the preliminary tests again within _____ days.
   A. 30 B. 20 C. 60 D. 15

   2._____

3. Driving licenses are NORMALLY issued for
   A. 1 year B. 2 years C. 6 months D. 3 years

   3._____

4. With an "unclassified" chauffeur's license, a driver can LEGALLY operate
   A. vehicles over 18,000 lbs.
   B. taxis and all vehicles for which an operator's license is required
   C. buses
   D. tractor-trailer and truck-trailer combinations

   4._____

5. The consequences that can result from driving under the influence of alcohol or other drugs are
   A. possible imprisonment
   B. a mandatory fine
   C. driver license revocation
   D. all of the above

   5._____

6. In New York State, what motor vehicles are subject to periodic inspection?
   A. All vehicles
   B. All vehicles over one year of age
   C. All vehicles over 4 years of age or those recently transferred
   D. Only vehicles which are transferred

   6._____

7. The law requires you to turn on the headlights one
   A. hour after sunset
   B. half hour before sunset
   C. half hour after sunset
   D. hour before sunset

   7._____

8. Financial security (compulsory insurance) requirements in New York State may be met by holding what type of insurance policy, and for how much coverage?
   A. Posting bonds worth $25,000
   B. Real estate in the amount of $25,000
   C. Auto liability insurance in the amount of 20/40/10
   D. Auto liability insurance in the amount of 10/20/5

   8._____

9. Under the state's point system, a driver must pay a Driver Responsibility Assessment fee if he/she has accumulated
    A. 10 points within 2 years
    B. 8 points within 2 years
    C. 6 points within 18 months
    D. 5 points within 1 year

9.____

10. The act that will result in IMMEDIATE failure of the road test is
    A. being unable to park
    B. refusing to follow instructions
    C. parking near a fire hydrant
    D. rolling on a grade

10.____

11. Three points will be charged against a driver's record for
    A. failure to keep right
    B. speeding or reckless driving
    C. going through a red light or stop sign
    D. failure to yield right of way

11.____

12. The Department of Motor Vehicles defines the hours of darkness by one
    A. hour after sunset to one half hour before sunrise
    B. half hour before sunset to one half hour before sunrise
    C. half hour after sunset to one half hour before sunset
    D. hour after sunset to one hour before sunrise

12.____

13. The accidents that must be reported are those over _____ damage or personal injury.
    A. $50   B. $250   C. $1,000   D. $5,000

13.____

14. You should report an accident to the
    A. nearest police precinct within 48 hours
    B. Commissioner of Motor Vehicles within 48 hours
    C. Commissioner of Highways within 48 hours
    D. Chief of Police within 72 hours

14.____

15. If you leave the scene of an accident in which you are involved,
    A. you will not collect for damages
    B. you may face criminal action
    C. you will not be admitted to a hospital if injured
    D. your automobile may be impounded

15.____

16. The MAXIMUM penalty possible for driving a vehicle without providing proof of financial security (compulsory insurance) is
    A. a fine of $1,000
    B. a fine of $100
    C. a fine of $1,500
    D. imprisonment up to 1 year

16.____

17. The definition of a motor vehicle under New York State law is
    A. gas-driven vehicles only
    B. diesel-powered vehicles only
    C. a vehicle operated by a power other than muscular power
    D. a vehicle which has the motor only up front

17.____

18. The MAXIMUM period of time after you become a New York State resident before you can register your car is _____ days.
    A. 20   B. 30   C. 60   D. 90

19. In New York State, a driver may LEGALLY drive a car which carries no insurance or other security coverage
    A. only when accompanied by a parent or guardian
    B. never
    C. if he is over 21 years of age
    D. if he is over 25 years of age

20. The MAXIMUM speed limit in New York State, unless otherwise posted, is _____ MPH.
    A. 40   B. 55   C. 60   D. 65

KEY (CORRECT ANSWERS)

1.	B	11.	B
2.	A	12.	C
3.	D	13.	C
4.	B	14.	B
5.	D	15.	B
6.	A	16.	C
7.	C	17.	C
8.	D	18.	B
9.	C	19.	B
10.	B	20.	B

EXAMINATION SECTION
TEST 1

DIRECTIONS: Each question or incomplete statement is followed by several suggested answers or completions. Select the one that BEST answers the question or completes the statement. *PRINT THE LETTER OF THE CORRECT ANSWER IN THE SPACE AT THE RIGHT.*

1. The problem with driving the car in neutral is that 1.____
   A. you lose needed motor control
   B. the car will not go fast enough
   C. the car would not ride as smooth
   D. you would not be able to go up a hill

2. At 40 MPH, you should allow _____ car lengths between your car and the one ahead. 2.____
   A. four   B. eight   C. twelve   D. sixteen

3. Your taillight must be visible at night for _____ feet. 3.____
   A. 200   B. 350   C. 500   D. 400

4. The driver's left hand and arm are extended upward. This hand signal means that the driver plans to 4.____
   A. turn left   B. turn right
   C. come to a stop   D. go straight ahead

5. Which of the following are used on some highways to direct drivers into the proper lanes for turns? 5.____
   A. Flashing red lights
   B. White lines on the side of the road
   C. White arrows sin the middle of the lanes
   D. Flashing yellow lights

6. When you want to overtake and pass another vehicle, you should 6.____
   A. change lanes quickly so the other driver will see you
   B. signal and pass when safe to do so
   C. wait for a signal from the other driver
   D. stay close behind so you need less time to pass

7. If you drive past your exit on an expressway, you should 7.____
   A. drive to the next exit and leave the expressway
   B. make a U-turn at the nearest emergency turn area
   C. make a U-turn at the next service area
   D. pull onto the shoulder, then back up to the exit

8. A flashing yellow light means
   A. come to a full stop
   B. proceed with caution
   C. merging traffic
   D. pedestrian crossing

   8.____

9. You are waiting in the intersection to complete a left turn. You should
   A. drive around the rear of a car if it blocks you
   B. signal and keep your wheels straight
   C. flash your headlights so the driver will let you get through
   D. signal and keep your wheels turned to the left

   9.____

10. Alcohol affects
    A. recovery from headlight glare
    B. judgment of distances
    C. reaction time
    D. all of the above

    10.____

11. A red and white triangular sign at an intersection means
    A. always come to a full stop at the intersection
    B. look both ways as you cross the intersection
    C. slow down and be prepared to stop if necessary
    D. slow down if an emergency vehicle is approaching

    11.____

12. When driving at 60 MPH, a driver will be able to stop his car in _____ feet.
    A. 67   B. 120   C. 190   D. 400

    12.____

13. After you have passed a car, you should return to the right lane when you
    A. see the front bumper of the other car in your mirror
    B. see the other car's headlights come on
    C. have put your turn signal on
    D. have turned your headlights on

    13.____

14. You may pass another vehicle on the right if it is waiting to
    A. park at the curb
    B. turn into a driveway on the right
    C. turn right
    D. turn left

    14.____

15. Expressways have *expressway entrance lanes* (acceleration lanes) so that drivers can
    A. reach the proper speed before blending with traffic
    B. test their brakes before driving at expressway speeds
    C. test the pickup of their cars
    D. stop at the end to wait for a traffic opening

    15.____

16. Night driving is dangerous because
    A. some traffic signs are less visible at night
    B. more vehicles are on the road at night
    C. street lights tend to blur our vision
    D. the distance we can see ahead is reduced

    16.____

17. Assuming that the street is level, after you have finished parallel parking in a space between two other cars, you should
    A. leave your front wheels turned toward the curb
    B. straighten your front wheels and leave room between cars
    C. move as far forward in the space as possible
    D. make sure your car almost touches the car behind you

17.____

18. You drive along a street and hear a siren. You cannot immediately see the emergency vehicle.
    You should
    A. pull to the curb until you are sure it is not on your street
    B. speed up and turn at the next intersection
    C. keep driving until you see the vehicle
    D. slow down but don't stop until you see it

18.____

19. If you leave ignition keys in an unattended vehicle,
    A. you must leave the meter running
    B. you commit a traffic infraction
    C. it is alright as long as you have your parking brake set
    D. you should leave them in the event the car has to be moved

19.____

20. The ones who ALWAYS have the right-of-way are
    A. motorists   B. pedestrians   C. cyclists   D. animals

20.____

21. On a road where there are no sidewalks, a pedestrian should walk
    A. on the shoulder of the road, facing traffic
    B. on the shoulder of the road, going with the traffic
    C. in the gutter alongside the road
    D. in the nearest clear space next to the road

21.____

22. To signal for help on the State Thruway,
    A. flash your headlights on and off
    B. flash your brake lights on and off
    C. tie a white cloth to the left-hand door handle of the car
    D. stand on the road and flag down the first oncoming car

22.____

23. The MAIN use to which a driver's horn should be put is
    A. to let the other driver know the light is green
    B. in passing other cars or as a warning
    C. if the driver is in a hurry
    D. so that pedestrians will give you the right-of-way

23.____

24. If a car is traveling at 40 MPH, it needs _____ feet to stop.
    A. 30   B. 67   C. 120   D. 190

24.____

4 (#1)

25. When a tire blows out, 25.____
    A. take your foot from the gas and hold the steering wheel as steadily as possible
    B. brake firmly until you bring the car to a stop
    C. disengage your clutch and use your brakes to reduce speed
    D. give more gas and hold the steering wheel as steadily as possible

---

KEY (CORRECT ANSWERS)

1.	A		11.	C
2.	A		12.	D
3.	C		13.	A
4.	B		14.	D
5.	C		15.	A
6.	B		16.	D
7.	A		17.	B
8.	B		18.	A
9.	B		19.	B
10.	D		20.	B

21.	A
22.	C
23.	B
24.	C
25.	A

TEST 2

DIRECTIONS: Each question or incomplete statement is followed by several suggested answers or completions. Select the one that BEST answers the question or completes the statement. *PRINT THE LETTER OF THE CORRECT ANSWER IN THE SPACE AT THE RIGHT.*

1. When a driver sees or hears a vehicle with a flashing red light on, siren blowing, or bell ringing, he should
    A. give it the right-of-way
    B. speed up and drive on
    C. stop in his lane
    D. stop and direct traffic, if there is no police officer

    1.____

2. When approaching a stopped school bus with red lights flashing, a driver should
    A. pass the bus with due caution
    B. pass the bus only on the left
    C. stop at least 8 feet behind and wait until the bus proceeds
    D. stop and then go if all is clear

    2.____

3. Before making a turn, a driver should signal for _____ feet.
    A. 50   B. 100   C. 150   D. 75

    3.____

4. The general rule with regard to right-of-way at intersections is that the car _____ has the right-of-way.
    A. going straight ahead   B. on the main road
    C. on the right   D. making a turn

    4.____

5. You should be _____ feet from a vehicle you are overtaking before switching your headlights to low beam.
    A. 100   B. 200   C. 250   D. 350

    5.____

6. Unless a sign indicates otherwise, a driver must park _____ feet from a fire hydrant.
    A. 5   B. 10   C. 15   D. 9

    6.____

7. When parking parallel to the curb, the wheels must be no more than _____ inches away.
    A. 6   B. 12   C. 18   D. 24

    7.____

8. If a police officer at an intersection gives a signal for you to proceed although the traffic signal is against you, the driver should obey
    A. the traffic signal   B. whichever he wants
    C. the police officer   D. the pedestrian who may be crossing

    8.____

9. An octagonal (8-sided) sign means to
    A. reduce speed   B. proceed with caution
    C. yield the right-of-way   D. stop and proceed with caution

    9.____

10. When approaching a flashing red traffic signal, a driver should 10.____
    A. proceed with caution   B. stop and then proceed with caution
    C. pull over to the side of the road   D. reduce speed

11. When nearing an intersection marked with a *Yield Right of Way* sign, the 11.____
    driver must
    A. yield the right-of-way to pedestrians
    B. yield the right-of-way to all commercial traffic
    C. yield the right-of-way to all horse-drawn vehicle
    D. slow down and allow all cross traffic to proceed before him

12. If a signal light changes from green to yellow as a driver nears an intersection, 12.____
    he should
    A. try to get through the intersection before the red light comes on
    B. prepare to stop
    C. keep his speed the same
    D. speed up and rush through the intersection

13. A flashing yellow or amber light differs in meaning from a flashing red light in 13.____
    that yellow means _____ while red means _____.
    A. proceed with caution; stop and then proceed
    B. try to stop; stop and then proceed
    C. proceed with caution; stop
    D. stop; proceed at will

14. Diamond-shaped signs indicate 14.____
    A. cattle crossing ahead
    B. stop and then proceed with caution
    C. reduce speed for curves, hills, or narrow bridges
    D. railroad crossing ahead

15. The rectangular (square) signs mean 15.____
    A. proceed with caution   B. railroad crossing ahead
    C. yield right-of-way   D. danger, slow down

16. A broken line painted on the highway means that a driver 16.____
    A. must not cross it at any time
    B. may cross it to pass provided traffic permits
    C. may cross it to pass, even on hills
    D. must not cross it on weekends

17. A double solid line on the highway means that a driver 17.____
    A. may cross it any time
    B. may cross it only if he is on the main road
    C. must never cross it
    D. must never cross it unless traffic permits

18. The highway sign shaped like an inverted pyramid means
    A. stop
    B. slow down, and proceed with
    C. danger
    D. yield right-of-way

19. The shape of the highway sign which means that a driver is approaching a railroad crossing is
    A. square   B. round   C. diamond   D. rectangular

20. A driver may follow a fire engine on its way to a fire _____ feet in a city, _____ feet in a rural area.
    A. 200; 500   B. 100; 500   C. 20; 400   D. 100; 50

21. Parking lights should be used when a driver
    A. is driving in well-lighted areas
    B. leaves the car parked in a driveway
    C. parks the car on a road facing traffic
    D. parks the car on a road going with the traffic

22. When passing a playground, park, or other area where children are playing or walking,
    A. stop and then proceed with caution
    B. slow down and proceed with caution
    C. blow horn and make sure they see you
    D. blow horn, stop, and then proceed with caution

23. If a driver is parked parallel to the curb on a busy street, he may open the doors on the traffic side
    A. when the traffic light turns red
    B. between the hours of sunrise and sunset
    C. if he looks very carefully
    D. when no traffic is approaching

24. When following another car on a superhighway,
    A. do not tailgate
    B. try to follow at the same speed
    C. watch out for littering
    D. make sure you do not lose sight of it

25. When driving in heavy fog at night, a driver should use his
    A. upper headlight beams   B. lower headlight beams
    C. uppers, in addition to fog lights   D. lowers, in addition to fog lights

26. A driver may drive at the MAXIMUM speed limit whenever
    A. his car is in good condition
    B. there is an emergency
    C. he is on a State road unless otherwise marked
    D. he is escorted by a state policeman

27. At night when you meet an oncoming vehicle with blinding, bright lights, the SAFEST action to take is to
    A. turn your head away so that you don't have to look at the lights
    B. cast your gaze at the right side of the road, stay near it and slow down
    C. put on your brightest lights so as to counteract his
    D. put on your dark glasses

28. To get a car out of a skid,
    A. press the gas gently as you turn the wheels in the direction of the skid
    B. press the brakes and try to stop the vehicle
    C. press the gas hard so as to pull out of the skid
    D. turn the wheels as fast as you can in the direction you want

29. A driver should stay at least _____ car length(s) behind the car ahead of him for every _____ MPH.
    A. 2; 20   B. 2; 10   C. 1; 20   D. 1; 10

30. A driver can avoid being poisoned by the monoxide gas from his exhaust by
    A. always making sure he keeps the car windows closed
    B. keeping a window of the car open to allow fresh air in
    C. making sure he always uses the best grade gasoline
    D. boring an extra hole in the exhaust pipe

KEY (CORRECT ANSWERS)

1.	A	11.	D	21.	C
2.	C	12.	B	22.	B
3.	B	13.	A	23.	D
4.	C	14.	C	24.	A
5.	B	15.	A	25.	B
6.	C	16.	B	26.	C
7.	B	17.	C	27.	B
8.	C	18.	D	28.	A
9.	D	19.	B	29.	D
10.	B	20.	A	30.	B

EXAMINATION SECTION
TEST 1

DIRECTIONS: Each question or incomplete statement is followed by several suggested answers or completions. Select the one that BEST answers the question or completes the statement. *PRINT THE LETTER OF THE CORRECT ANSWER IN THE SPACE AT THE RIGHT.*

1. Your car's brakes transform one type of energy into another. Which of the following BEST describes the change?

    A. Kinetic energy into heat
    B. Centrifugal force into force of impact
    C. Gravity into kinetic energy
    D. Centrifugal force into heat

2. Which of the following qualities is MOST important in driving a motor vehicle?

    A. Fast reaction time
    B. Courage
    C. Skill
    D. Judgment

3. Glaring headlights add to night driving hazards. Which of the following should you NOT do?

    A. Lower your headlight beams in advance of meeting other cars
    B. Reduce your speed when facing headlight glare
    C. Focus your eyes downward on the center line of the road instead of up into the oncoming lights
    D. Lower your headlight beams when following another car

4. The following institutions lend money for the purchase of cars. Which charges the LOWEST rate of interest?

    A. Banks
    B. Pawnshops
    C. Installment finance companies
    D. Personal loan companies

5. Under what conditions do we find the GREATEST traction?

    A. Wet concrete pavement
    B. Dry concrete pavement
    C. Dry concrete pavement with sand on it
    D. Bumpy, uneven pavement

6. Your danger zone is

    A. the longest distance at which you can see and recognize danger
    B. your stopping distance
    C. the distance at which a vehicle in back of your car is following
    D. your braking distance

7. For sound financing of a purchase of an automobile, you would have to raise a down payment of AT LEAST _____ of the value of the car.

   A. 10 percent
   B. 25 percent
   C. one-third
   D. one-half

8. Which of the following is characteristic of older paved roads and not of modern highways?

   A. Median strips
   B. High road crowns
   C. Road banking
   D. Long sight distances

9. Designed especially for slowing down to prepare to leave the freeway is the

   A. deceleration lane
   B. median strip
   C. ramp
   D. road shoulder

10. When you find yourself getting very sleepy while driving on a long trip, the BEST remedy is

    A. black coffee
    B. fresh air
    C. Benzedrine
    D. sleep

11. Which of these four types of insurance does a bank or other lender require the purchaser to have?

    A. Collision
    B. Comprehensive
    C. Liability
    D. Medical payment

12. The professional specialist who plans the operation of highways is the

    A. Commissioner of Motor Vehicles
    B. highway engineer
    C. traffic engineer
    D. Commissioner of State Police

13. Which of the following is the CORRECT formula?

    A. Braking distance + stopping distance = reaction distance
    B. Reaction distance + stopping distance = braking distance
    C. Reaction distance + braking distance = stopping distance
    D. Reaction distance + danger zone = stopping distance

14. Which of the following is a YIELD sign?

    A.   B.   C.   D.

15. When you drive around a curve, which of the following helps you to do it safely?

    A. Centrifugal force
    B. Friction
    C. Kinetic energy
    D. Force of impact

16. If you are involved in an accident, which of the following things should you NOT do? 16._____

    A. Show your driver's license and vehicle registration card and make note of the information on those of the driver of the other car.
    B. If any person seems to be seriously injured, place him in your car immediately and proceed at once to the nearest hospital.
    C. Submit accident reports as indicated by your state and local regulations.
    D. Notify your insurance company.

17. No person should drive in dense fog unless it is absolutely necessary. When it does prove necessary, he should use 17._____

    A. parking lights
    B. high-beam headlights
    C. low-beam headlights
    D. no lights, to avoid distortion of vision

18. Under which of the following would you classify the wearing of glasses to aid vision? 18._____

    A. Compensation
    B. Field of vision
    C. Correction
    D. Adjustment

19. The key words for driving on a slippery surface are 19._____

    A. firmly and accurately
    B. gently and gradually
    C. strongly and steadily
    D. quickly and surely

20. Which of the following types of insurance is MOST important to a car owner? 20._____

    A. Collision
    B. Liability
    C. Comprehensive
    D. Medical payment

KEY (CORRECT ANSWERS)

1.	C	11.	A
2.	D	12.	C
3.	D	13.	C
4.	A	14.	D
5.	B	15.	A
6.	B	16.	B
7.	C	17.	C
8.	B	18.	C
9.	A	19.	B
10.	D	20.	B

TEST 2

DIRECTIONS: Each question or incomplete statement is followed by several suggested answers or completions. Select the one that BEST answers the question or completes the statement. *PRINT THE LETTER OF THE CORRECT ANSWER IN THE SPACE AT THE RIGHT.*

1. Which of these four items is a *grade separation*? 1.____

   A. A divided highway
   B. A change in the slope of a hill
   C. Bushes planted between two roadways on which traffic moves in opposite directions
   D. A cloverleaf

2. Which of the following blood alcohol concentrations should be used to establish that a driver is *under the influence of alcohol*? 2.____

   A. 0.05%   B. 0.10%   C. 0.15%   D. 0.6%

3. Three of the following four statements are true of freeways. Which statement is NOT true? 3.____

   A. They have a limited number of interchanges at which vehicles may enter or leave the freeway.
   B. They have a limited number of STOP and GO signals.
   C. Traffic moving in opposite directions is not separated by a median strip.
   D. Crossing the median strip is not permitted.

4. To correct a skid, you should 4.____

   A. steer in the direction in which the rear of the car is skidding
   B. steer in the direction opposite that in which the rear of the car is skidding
   C. hold the steering wheel firmly in the straight-ahead position
   D. use the parking or handbrake so that only the rear wheels will lock while the front wheels turn freely

5. The MOST dangerous effects of alcohol on the driver are those concerned with 5.____

   A. vision
   B. reaction time
   C. behavior
   D. coordination and driving skill

6. The *Three E's* of traffic safety are included in the following four words. Which of them is NOT one of the *Three E's*? 6.____

   A. Education   B. Engineering
   C. Enforcement   D. Efficiency

7. Which of the following BEST describes the true meaning of the word *courage*? 7.____

   A. Ability to overcome fear
   B. Absence of fear
   C. Taking chances to gain a reputation as a daredevil
   D. Lack of realization of the true nature of danger

8. Which of the following types of insurance is of GREATEST importance to you when you own a car?   8.____

   A. Liability
   B. Collision
   C. Comprehensive
   D. Medical payment

9. Which of the following statements is NOT correct?   9.____

   A. Most states have legalized the use of electric directional signals to signal turns.
   B. Overheating is always due to failures in the cooling system.
   C. Power brakes do not decrease the stopping distance.
   D. The horn should never be sounded except in the interest of safety.

10. Three of the following are good safety features. Which is NOT a safety feature?   10.____

    A. Door locks
    B. Rear-view mirror inside the car
    C. Eye-level outside mirror
    D. Ventilation of the inside of the car

11. The MOST important factor in good car maintenance is   11.____

    A. an honest, dependable service station or garage
    B. a skilled mechanic
    C. high quality, reliable parts
    D. a responsible car owner

12. Three of the following procedures will add to tire traction in starting your car on ice. Which one will NOT help?   12.____

    A. Letting some air out of the rear tires
    B. Sprinkling sand on the ice
    C. Slipping the clutch
    D. Feeding gas more gently and more gradually

13. The four-stroke cycle includes THREE of the following. Which of the following is NOT part of the cycle? _____ stroke.   13.____

    A. Intake
    B. Compression
    C. Power
    D. Completion

14. Vehicles A, C, and D in the illustration shown at the right have stopped to allow vehicle B to turn.
    Which vehicle, A, C, or D, would be the FIRST to cross the intersection, considering right-of-way rules?   14.____

    A. A
    B. C
    C. D
    D. None of the above

15. What part of the cost of planning, designing, and constructing the National System of Interstate and Defense Highways is paid for by Federal-aid funds?   15.____

    A. 90%   B. 50%   C. 10%   D. 100%

16. When you leave a freeway and drive on a city street, you must check your speed frequently because you may be   16.____

    A. accelerated
    B. suffering from highway hypnosis
    C. velocitized
    D. suffering impairment of vision due to carbon monoxide

17. Which of the following statements is CORRECT?   17.____

    A. Certain drugs, like Benzedrine in *keep-awake* pills, actually make driving at night safe.
    B. A driver should trust no one but a physician to determine whether or not he should drive after taking any kind of drug.
    C. The Federal Food and Drug Act does not permit the sale of any drug dangerous to a driver without a prescription from a registered physician.
    D. The individual driver must rely entirely upon his judgment and knowledge of how a specific drug will affect him.

18. Three of the following four maintenance procedures are good.   18.____
    Which is NOT a good procedure?

    A. Rotate your tires to avoid uneven wear.
    B. Avoid letting oil or gasoline come into contact with your tires.
    C. For driving in very hot weather, underinflate your tires to avoid building up excessive pressure in them.
    D. Keep the battery terminals covered with a light layer of grease.

19. Drivers should be able to recognize traffic signs by their shape.   19.____
    Which of the following signs warns drivers that they are approaching a railroad grade crossing?

    A.   B.   C.   D.

20. Imagine that the steering wheel is the face of a clock.   20.____
    The driver's hands should grasp it at _____ and _____ o'clock.

    A. 8; 4   B. 9; 3   C. 10; 2   D. 11; 1

KEY (CORRECT ANSWERS)

1. D
2. A
3. B
4. A
5. D

6. C
7. A
8. A
9. B
10. C

11. C
12. A
13. D
14. C
15. A

16. C
17. B
18. C
19. B
20. C

EXAMINATION SECTION
TEST 1

DIRECTIONS: Each question or incomplete statement is followed by several suggested answers or completions. Select the one that BEST answers the question or completes the statement. *PRINT THE LETTER OF THE CORRECT ANSWER IN THE SPACE AT THE RIGHT.*

1. You are driving in the middle lane on a three-lane expressway; a car begins to pass you on the right.
   The actions of that driver are
   A. *permissible* if there are no signs that forbid passing on the right
   B. *impermissible* because he is passing you in your blind spot
   C. *impermissible* because *pass to the left* is a firm rule
   D. *permissible* as long as he does it on a limited access highway

   1.____

2. The driver's left hand and arm are extended downward.
   This hand signal means that the driver plans to
   A. turn right   B. stop
   C. go straight ahead   D. turn left

   2.____

3. The driver's left hand and arm are extended upward.
   This hand signal means that the driver plans to
   A. go straight ahead   B. come to a stop
   C. turn right   D. turn left

   3.____

4. You have the right-of-way when you are
   A. entering a traffic circle   B. leaving a parking space
   C. already in a traffic circle   D. backing out of a private driveway

   4.____

5. You MUST yield the right-of-way to an approaching vehicle
   A. turning left   B. already in a traffic circle
   C. already in an intersection D. going straight ahead

   5.____

6. You come to an intersection which is blocked by other traffic.
   You should
   A. get as close as possible to the other car
   B. sound your horn to make the cars move up
   C. stay out of the intersection until you can pass through
   D. go slowly until the traffic ahead moves

   6.____

7.

Figure number 3 shown above is the shape of the _____ sign.
A. stop
B. railroad crossing
C. road hazard
D. yield

8. What does a *stop* sign mean?
A. Roll carefully through the intersection to avoid traffic
B. Stop only when cars are approaching you
C. Stop only for traffic on an intersecting road
D. Come to a full stop, then go when it is safe to do so

9. What are the colors of a *stop* sign? _____ letters on a _____ background
A. White; green
B. Black; yellow
C. Yellow; black
D. White; red

10. As you get near the intersection, the traffic light changes from green to yellow. You should
A. stop in the center of the intersection if the light turns red
B. speed up to beat the red light
C. stop at the intersection even if the light is still yellow
D. slow down and get ready to stop if the light turns red

11. A traffic light which has a green arrow and a red light means
A. wait for a green light, then move only as the arrow points
B. move only as the arrow points
C. vehicles moving in any direction must stop
D. move immediately straight or as the arrow points

12. You may cross a double solid yellow line to
A. pass a slow moving truck
B. pass a car if traffic is light
C. turn around if you want to go the other way
D. turn into a driveway

13. What does a single solid white line in the highway mean? Cross it
A. *only* to turn into a driveway
B. when it is safe to do so
C. whenever it is necessary to do so
D. *only* to make a U-turn

14. What does a NO STOPPING sign mean? You may
A. stop when ordered to do so by a policeman
B. not stop for longer than 5 minutes
C. stop long enough to unload packages
D. not stop your vehicle at all

15. You can NEVER park   15.____
    A. in a crosswalk   B. at the entrance of a building
    C. on a one-way street   D. within 50 feet of a fire hydrant

16. A blind person legally has the right-of-way when he is   16.____
    A. helped by another person
    B. wearing light-colored clothing
    C. wearing black-lens glasses
    D. being led by a seeing-eye dog or using a white cane

17. On a road which has no sidewalks, a pedestrian should walk on the   17.____
    A. side of the road facing oncoming traffic
    B. side of the road which has the lightest traffic
    C. same side of the road as traffic is moving
    D. right side of the road

18. One of the rules of defensive driving is to   18.____
    A. maintain confidence that you can avoid danger at the last minute
    B. know what is going on around you as you drive
    C. look straight ahead as you drive
    D. feel assured that other drivers will make up for your errors

19. Why is driving on an expressway different from driving on an ordinary street?   19.____
    A. Your field of vision is narrowed at high speeds.
    B. You must get used to high speed driving.
    C. Trucks have to go slower on the expressways.
    D. Motorcycle can be used only in the right lane.

20. You have just left an expressway and are starting to drive on an ordinary   20.____
    highway.
    You should
    A. stay twice as far behind other cars
    B. check your speedometer to keep at the lower speed limit
    C. change gradually to the lower speed limit
    D. check your tires for correct pressure

KEY (CORRECT ANSWERS)

1.	A	11.	B
2.	B	12.	D
3.	C	13.	B
4.	C	14.	A
5.	A	15.	A
6.	C	16.	D
7.	A	17.	A
8.	D	18.	B
9.	D	19.	B
10.	D	20.	B

TEST 2

DIRECTIONS: Each question or incomplete statement is followed by several suggested answers or completions. Select the one that BEST answers the question or completes the statement. *PRINT THE LETTER OF THE CORRECT ANSWER IN THE SPACE AT THE RIGHT.*

1. You may pass another vehicle on the right if it is waiting to
   A. turn into a driveway on the right   B. park at the curb
   C. turn right   D. turn left

   1.____

2. When you want to overtake and pass another vehicle, you should
   A. stay closely behind so you may need less time to pass
   B. change lanes quickly so the other driver will see you
   C. wait for a signal from the other driver
   D. signal and pass when safe to do so

   2.____

3. In general, you should pass vehicles going in the same direction as you are going
   A. at intersections where you have more space
   B. on the right
   C. on the left
   D. whenever you have the opportunity to do so

   3.____

4. You drive along a street and hear a siren, but you cannot immediately see the emergency vehicle.
   You should
   A. slow down but don't stop until you see it
   B. speed up and turn at the next intersection
   C. keep driving until you see the vehicle
   D. pull to the curb until you are sure it is not on your street

   4.____

5. What should you do when you are going to enter a highway from a private road?
   A. Yield the right-of-way to highway traffic or pedestrians.
   B. Stop completely even if there is no traffic.
   C. Stop with part of the car on the highway to warn other drivers.
   D. Drive out fast to keep up with other cars.

   5.____

6. Your car and another car both reach an intersection at the same time. There is no traffic signal.
   Which vehicle has the right-of-way?
   The car
   A. making a turn   B. on the left   C. on the right   D. opposite you

   6.____

7. [figure: row of shapes numbered 1–5: diamond, inverted triangle, octagon, rectangle, circle]

Figure number 2 shown above is the shape of the _____ sign.
A. yield   B. stop   C. road hazard   D. speed limit

8. What does a YIELD sign mean?
A. Look both ways as you cross the intersection.
B. Always come to a full stop at the intersection.
C. Slow down and be prepared to stop if necessary.
D. Slow down if an emergency vehicle is approaching.

9. You come to an intersection which has a flashing red light. You should
A. stop only if cars are already in the intersection
B. go through the intersection slowly
C. stop only if cars are approaching the intersection
D. come to a full stop, then go when safe to do so

10. You may cross a single broken white line ONLY
A. when you will not interfere with traffic
B. on the order of a policeman
C. when the car in front is disabled
D. to make a U-turn

11. The road is marked with a single solid yellow line and a broken white line next to it; the broken white line is on your side of the solid yellow line. You may cross
A. if the traffic is clear
B. only at an intersection
C. if you are on an expressway
D. only in an emergency

12. What should you do after you have finished backing your car into a parallel parking space between two other cars? (Assume that the street is on level ground.)
A. Leave your front wheels turned toward the road.
B. Straighten your front wheels and leave room between cars.
C. Make sure your car almost touches the car behind you.
D. Move as far forward in the space as possible.

13. You are parking your car on the right side of a street, the car is facing downhill, and there is no curb.
You should set the parking brake and ALSO
A. turn the front wheels to the left
B. park on the shoulder
C. point the front wheels straight
D. turn the front wheels to the right

14. When can motorcycles ride three abreast in the same traffic lane? 14.____
    A. During daylight hours   B. On an open highway
    C. At no time   D. On a city street

15. Minimum speed signs are designed to 15.____
    A. test future traffic signal needs   B. show current local road conditions
    C. keep traffic flowing smoothly   D. assure pedestrian safety

16. When there is no posted speed limit in the state, what is the FASTEST you may drive? 16.____
    A. 55   B. 65   C. 60   D. 40

17. Expressways have *expressway entrance lanes* (acceleration lines) so that drivers can 17.____
    A. pass slower moving vehicles
    B. test their brakes before driving at expressway speeds
    C. reach the proper speed before entering traffic
    D. test the pickup of their cars

18. If you drive past your exit on an expressway, you should 18.____
    A. make a U-turn at the next service area
    B. pull onto the shoulder, then back up to the exit
    C. drive to the next exit and get off the highway
    D. make a U-turn at the nearest emergency turn area

19. You are getting on a highway which has a very short entrance lane. The SAFEST way for you to enter the flow of traffic would be to 19.____
    A. use the left lane of the highway to get up cruising speed
    B. wait for a large gap in traffic, then speed up quickly
    C. get up to cruising speed gradually soother cars will see you
    D. use as much ramp as possible to get up to cruising speed

20. When you get ready to leave an expressway, you should begin to use your turn signal _____ the exit lane. 20.____
    A. when you see cars behind you in
    B. before you reach
    C. once you are in
    D. just as you get to

KEY (CORRECT ANSWERS)

1.	D	11.	A
2.	D	12.	B
3.	C	13.	D
4.	D	14.	C
5.	A	15.	C
6.	C	16.	B
7.	A	17.	C
8.	C	18.	C
9.	D	19.	B
10.	A	20.	B

TEST 3

DIRECTIONS: Each question or incomplete statement is followed by several suggested answers or completions. Select the one that BEST answers the question or completes the statement. *PRINT THE LETTER OF THE CORRECT ANSWER IN THE SPACE AT THE RIGHT.*

1. In which of the following situations is passing ALWAYS forbidden? 1.____
   A. The vehicle ahead is making a left turn
   B. You are on a one-way street which has two lanes
   C. When a pedestrian is in a crosswalk
   D. The vehicle ahead is going to park parallel to the curb

2. After you have passed a car, you should return to the right lane when you 2.____
   A. have turned your headlights on
   B. see the other car's headlights come on
   C. have put your turn signal on
   D. see the front bumper of the other car in your mirror

3. You are driving outside of the city and you see a school bus which is stopped and its red lights are flashing. 3.____
   You may
   A. pass if no children are on the road
   B. pass if it is on the other side of a divided highway
   C. not pass if you are behind it
   D. not pass while the lights flash

4. You are waiting in the intersection to complete a left turn. 4.____
   You should
   A. signal and keep your wheels turned to the left
   B. flash your headlights so the driver will let you get through
   C. signal and keep your wheels straight
   D. drive around the rear of a car if it blocks you

5. You want to turn left at an intersection. The light is green, but oncoming traffic is heavy. 5.____
   You should
   A. use the next intersection
   B. take the right-of-way since you have the light
   C. wait at the crosswalk for traffic to clear
   D. wait in the intersection for traffic to clear

6. You are driving on a street that several driveways on your right. You want to turn right at the next intersection. 6.____
   You should begin to use your turn signal
   A. at least 100 feet before the turn
   B. as soon as you get to the intersection where you want to turn
   C. as soon as you see cars behind you
   D. about halfway down the street

Questions 7-9.

DIRECTIONS: Questions 7 through 9 are to be answered on the basis of the traffic signs shown below.

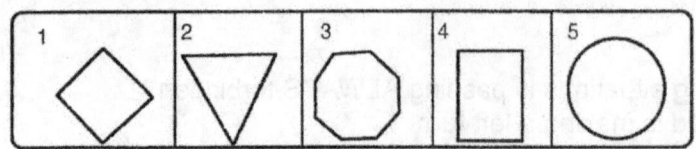

7. Figure number 5 shown above is the shape of the _____ sign.
   A. road hazard   B. stop   C. yield   D. railroad crossing

8. Figure number 4 shown above is the shape of the _____ sign.
   A. no U turn
   B. road hazard
   C. railroad crossing
   D. stop

9. Figure number 4 shown above is the shape of the _____ sign.
   A. railroad crossing
   B. stop
   C. no parking
   D. road hazard

10. What does a flashing yellow light mean?
    A. Come to a full stop
    B. Proceed with caution
    C. Pedestrian crossing
    D. Merging traffic

11. A solid white line on the right edge of the highway slants in towards your left. This means that
    A. you will be required to turn left just ahead
    B. there is an intersection just ahead
    C. you are approaching a construction area
    D. the road will get narrower

12. Which of the following is used on some highways to direct drivers into the proper lanes for turns?
    A. Flashing red lights
    B. White arrows in the middle of the lanes
    C. White lines on the side of the road
    D. Flashing yellow lights

13. Which of the following should you do after parking your vehicle on level ground?
    A. Apply the parking or emergency brake
    B. Put the car in drive or firsts gear
    C. Turn the wheels to the right
    D. Leave the wheels straight

14. You are parking facing uphill on the right side of the street, and there is a curb on the right side.
    You should leave the car with the front wheels
    A. turned to the left with the shift lever in neutral
    B. straight with the parking brake set on
    C. turned to the right with the shift lever in park
    D. turned to the left and set the parking brake

14.____

15. If you are parked parallel to the curb, you may get out of the car on the traffic side
    A. during the daytime when other drivers can see you
    B. when you won't interfere with oncoming vehicles
    C. if you use your four-way flasher first
    D. when the traffic light at the closest intersection turns red

15.____

16. When are motorcycle operators required to use signals?
    For
    A. stops only
    B. all turns and stops
    C. turns only
    D. left turns and stops only

16.____

17. A safe speed to drive your car
    A. is the posted speed limit
    B. depends on the weather and road conditions
    C. is less than the posted speed limit
    D. depends on the mechanical skill of the driver

17.____

18. What does alcohol do to your driving skills and judgment?
    It
    A. harms both driving skills and judgment
    B. has no effect on either driving skills or judgment
    C. has no effect on judgment, but it harms driving skills
    D. helps your driving skills but harms your judgment

18.____

19. Night driving is dangerous because
    A. more vehicles are on the road at night
    B. the distance we can see ahead is reduced
    C. some traffic signs are less visible at night
    D. street lights tend to blur our vision

19.____

20. In order to drive with the same margin of safety at night as in the daytime, it is MOST important for you to
    A. be ready to brake more quickly
    B. use your high beams at all times
    C. reduce your driving speed
    D. watch for cars at intersections

20.____

KEY (CORRECT ANSWERS)

1.	C	11.	D
2.	D	12.	B
3.	D	13.	A
4.	C	14.	D
5.	D	15.	B
6.	A	16.	B
7.	D	17.	B
8.	A	18.	A
9.	C	19.	B
10.	B	20.	C

TEST 4

DIRECTIONS: Each question or incomplete statement is followed by several suggested answers or completions. Select the one that BEST answers the question or completes the statement. *PRINT THE LETTER OF THE CORRECT ANSWER IN THE SPACE AT THE RIGHT.*

1. You are driving outside of the city. A school bus is stopped with its red lights flashing, and the driver waves you on.
   You may
   A. wait until the bus moves, then drive by
   B. drive by the bus slowly or carefully
   C. drive by slowly as soon as the lights go off
   D. drive by the bus if you are on a divided highway

2. The car behind you wants to pass.
   You should
   A. maintain your speed so traffic will flow smoothly
   B. slow down slightly and stay in your lane
   C. blow your horn to allow him to pass
   D. pull to the right and stop so he can pass

3. If you are in the left lane on an expressway and you see cars coming up behind, you should
   A. pull to the right lane as soon as it is safe
   B. continue driving at the speed limit
   C. motion to the drivers to pass you on the right
   D. speed up to keep traffic moving smoothly

4. Before you make any turn, you should
   A. signal two car lengths before the turn
   B. maintain your normal speed
   C. look around to make sure it is safe to turn
   D. honk your horn to warn other drivers

5. When you want to make a right turn, your car must be
   A. near the center of the street
   B. close to the right side of the street
   C. close to the left side of the street
   D. past the center of the intersection when you begin to turn

6. You are making a left turn from a two-way street into a one-way street.
   When you have completed the turn, your car should be in
   A. either the right or left lane, depending on traffic
   B. the left lane of the street
   C. the right lane of the street
   D. the center of the street, between the two lanes

49

Questions 7-8.

DIRECTIONS: Questions 7 and 8 are to be answered on the basis of the traffic signs shown below.

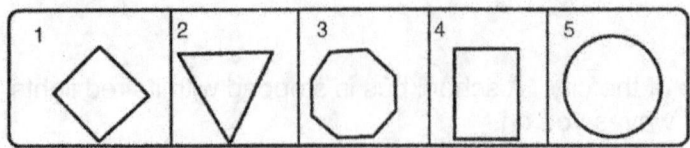

7. Figure number 4 shown above is the shape of the _____ sign.
   A. stop   B. yield   C. speed limit   D. railroad crossing

8. Figure number 1 shown above is the shape of the _____ sign.
   A. speed limit
   B. road hazard
   C. railroad crossing
   D. yield

9. What are the colors of a sign which tells you the distance to the next exit of a highway?
   _____ with _____ letters
   A. Yellow; black
   B. Red; white
   C. Black; white
   D. Green; white

10. Which of the following MUST you obey over the other three?
    A
    A. steady red light
    B. policeman
    C. flashing red light
    D. stop sign

11. An intersection has a stop sign, crosswalk, but no stop line. You MUST stop
    A. with your front wheels in the crosswalk
    B. before the crosswalk
    C. 50 feet before the intersection
    D. where you think the stop line would be

12. Before you leave a parking space which is parallel to the curb, you should
    A. sound your horn
    B. turn on your four-way flasher
    C. look for traffic by turning your head
    D. look for traffic by using your inside rear-view mirror

13. You want to back out of your driveway but you see children playing nearby. Before you start to move your car, you should
    A. race your motor to warn the children that you are moving
    B. walk to the back of the car to be sure the way is clear
    C. sound your horn so the children will hear you
    D. tell the children to stay away from the driveway

14. What does a *slow moving vehicle* emblem look like? 14.____
    A _____ sign.
    A. diamond-shaped yellow
    B. round green
    C. square red
    D. triangular orange

15. If you become drowsy while on a long drive, 15.____
    A. move your eyes from side to side to change your view
    B. slow down so you will be able to react better
    C. stop at a rest area and take a short walk
    D. turn on your car radio

16. On long trips, you can prevent drowsiness by 16.____
    A. turning on your car radio
    B. moving your eyes from side to side as you drive
    C. slowing down so you can react better
    D. stopping at regular intervals for a rest

17. Seat belts can be MOST effective as injury preventive devices when they are worn by 17.____
    A. passengers when they are on a long drive
    B. all occupants of a car being driven on an expressway
    C. the person driving the car
    D. passengers and the driver whenever they are in the car

18. When you drive at night, you can reduce the problem of glare from the headlights of an approaching car by 18.____
    A. looking at a spot on the lower edge of the steering wheel
    B. wearing glasses with lightly tinted lenses
    C. looking to the lower right side of your lane
    D. having the inside lights on to make the amount of light equal

19. When you drive at night on the open highway, you should use your low beam headlights when 19.____
    A. the sky is not completely dark
    B. approaching an intersection
    C. following closely behind another vehicle
    D. street lights are provided

20. Your car starts to skid on a slipper road. 20.____
    You should
    A. steer away from the skid and pump the brakes
    B. steer the same way as the rear of the car is skidding
    C. pump your brakes with light taps on the pedal
    D. brake quickly and the wheel straight

KEY (CORRECT ANSWERS)

1. B   11. B
2. B   12. C
3. A   13. B
4. C   14. D
5. B   15. C

6. B   16. D
7. C   17. D
8. B   18. C
9. D   19. C
10. B   20. B

TEST 5

DIRECTIONS: Each question or incomplete statement is followed by several suggested answers or completions. Select the one that BEST answers the question or completes the statement. *PRINT THE LETTER OF THE CORRECT ANSWER IN THE SPACE AT THE RIGHT.*

1. What are the colors of a *stop* sign? _____ letters on a _____ background.
   A. White; green
   B. Yellow; black
   C. White; red
   D. Black; yellow

   1.____

2. Figure number 4 shown above is the shape of the _____ sign.
   A. stop
   B. railroad crossing
   C. no parking
   D. road hazard

   2.____

3. What does a *no stopping* sign mean? You may
   A. stop long enough to unload packages
   B. not stop your vehicle at all
   C. stop when ordered to do so by a policeman
   D. not stop for longer than 5 minutes

   3.____

4. Which of the following statements applies to all driving emergency situations?
   A. Always slow down gradually
   B. Don't panic
   C. Apply your brakes immediately
   D. Your first reaction is the best reaction

   4.____

5. When braking on a slippery road, you should
   A. pump the brakes with light taps
   B. shift to a lower gear and not use the brakes
   C. apply the brakes firmly
   D. shift into neutral and not use the brakes

   5.____

6. Before you leave a parking space which is parallel to the curb, you should
   A. turn on your four-way flasher
   B. look for traffic by turning your head
   C. look for traffic by using your inside rear-view mirror
   D. sound your horn

   6.____

7. In addition to signaling, before you make any turn, you should
   A. honk your horn to warn other drivers
   B. maintain your normal speed
   C. flash your headlights
   D. look around to make sure it is safe to turn

   7.____

53

8. What should you do when you are going to enter a highway from a private road?
   A. Yield the right-of-way to highway traffic or pedestrians
   B. Stop with part of the car on the highway to warn other drivers
   C. Drive out fast to keep up with other cars
   D. Stop completely even if there is no traffic

8.____

9. When you drive at night, you can reduce the problem of glare from the headlights of an approaching car by
   A. looking at a spot on the lower edge of the steering wheel
   B. looking to the lower right side of your lane
   C. having the inside lights on to make the amount of light equal
   D. wearing glasses with lightly tinted lenses

9.____

10. The driver's left hand and arm is extended downward. His hand signal means that the driver plans to
    A. stop
    B. go straight ahead
    C. turn left
    D. turn right

10.____

11. You are driving outside the city. A school bus is stopped with its red lights flashing, and the driver waves you on.
    You may
    A. wait until the bus moves, then drive by
    B. drive by the bus slowly
    C. drive by the bus if you are on a divided highway
    D. drive by slowly as soon as the lights go off

11.____

12. What does a single solid white line in the highway mean?
    Cross it
    A. whenever it is necessary to do so
    B. when it is safe to do so
    C. only to make a U-turn
    D. only to turn into a driveway

12.____

13. What does a flashing yellow light mean?
    A. Merging traffic
    B. Come to a full stop
    C. Pedestrian crossing
    D. Proceed with caution

13.____

14. Which of the following must you obey over the other three?
    A
    A. police officer
    B. flashing red light
    C. steady red light
    D. stop sign

14.____

15. You may NEVER park
    A. on a one-way street
    B. at the entrance of a building
    C. in a crosswalk
    D. within 50 feet of a fire hydrant

15.____

16. When you drive in heavy fog during daylight hours, you should drive with your
    A. headlights off
    B. headlights on low beam
    C. headlights on high beam
    D. parking lights on

16.____

3 (#5)

17. You must yield the right-of-way to an approaching vehicle when you are   17._____
    A. already in an intersection   B. going straight ahead
    C. already in a traffic circle   D. turning left

18. You drive along a street and hear a siren. You cannot immediately see the   18._____
    emergency vehicle.
    You should
    A. pull to the curb until you are sure it is not on your street
    B. slow down but do not stop until you see it
    C. speed up and turn at the next intersection
    D. keep driving until you see the vehicle

19. If you drive past your exit on an expressway, you should   19._____
    A. make a U-turn at the next service area
    B. drive to the next exit and get off the highway
    C. pull onto the shoulder, then back up to the exit
    D. make a U-turn at the nearest emergency turn area

20. The car behind you wants to pass.   20._____
    You should
    A. blow your horn to allow him to pass
    B. pull to the right and stop so he can pass
    C. slow down slightly and stay in your lane
    D. maintain your speed so traffic will flow smoothly

KEY (CORRECT ANSWERS)

1.	C	11.	B
2.	C	12.	B
3.	C	13.	D
4.	B	14.	A
5.	A	15.	C
6.	B	16.	B
7.	D	17.	D
8.	A	18.	A
9.	B	19.	B
10.	A	20.	C

EXAMINATION SECTION
TEST 1

DIRECTIONS: Each question or incomplete statement is followed by several suggested answers or completions. Select the one that BEST answers the question or completes the statement. *PRINT THE LETTER OF THE CORRECT ANSWER IN THE SPACE AT THE RIGHT.*

Questions 1-9.

DIRECTIONS: Questions 1 through 9, inclusive, are based on the STATE MOTOR VEHICLE BUREAU'S POINT SYSTEM given below. Read this point carefully before answering these items.

STATE MOTOR VEHICLE BUREAU'S POINT SYSTEM

The newly revised point system was effective April 1. After that date, a driver having offenses resulting in an accumulation of eight points within two years, ten points within three years, or twelve points within four years, is to be summoned for a hearing which may result in the loss of his license. Under the point system, three points are charged for speeding, two points for passing a red light or crossing a double line or failing to stop at a stop sign, one and a half points for inoperative horn or insufficient lights, and one point for improper turn or failure to notify Bureau of change of address. The Commissioner of Motor Vehicles is required to revoke a driver's license if he has three speeding violations in a period of 18 months, or drives while intoxicated or leaves the scene of an accident or makes a false statement in his application for a driver's license. This system is necessary because studies show violations of traffic laws cause four out of five fatal accidents in the state.

1. The traffic offense which calls for license revocation if repeated three times within a period of 1½ years is
   A. passing a red light
   B. passing a stop sign
   C. crossing a double line
   D. speeding

   1.____

2. The individual who has the power to revoke a driver's license is the
   A. traffic officer
   B. motor vehicle inspector
   C. Commissioner of Motor Vehicles
   D. Traffic Commissioner

   2.____

3. Crossing a double line has a penalty of twice as many points as for
   A. making an improper turn
   B. speeding
   C. passing a red light
   D. an inoperative horn

   3.____

4. Failure of a driver to properly notify the Bureau of Motor Vehicles of a change in his address carries a penalty of _____ point(s).
   A. ½   B. 1   C. 1½   D. 2

   4.____

5. The point system is specifically designed to penalize the driver who
   A. is inexperienced
   B. repeatedly violates traffic laws
   C. is overage
   D. ignores parking violations

   5.____

6. A false statement on a driver's license application calls for a penalty of
   A. 10 points
   B. 8 points
   C. license suspension
   D. license revocation

7. Insufficient lights carries a penalty of _____ point(s).
   A. ½
   B. 1
   C. 1½
   D. 2

8. A driver is summoned for a hearing if, within a period of three years, he accumulates _____ points.
   A. 6
   B. 8
   C. 10
   D. 12

9. The percentage of fatal accidents caused by traffic violations is
   A. 80%
   B. 70%
   C. 60%
   D. 50%

Questions 10-11.

DIRECTIONS: Questions 10 and 11 are to be answered ONLY according to the information given in the following passage.

The State Vehicle and Traffic law was changed effective October 1, 2005 to provide for all new driving licenses to be issued on a six-month probationary basis. The probationary license will be cancelled if during this six-month period the driver is found guilty of tailgating, speeding, reckless driving, or driving while his ability is impaired by alcohol. The license will also be cancelled if the driver is found guilty of two other moving violations. If a probationary license is cancelled, the driver must wait for sixty days after the date of cancellation before applying for another license; and if the application is approved, the applicant must meet certain additional requirements including a new road test before a new license will be issued.

10. It is MOST reasonable to assume that the main purpose of the change in the law referred to above was to
    A. find out who is responsible for most traffic accidents
    B. make the road tests more difficult for new drivers to pass
    C. make it harder to get a driver's license
    D. serve as a further check on the competence of new drivers

11. According to the above passage, we may assume that a probationary license will NOT be cancelled if a driver is found guilty of
    A. passing a red light and failing to keep to the right on a road
    B. following another vehicle too closely
    C. overtime parking at a meter on two or more occasions
    D. driving at 60 miles an hour on a road where the speed limit is 50 miles an hour

Questions 12-13.

DIRECTIONS: Questions 12 and 13 are to be answered ONLY on the basis of the following passage.

   If a motor vehicle fails to pass inspection, the owner will be given a rejection notice by the inspection station. Repairs must be made within ten days after this notice is issued. It is not necessary to have the required adjustment or repairs made at the station where the inspection occurred. The vehicle may be taken to any other garage. Re-inspection after repairs may be made at any official inspection station, not necessarily the same station which made the initial inspection. The registration of any motor vehicle for which an inspection sticker has not been obtained as required, or which is not repaired and inspected within ten days after inspection indicates defects, is subject to suspension. A vehicle cannot be used on public highways while its registration is under suspension.

12. According to the above passage, the owner of a car which does NOT pass inspection must
    A. have repairs made at the same station which rejected this car
    B. take the car to another station and have it re-inspected
    C. have repairs made anywhere and then have the car re-inspected
    D. not use the car on a public highway until the necessary repairs have been made

12._____

13. According to the above passage, the one of the following which may be cause for suspension of the registration of a vehicle is that
    A. an inspection sticker was issued before the rejection notice had been in force for ten days
    B. it was not re-inspected by the station that rejected it originally
    C. it was not re-inspected either by the station that rejected it originally or by the garage which made the repairs
    D. it has not had defective parts repaired within ten days after inspection

13._____

Questions 14-18.

DIRECTIONS: Questions 14 through 18 are to be answered ONLY on the basis of the following passage.

   Under the Vehicular Responsibility Law of a certain state, an insurance carrier who has previously furnished the Division of Roads and Vehicles with evidence of a vehicle registrant's financial responsibility (Form VR-1, VR-1A, VR-2B or VR-11) must, in case of termination of insurance, first notify the insured registrant at least 10 days in advance if the termination is due to failure to pay the insurance premium and at least 20 days if the termination is due to any other reason. The insurance carrier must then notify the Division not later than 30 days following the effective date of actual termination of insurance coverage. The only acceptable proof of such termination is Form VR-4.

   Upon receipt of Form VR-4 by the Division, a search will be made for any superseding coverage or a record of voluntary surrender of plates and registration certificate on or prior to the effective date of termination. If such a record is found, no further action is taken by the

Division. If the Division finds no record of acceptable superseding coverage or timely surrender of plates and registration, Form Letter VR-7T is sent to the registrant with a photostatic copy of Form VR-4, providing him with an opportunity to invalidate the proceeding to cancel his registration by submitting additional evidence, which may take the form of proof of continuous financial responsibility, timely sale of the vehicle, or evidence of voluntary surrender of plates and registration certificate. Only after the registrant has failed to comply by one of the above three methods is an order to cancel registration (Form VR-8) issued.

Upon the issuance of a cancellation order, a copy of the order is mailed to the registrant directing him to immediately surrender his plates and registration certificate to a specified area office of the Division. At the same time, two copies of the cancellation order are sent to the area office, where they are held for 15 days. If the registrant complies with the order, he is issued a notice of compliance (Form VR-3). If he fails to comply within the 15 days, two more copies of the order are mailed to the Highway Patrol for enforcement of the cancellation order. No further action is taken for a period of 30 days. If no record of enforcement is received, another copy of the cancellation order is sent to the Police Department as a follow-up.

14. When the Division of Roads and Vehicles receives acceptable evidence that the insurance coverage on a particular registrant has been terminated, it is required FIRST to
    A. cancel the registration if the insurance was terminated because of failure to pay the insurance premium
    B. notify the registrant to voluntarily surrender his plates and registration certificate on or prior to a certain date
    C. determine whether the registrant has obtained other insurance for that vehicle
    D. send the registrant Form Letter VR-7T stating that he must submit evidence to prevent cancellation of his registration

15. In order to comply with the above procedure, the MINIMUM number of copies of the cancellation order that must be prepared, including one to be kept in the central Division of Roads and Vehicles file, is
    A. 3   B. 4   C. 5   d. 6

16. The one of the following which is required before steps
    A. the insurance carrier to notify the Division of Roads and Vehicles in writing (VR-11) that the insured registrant's premium payment is 30 days overdue
    B. the registrant to notify the Division of Roads and Vehicles that he either intends to sell or has sold his vehicle
    C. Form VR-8 to be sent to the insured registrant by the Division of Roads and Vehicles
    D. Form VR-4 to be sent by the insurance carrier to the Division of Roads and Vehicles

17. The MAXIMUM amount of time a vehicle registrant is allowed in which to comply with a cancellation order before the police are asked to enforce the order is _____ days.
    A. 30   B. 35   C. 40   D. 45

18. It would be MOST accurate to state with regard to the issuance of a certificate of compliance that the
    A. Division of Roads and Vehicles issues one to the registrant after he has submitted the additional evidence in response to Form Letter VR-7T
    B. Division of Roads and Vehicles may issue one to the registrant at any time after he has been mailed a copy of the cancellation order and before the Highway Patrol is notified
    C. Highway Patrol may issue one to the registrant if he surrenders his plates and registration to them during the 30 days following their receipt of the request for enforcement
    D. Highway Patrol may issue one to the registrant at any time before the Police Department is notified

18.____

Questions 19-22.

DIRECTIONS: Questions 19 through 22 are to be answered ONLY on the basis of the information given in the following passage.

All automotive accidents, no matter how slight, are to be reported to the Safety Division by the employee involved on Accident Report Form S-23 in duplicate. When the accident is of such a nature that it requires the filling out of the State Motor Vehicle Report Form MV-104, this form is also prepared by the employee in duplicate and sent to the Safety Division for comparison with Form S-23. The Safety Division forwards both copies of Form MV-104 to the Corporation Counsel, who sends one copy to the State Bureau of Motor Vehicles. When the information on the Form S-23 indicates that the employee may be at fault, an investigation is made by the Safety Division. If this investigation shows that the employee was at fault, the employee's dispatcher is asked to file a complaint on Form D-11. The foreman of mechanics prepares a damage report on Form D8 and an estimate of the cost of repairs on Form D-9. The dispatcher's complaint, the damage report, the repair estimate, and the employee's previous accident record are sent to the Safety Division where they are studied together with the accident report. The Safety Division then recommends whether or not disciplinary action should be taken against the employee.

19. According to the above passage, the Safety Division should be notified whenever an automotive accident has occurred by means of Form(s)
    A. S-23
    B. S-23 and MV-104
    C. S-23, MV-104, D-8, D-9, and D-11
    D. S-23, MV-104, D-8, D-9, D-11, and employee's accident report

19.____

20. According to the above passage, the forwarding of the Form MV-104 to the State Bureau of Motor Vehicles is done by the
    A. Corporation Counsel
    B. dispatcher
    C. employee involved in the accident
    D. Safety Division

20.____

21. According to the above passage, the Safety Division investigates an automotive accident if the
    A. accident is serious enough to be reported to the State Bureau of Motor Vehicles
    B. dispatcher files a complaint
    C. employee appears to have been at fault
    D. employee's previous accident report is poor

22. Of the forms mentioned in the above passage, the dispatcher is responsible for preparing the
    A. accident report form
    B. complaint form
    C. damage report
    D. estimate cost of repairs

Questions 23-25.

DIRECTIONS: Questions 23 through 25 are to be answered ONLY on the basis of the information given in the following passage.

One of the major problems in the control of city motor equipment, and especially passenger equipment, is keeping the equipment working for the city and for the city alone for as many hours of the day as is practical. Even when most city employees try to get the most out of the cars, a poor system of control will result in wasted car hours. Some city employees have a legitimate use for a car all day long while others use a car only a small part of the day and then let it stand. As a rule, trucks are easier to control than passenger cars because they are usually assigned to a specific job where a foreman continually oversees them. Even though trucks are usually fully utilized, there are times when the normal work assignment cannot be carried out because of weather conditions or seasonal changes. At such times, a control system could plan to make the trucks available for other uses.

23. According to the above passage, a problem connected with controlling the use of city motor equipment is
    A. increasing the life span of the equipment
    B. keeping the equipment working all hours of the day
    C. preventing the overuse of the equipment to avoid breakdowns
    D. preventing the private use of the equipment

24. According to the above passage, a good control system for passenger equipment will MOST likely lead to
    A. better employees being assigned to operate the cars
    B. fewer city employees using city cars
    C. fewer wasted car hours for city cars
    D. insuring that city cars are used for legitimate purposes

25. According to the above passage, a control system for trucks is useful because
    A. a foreman usually supervises each job
    B. special conditions sometimes prevent the planned use of a truck
    C. trucks are easier to control than passenger cars
    D. trucks are usually assigned to specific jobs where they cannot be fully utilized

Question 26.

DIRECTIONS: Question 26 is to be answered SOLELY on the basis of the following passage.

Whereas automobile travel in general corresponds to the general motor vehicles index, as represented by total gas usage. Traffic trends on one particular road may vary from average. Comparison of the records of various main arteries indicates that automobile travel on some highways has gone up much faster than the general trend of gas usage. The conclusion is that the bulk of local travel remains stable, but a very large share of the total increase in travel is concentrated on main highways. This would be especially true on new highways which provide better means of travel and foster trips which would not have been made if the new route has not been constructed.

26. According to the above passage, which one of the following is MOST likely to result in increased automobile travel? 26.____
    A. A new roadway
    B. Stable local conditions
    C. A choice of routes
    D. Traffic trends

Questions 27-30.

DIRECTIONS: Questions 27 through 30 are to be answered ONLY on the basis of the following passage.

Analysis of current data reveals that motor vehicle transportation actually requires less space than was used for other types of transportation in the pre-automobile era, even including the substantial area taken by freeways. The reason is that when the fast-moving through traffic is put on built-for-the-purpose arterial roads, then the amount of ordinary space needed for strictly local movement and for access to property drops sharply. Even the amount of land taken for urban expressways turns out to be surprisingly small in terms either of total urban acreage or of the volume of traffic they carry. No existing or contemplated urban expressway system requires as much as 3 percent of the land in the areas it serves, and this would be exceptionally high. The Los Angeles freeway system, when complete, will occupy only 2 percent of the available land; the same is true of the District of Columbia, where only 0.75 percent will be pavement, with the remaining 1.25 percent as open space. California studies estimate that, in a typical California urban community, 1.6 to 2 percent of the area should be devoted to freeways, which will handle 50 to 60 percent of all traffic needs, and about ten time as much land to the ordinary roads and streets that carry the rest of the traffic. By comparison, when John A. Sutter laid out Sacramento in 1850, he provided 38 percent of the area for street and sidewalks. The French architect, Pierre L'Enfant, proposed 59 percent of the area of the District of Columbia for roads and streets; urban renewal in Southwest Washington, incorporating a modern street network, reduced the acreage of space for pedestrian and vehicular traffic in the renewal area from 48.2 to 41.5 percent of the total. If we are to have a reasonable consideration of the impact of highway transportation on contemporary urban development, it would be well to understand these relationships.

27. The author of this passage says that
    A. modern transportation uses less space than was used for transportation before the auto age
    B. expressways require more space than streets in terms of urban acreage
    C. typical urban communities were poorly designed in terms of relationship between space used for traffic and that used for other purposes
    D. the need for local and access roads would increase if the number of expressways were increased

28. According to the above passage, it was originally planned that the percent of the area to be used for roads and streets in the District of Columbia should be MOST NEARLY
    A. 40%   B. 45%   C. 50%   D. 60%

29. The above passage states that the amount of space needed for local traffic
    A. *increases* when arterial highways are constructed
    B. *decreases* when arterial highways are constructed
    C. *decreases* when there is more land available
    D. *increases* when there is more land available

30. According to the above passage, studies estimate that, land devoted to in a typical California urban community, the amount of ordinary roads and streets as compared with that devoted to freeways should be MOST NEARLY as much.
    A. One-half   B. One-tenth   C. Twice   D. Ten times

KEY (CORRECT ANSWERS)

1.	D	11.	C	21.	C
2.	C	12.	C	22.	B
3.	A	13.	D	23.	D
4.	B	14.	C	24.	C
5.	B	15.	B	25.	B
6.	D	16.	D	26.	A
7.	C	17.	D	27.	A
8.	C	18.	B	28.	D
9.	A	19.	A	29.	B
10.	D	20.	A	30.	D

TEST 2

DIRECTIONS: Each question or incomplete statement is followed by several suggested answers or completions. Select the one that BEST answers the question or completes the statement. *PRINT THE LETTER OF THE CORRECT ANSWER IN THE SPACE AT THE RIGHT.*

Questions 1-5.

DIRECTIONS: Questions 1 through 5 are to be answered ONLY on the basis of information given in the following passage.

Fatigue can make a driver incompetent. He may become less vigilant. He may lose judgment as to the speed and distance of other cars. His reaction time is likely to be slowed down, and he is less able to resist glare. With increasing fatigue, driving efficiency falls. Finally, nodding at the wheel results, from which accidents follow almost invariably.

Accidents that occur with the driver asleep at the wheel are generally very serious. With the driver unconscious, no effort is made either to prevent the accident or to lessen its seriousness. Accidents increase as day wears on and reach their peak in the early evening and during the first half of the night. Driver fatigue undoubtedly plays a significant part in causing these frequent night accidents.

1. Among the results of fatigue, the passage does NOT indicate   1._____
   A. lessened hearing effectiveness   B. lessened vigilance
   C. loss of driving efficiency   D. increased reaction time

2. According to the passage, accidents almost always follow as a result of   2._____
   A. fatigue   B. slowed down reaction time
   C. nodding at the wheel   D. lessened vigilance

3. According to the passage, accidents that occur in the early evening and during   3._____
   the first half of the night are
   A. always caused by driver fatigue
   B. very frequently the result of lessened resistance to glare
   C. usually due to falling asleep at the wheel
   D. more frequent than accidents in the afternoon

4. According to the passage, very serious accidents result from   4._____
   A. falling asleep at the wheel   B. poor driving
   C. lack of judgment   D. poor vision

5. Referring to the passage, which of the following conclusions is NOT correct?   5._____
   A. There are only two paragraphs in the entire passage.
   B. One paragraph contains four sentences.
   C. There are six words in the first sentence.
   D. There is no sentence of less than six words.

Questions 6-8.

DIRECTIONS: Questions 6 through 8 are to be answered ONLY according to the information given in the following passage.

Drivers and pedestrians face additional traffic hazards during the fall months. Changing autumn weather conditions, longer hours of darkness, and the abrupt nightfall during the evening rush hour can mean more traffic deaths and injuries unless drivers and pedestrians exercise greater care and alertness. Drivers must adjust to changing light conditions; they cannot use the same driving habits and attitudes at dusk as they do during daylight. Moderate speed and continual alertness are imperative for safe city driving at this time of year.

6. According to the above passage, two new traffic risks which motorists face in the fall are 6.____
   A. changing weather conditions and more traffic during the evening rush hour
   B. fewer hours of daylight and sudden nightfall
   C. less care by pedestrians and a change in autumn weather conditions
   D. more pedestrians on the street and longer hours of darkness

7. According to the above passage, there may be more traffic deaths and injuries in the fall MAINLY because both pedestrians and drivers are 7.____
   A. distracted by car lights being turned on earlier
   B. hurrying to get home from work in the evening
   C. confronted with more traffic dangers
   D. using the streets in greater numbers

8. According to the above passage, an ESSENTIAL requirement of driving safely in the city in the fall is 8.____
   A. eyes down on the road at all times
   B. very slow speed
   C. no passing
   D. reasonable speed

Questions 9-11.

DIRECTIONS: Questions 9 through 11 are to be answered ONLY according to the information given in the following passage.

A traffic sign is a device mounted on a fixed or portable support through which a specific message is conveyed by means of words or symbols. It is erected through which a specific purpose of regulating, warning, or guiding traffic.

A regulatory sign is used to indicate the required method of traffic movement or the permitted use of a highway. It gives notice of traffic regulations that apply only at specific places or at specific times that would not otherwise be apparent.

A warning sign is used to call attention to conditions on or near a road that are actually or potentially hazardous to the safe movement of traffic.

A guide sign is used to direct traffic along a route or toward a destination, or to give directions, distances, or information concerning places or points of interest.

9. According to the above passage, which one of the following is NOT a *regulatory* sign?   9.____
   A. Right turn on red signal permitted
   B. Trucks use right lane
   C. Slippery when wet
   D. Speed limit 60

10. According to the above passage, which one of the following LEAST fits the description of a *warning* sign?   10.____
    A. No right turn
    B. Falling rock zone
    C. Low clearance, 12 ft. 6 in.
    D. Merging traffic

11. According to the above passage, which one of the following messages is LEAST likely to be conveyed by a *guide* sign?   11.____
    A. Southbound
    B. Signal ahead
    C. Bridge next exit
    D. Entering city

Questions 12-14.

DIRECTIONS: Questions 12 through 14 are to be answered ONLY on the basis of the information given in the following passage.

A National Safety Council study of 685,000 traffic accidents reveals that most accidents happen under *safe* conditions—in clear, dry weather, on straight roads, and when traffic volumes are low. The point is most accidents can be attributed to lapses on the part of the drivers rather than traffic or road conditions or deliberate law violations. Most drivers try to avoid accidents. Why, then, do so many get into trouble? A major cause is the average motorist's failure to recognize a hazard soon enough to avoid it entirely. He does not, by habit, notice the clues that are there for him to see. He takes constant risks in traffic without even knowing it. These faulty seeing habits plus the common distractions that all drivers must deal with, such as hurry, worry daydreaming, impatience, concentration on route problems, add up to a guaranteed answer—an accident.

12. According to a study by the National Safety Council, MOST accidents can be blamed on   12.____
    A. curving, hilly roads
    B. errors made by drivers
    C. heavy streams of traffic
    D. wet, foggy weather

13. According to the above passage, an IMPORTANT reason why the average motorist gets into an accident is that he   13.____
    A. does not see the danger of an accident soon enough
    B. does not try to avoid accidents
    C. drives at too great a speed
    D. purposely takes reckless chances

14. According to the above passage, it is NOT reasonable to say that drivers are distracted from their driving and possibly involved in an accident because they
    A. are impatient about something
    B. concentrate on the road ahead
    C. hurry to get to where they are going
    D. worry about some problem

14._____

Questions 15-18.

DIRECTIONS: Questions 15 through 18 are to be answered ONLY on the basis of the information given in the following passage.

If a good automobile road map is studied thoroughly before a trip is started, much useful information can be learned. This information may help to decrease the cost of and the time required for the trip and, at the same time, increase the safety and comfort of the trip. The legend found on the face of the map explains symbols and markings and the kind of roads on various routes. The legend also explains how to tell by width, color, or type of line whether the road is dual- or multiple-lane, and whether it is paved, all-weather, graded, earth, under construction, or proposed for construction. Federal routes are usually shown by a number within a shield, and state routes by a number within a circle. The legend also shows scale of miles on a bar marked to indicate the distance each portion of the bar represents on the earth's surface. Distances between locations on the map are shown by plain numerals beside the route lines; they indicate mileage between marked points or intersections. Add the mileage numbers shown along a route to determine distances.

15. According to the above passage, the markings on the road map will show
    A. a different color for a road proposed for construction than for one under construction
    B. a double line if a road is a dual-lane road
    C. what part of a road is damaged or being repaired
    D. which roads on state routes have more than two lanes

15._____

16. The above passage does NOT mention as a possible advantage of studying a good road map before beginning a trip the
    A. increase in interest of the trip
    B. reduction in the chance of an accident on the trip
    C. saving of money
    D. saving of time

16._____

17. According to the above passage, in order to find the total mileage of a certain route, a motorist should add the numbers
    A. on the bar scale in the legend
    B. between marked points beside the route lines
    C. inside a shield along the route
    D. within a circle along the route

17._____

18. According to the above passage, the legend on a road map includes information   18.____
    which a motorist could use to
    A. choose the best paved route   B. figure the toll charges
    C. find the allowable speed limits   D. learn the location of bridges

Questions 19-30.

DIRECTIONS: The following is an accident report similar to those used by departments for reporting accidents. Questions 19 through 30 are to be answered ONLY on the basis of the information contained in this accident report.

ACCIDENT REPORT

Date of Accident: April 12, _____
Place of Accident: 17th Ave. & 22nd St.
Time of Accident: 10:15 A.M.
City Vehicle:
Operator's Name: John Smith
Title: Motor Vehicle Operator
Badge No.: 17-5427
Operator License No.: S2874-7513-3984
Vehicle Code No.: B7-8213
License Plate No.: BK-4782
Damage to Vehicle: Left front fender dented; broken left front headlight and parking light; windshield wipers not operating

Date of Report: April 15, _____ Friday
Vehicle No. 2:
Operator's Name: James Jones
Operator's Address: 427 E. 198th St.
Operator License No.: J0837-0882-7851
Owner's Name: Michael Greene
Owner's Address: 582 E. 92nd St.
License Plate No.: 6Y-3916
Damage to Vehicle: Left front bumper bent inward; broken left front headlight; grille broken in three places

DESCRIPTION OF ACCIDENT: I was driving on 17th Avenue, a southbound one-way street and made a slow, wide turn west into 22nd Street, a two-way street, because a moving van was parked near the corner of 22nd Street. As I completed my turn, a station wagon going east on 22nd Street hit me. The driver of the station wagon said he put on his brakes but he skidded on some oil that was on the street. The driver of the van saw the accident from his cab and told me that the station wagon skidded as he put on his brakes. Patrolman Jack Reed, Badge #24578, who was at the southeast corner of the intersection, saw what happened and made some notes in his memo book.

   Persons Injured – Names and Addresses. If none, state NONE:
   Witnesses – Names and Addresses: If none, state NONE:
     Jack Reed, 33-47 83rd Drive
     Thomas Quinn: 527 Flatlands Avenue

                               Report prepared by: John Smith
                               Title: Motor Vehicle Operator

19. According to the report, the accident happened on
    A. Friday, between 6:00 A.M. and 12:00 Noon
    B. Friday, between 12:00 Noon and 6:00 P.M.
    C. Tuesday, between 6:00 A.M. and 12:00 Noon
    D. Monday, between 12:00 Noon and 6:00 P.M.

20. Which one of the following numbers is part of the driver's license of the operator of the city vehicle?
    A. 3984   B. 5247   C. 4782   D. 7851

21. The address of the driver of the city vehicle is
    A. not given in the report
    B. 427 E. 198th Street
    C. 582 E. 92nd Street
    D. 33-47 83rd Drive

22. A section of the report that is NOT properly filled out is
    A. Witnesses
    B. Description of Accident
    C. Persons Injured
    D. Damage to Vehicle

23. According to the accident report, if the only witnesses were the patrolman and the van driver, then the van driver's name is
    A. Reed   B. Quinn   C. Jones   D. Greene

24. According to the report, the diagram that would BEST show where the cars collided and where the moving van ([v]) was parked at the time of the accident is

25. According to the information in the report, it would be MOST correct to say that Michael Greene was
    A. the driver of the station wagon
    B. a passenger in the station wagon
    C. the owner of the moving van
    D. the owner of the station wagon

26. According to the information in the report, a factor which contributed to the accident was 26.____
    A. a slippery road condition
    B. bad brakes of one car
    C. obstructed view of traffic light caused by parked van
    D. windshield wipers on the city car not operating properly

27. When a driver makes a report such as this, it is MOST important that he 27.____
    A. print the information so that his supervisor can read it quickly
    B. keep it short because a long report makes it look as though he is hiding a mistake behind many words
    C. show clearly why the accident isn't his fault
    D. give all the facts accurately and completely

28. The first two letters or numbers in the City Vehicle Code Number indicate the type of vehicle. Two letters indicate an 8 passenger 8-cylinder car; two numbers indicates a 6 passenger, 8-cylinder car; a letter followed by a number indicates a 6 passenger 6-cylinder car; a number followed by a letter indicate an 8-cylinder station wagon. 28.____
    The city car involved in this accident is, therefore, a(n)
    A. 8-cylinder station wagon   B. 6 passenger 6-cylinder car
    C. 6 passenger 8-cylinder car   D. 8 passenger 8-cylinder car

29. From the information in the report, the driver of the city vehicle may have been partially at fault because he 29.____
    A. appears to have begun his turn from the wrong lane
    B. appears to have entered the wrong lane of traffic
    C. did not blow his horn as he made the turn
    D. should have braked as he made the turn

30. What evidence is there in the report that the two vehicles collided in front, driver's side? 30.____
    A. The description of the accident
    B. There is no such evidence
    C. The type of damage to the vehicles
    D. The van driver's statement

KEY (CORRECT ANSWERS)

1.	A	11.	B	21.	A		
2.	C	12.	B	22.	C		
3.	D	13.	A	23.	B		
4.	A	14.	B	24.	D		
5.	D	15.	D	25.	D		
6.	B	16.	A	26.	A		
7.	C	17.	B	27.	D		
8.	D	18.	A	28.	B		
9.	C	19.	C	29.	B		
10.	A	20.	A	30.	C		

TEST 3

DIRECTIONS: Each question or incomplete statement is followed by several suggested answers or completions. Select the one that BEST answers the question or completes the statement. *PRINT THE LETTER OF THE CORRECT ANSWER IN THE SPACE AT THE RIGHT.*

Questions 1-7.

DIRECTIONS: Questions 1 through 7, inclusive, are to be answered on the basis of the following passage.

DRINKING AND DRIVING

In fatal traffic accidents, a drinking driver is involved more than 30% of the time; on holiday weekends, more than 50% of the fatal accidents involve drinking drivers. Drinking to any extent reduces the judgment, self-control, and driving ability of any driver. Social drinkers, especially those who think they drive better after a drink, are a greater menace than commonly believed, and they outnumber the obviously intoxicated. Two cocktails may reduce visual acuity as much as wearing dark glasses at night. Alcohol is not a stimulant; it is classified medically as a depressant. Coffee or other stimulants will not offset the effects of alcohol; only time can eliminate alcohol from the bloodstream. It takes at least three hours to eliminate one ounce of pure alcohol from the bloodstream.

1. Alcohol is classified by doctors as a
   A. stimulant   B. sedative   C. depressant   D. medicine

2. Social drinkers
   A. never become obviously intoxicated
   B. always drink in large groups
   C. drive better after two cocktails
   D. are a greater menace than commonly believed

3. Alcohol will BEST be eliminated from the bloodstream by
   A. fresh air   B. a stimulant   C. coffee   D. time

4. More than half of the fatal accidents on holiday weekends involve _____ drivers.
   A. inexperienced   B. drinking   C. fast   D. slow

5. Drinking to any extent does NOT
   A. impair judgment
   B. decrease visual acuity
   C. reduce accident potential
   D. affect driving ability

6. In traffic accidents resulting in death, a drinking driver is involved
   A. about one-third of the time
   B. mainly at night
   C. more than 80% of the time
   D. practically all the time on weekends

73

7. After taking two alcoholic drinks, it is BEST not to drive until you have   7._____
   A. had a cup of black coffee   B. waited three hours
   C. eaten a full meal   D. taken a half-hour nap

Questions 8-12.

DIRECTIONS: Questions 8 through 12 are to be answered ONLY on the basis of the information contained in the following accident report.

REPORT OF ACCIDENT

Date of Accident: Nov. 27, _____
Department Vehicle
Operator's Name: John Doe
Title: Motor Vehicle Operator
Vehicle Code No.: 17-129
License Plate No.: IN-2345
Damage to Vehicle: Crumpled and torn front left fender, broken left headlight, front bumper bent outward on left side, hubcap dented badly and torn off

Time: 2:20 P.M.   Date of Report: 11/28
Vehicle No. 2
Operator's Name: Richard Roe
Operator's Address: 983 E. 84th St.
Owner's Name: Robert Roe
Owner's Address: 983 E. 84th St.
License Plate No.: 9Y-8765
Damage to Vehicle: Crumpled right front fender, broken right headlight and parking light, right left front side of front bumper badly bent

Place of Accident: 71st & 3rd Ave.

DESCRIPTION OF ACCIDENT: I was driving west on 71st St. and started to turn north into 3rd Avenue since the light was still green for me. I stopped at the crosswalk because a woman was in the middle of 3rd Avenue crossing from west to east. She had just cleared my car when a Ford sedan, going north, crashed into my left front fender. The light was green on 3rd Ave. when he hit me. The woman who had crossed the avenue in front of me, and whose name I got as a witness, was standing on the corner when I got out of the car.

Persons Injured

_____   _____
Mrs. Mary Brown   Witness   215 E. 71 St.

Report prepared by: John Doe
Title: Motor Vehicle Operator
Badge #17832

3 (#3)

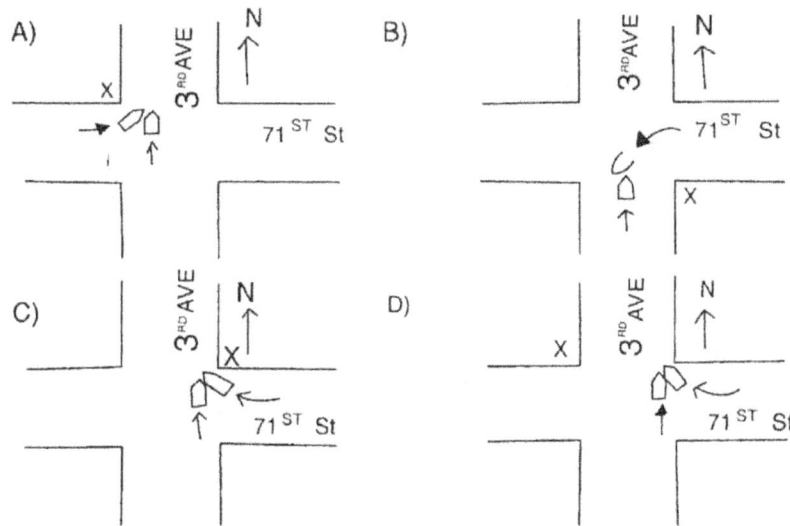

8. According to the description of the accident, the diagram that would BEST show how and where the vehicles crashed and the position of the witness (X) is
   A. A   B. B   C. C   D. D

9. The pedestrian mentioned in the description of the accident was
   A. an unknown woman
   B. Mary Brown
   C. an unknown man
   D. Robert Roe

10. According to the information in the report, the one of the following statements which is INCORRECT is:
    A. Both cars were moving when the accident happened
    B. One car was moving when the accident happened
    C. The Department car was headed northwest when the accident happened
    D. The traffic lights had changed just before the accident happened

11. From the description of the accident as given in the report, the accident would PROBABLY be classified as
    A. premeditated   B. calamitous   C. minor   D. fatal

12. From a reading of the accident report, it can be seen that
    A. the witness was completely unfamiliar with the neighborhood in which the accident took place
    B. the accident occurred in the early hours of the morning
    C. neither driver owned the vehicle he was driving
    D. it was raining when the accident took place

Questions 13-24.

DIRECTIONS: Questions 13 through 24 are based on the description of an automobile accident given below. Read the description carefully before answering these questions.

DESCRIPTION OF AUTOMOBILE ACCIDENT

Ten persons were injured, two critically, when a driverless auto—its accelerator jammed-up ran wild through the busy intersection at 8th Ave. and 42nd Street at 11:30 A.M. yesterday. The car struck a truck, overturned it, and mounted the sidewalk. Several persons were bowled over before the car was finally stopped by collision with a second truck. Police Officer Fred Black, Badge No. 82143, said that the freak accident occurred after the car's driver, Mrs. Mary Jones, 39, of Queens, got out of the car with her daughter, Gloria, aged 3, while the engine was still running. Mr. Herbert Field, 64, of the Bronx, a passenger in the car, accidentally stepped on the accelerator when he tried to get out. This caused the car to shoot forward because the shift was in *drive*, and 5 pedestrians were thrown to the ground.

13. This accident occurred
    A. late in the morning
    B. early in the morning
    C. early in the afternoon
    D. late in the evening

14. The number of persons who were injured, but not critically, is
    A. 2   B. 5   C. 8   D. 10

15. This accident occurred a block away from
    A. Grand Central Terminal
    B. Times Square
    C. Union Square
    D. Pennsylvania Station

16. The runaway car was finally stopped just after it
    A. mounted the sidewalk
    B. collided with a second truck
    C. crossed the intersection
    D. bowled over several persons

17. It can be inferred from the description that the driverless auto had
    A. power brakes
    B. power steering
    C. a turn indicator
    D. an automatic shift

18. The number on the police officer's badge is
    A. 82314   B. 82413   C. 82143   D. 82341

19. The first name of the driver of the car is
    A. Mary   B. Fred   C. Gloria   D. Herbert

20. According to the accident description, the adult passenger lives in
    A. the Bronx, and so does the driver
    B. Queens, and so does the driver
    C. the Bronx, and the driver in Queens
    D. Queens, and the driver in the Bronx

21. The number of pedestrians who were thrown to the ground is 21.____
    A. 2   B. 5   C. 7   D. 10

22. The person who made a statement about the runaway car was 22.____
    A. Herbert Field   B. Mary Jones
    C. Gloria Jones   D. Fred Black

23. Herbert Field is older than Mary Jones by about _____ years. 23.____
    A. 25   B. 35   C. 51   D. 61

24. The car shot forward immediately after 24.____
    A. Mrs. Jones placed the shift in *drive*
    B. Mr. Field stepped on the accelerator
    C. Mrs. Jones stepped out of the car
    D. Mr. Field got out of the car

Questions 25-28.

DIRECTIONS: Questions 25 through 28 are to be answered ONLY on the basis of the information given in the following passage.

ACCIDENT PRONESS

Accident proneness is a subject deserving much more attention than it has received. Studies have shown a high incidence of accidents to be associated with particular employees who are called accident prone. Such employees, according to these studies, behave on their jobs in ways which make them likely to have more accidents than would normally be expected.

It is important to point out the difference between the employee who is a *repeater* and the one who is truly accident prone. It is obvious that any person assigned to work about which he knows little will be liable to injury until he does learn the *how* of the job. Few workers left completely on their own will develop adequate safe practices. Therefore, they must be trained. Only those who fail to respond to proper training should be regarded as accident prone.

The dangers of an occupation should also be considered when judging an accident record. For a crane operator, a record of five accidents in a given period of time may not indicate accident proneness, while, in the case of a clerk, two accidents over the same period of time may be excessive. There are the reporters whose accident records can be explained by correctible physical defects, by correctible unsafe plant or machine conditions, or by assignment to work for which they are not suited because they cannot meet all the job's physical requirements. Such repeaters cannot be fairly called *accident prone*. A diagnosis of accident proneness should not be lightly made but should be based on all of these considerations.

25. According to the above passage, studies have shown that accident prone 25.____
    employees
    A. work under unsafe physical conditions
    B. act in unsafe ways on the job
    C. are not usually physically suited for their jobs
    D. work in the more dangerous occupations

26. According to the above passage, a person who is accident prone
    A. has received proper training which has not reduced his tendency toward accidents
    B. repeats the same accident several times over a short period of time
    C. experiences excessive anxiety about dangers in his occupation
    D. ignores unsafe but correctible machine conditions

26.____

27. According to the above passage, MOST persons who are given work they know little about
    A. will eventually learn on their own sufficient safety practices to follow
    B. work safely if they are not accident prone
    C. must be trained before they develop adequate safety methods
    D. should be regarded as accident prone until they become familiar with the job

27.____

28. According to the above passage, to effectively judge the accident record of an employee, one should consider
    A. the employee's age and physical condition
    B. that five accidents are excessive
    C. the type of dangers that are natural to his job
    D. the difficulty level of previous occupations held by the employee

28.____

Questions 29-30.

DIRECTIONS: Questions 29 and 30 are to be answered ONLY on the basis of the information given in the following passage.

When heavy rain beats on your windshield, it becomes hard for you to see ahead and even harder to see objects to the side—despite good windshield wipers. Also, the danger zone becomes longer when it is raining because the car takes longer to stop on wet streets. Remember that the danger zone of your car is the distance within which you can't stop after you have seen something on the road ahead of your car. The way to reduce the length of the danger zone of your car while driving is to reduce speed.

29. From the information in the above passage, you cannot tell if the danger zone of your car
    A. can be made smaller
    B. is greater on a rainy day
    C. is greater on cloudy days than on clear days
    D. is the distance in back of the car or in front of the car

29.____

30. According to the above passage, the danger zone of a moving car is affected by
    A. the condition of the street and the speed of the car
    B. many things which cannot be pinned down, in addition to the mechanical condition of the car
    C. the number of objects to the front and to the side
    D. visibility of the road and the reaction time of the driver

30.____

KEY (CORRECT ANSWERS)

1.	C	11.	C	21.	B
2.	D	12.	C	22.	D
3.	D	13.	A	23.	A
4.	B	14.	C	24.	B
5.	C	15.	B	25.	B
6.	A	16.	B	26.	A
7.	B	17.	D	27.	C
8.	C	18.	C	28.	C
9.	B	19.	A	29.	C
10.	A	20.	C	30.	A

PREPARING WRITTEN MATERIAL

PARAGRAPH REARRANGEMENT
COMMENTARY

The sentences that follow are in scrambled order. You are to rearrange them in proper order and indicate the letter choice containing the correct answer at the space at the right.

Each group of sentences in this section is actually a paragraph presented in scrambled order. Each sentence in the group has a place in that paragraph; no sentence is to be left out. You are to read each group of sentences and decide upon the best order in which to put the sentences so as to form a well-organized paragraph.

The questions in this section measure the ability to solve a problem when all the facts relevant to its solution are not given.

More specifically, certain positions of responsibility and authority require the employee to discover connection between events sometimes, apparently, unrelated. In order to do this, the employee will find it necessary to correctly infer that unspecified events have probably occurred or are likely to occur. This ability becomes especially important when action must be taken on incomplete information.

Accordingly, these questions require competitors to choose among several suggested alternatives, each of which presents a different sequential arrangement of the events. Competitors must choose the MOST logical of the suggested sequences.

In order to do so, they may be required to draw on general knowledge to infer missing concepts or events that are essential to sequencing the given events. Competitors should be careful to infer only what is essential to the sequence. The plausibility of the wrong alternatives will always require the inclusion of unlikely events or of additional chains of events which are NOT essential to sequencing the given events.

It's very important to remember that you are looking for the best of the four possible choices, and that the best choice of all may not even be one of the answers you're given to choose from.

There is no one right way to solve these problems. Many people have found it helpful to first write out the order of the sentences, as they would have arranged them, on their scrap paper before looking at the possible answers. If their optimum answer is there, this can save them some time. If it isn't, this method can still give insight into solving the problem. Others find it most helpful to just go through each of the possible choices, contrasting each as they go along. You should use whatever method feels comfortable and works for you.

While most of these types of questions are not that difficult, we've added a higher percentage of the difficult type, just to give you more practice. Usually there are only one or two questions on this section that contain such subtle distinctions that you're unable to answer confidently. And you then may find yourself stuck deciding between two possible choices, neither of which you're sure about.

EXAMINATION SECTION

TEST 1

DIRECTIONS: The sentences that follow are in scrambled order. You are to rearrange them in proper order and indicate the letter choice containing the correct answer. *PRINT THE LETTER OF THE CORRECT ANSWER IN THE SPACE AT THE RIGHT.*

1. Below are four statements labeled W, X, Y and Z. 1.____
   W. He was a strict and fanatic drillmaster.
   X. The word is always used in a derogatory sense and generally shows resentment and anger on the part of the user.
   Y. It is from the name of this Frenchman that we derive our English word, martinet.
   Z. Jean Martinet was the Inspector-General of Infantry during the reign of King Louis XIV.
   The PROPER order in which these sentences should be placed in a paragraph is:
   A. X, Z, W, Y   B. X, Z, Y, W   C. Z, W, Y, X   D. Z, Y, W, X

2. In the following paragraph, the sentences, which are numbered, have been jumbled. 2.____
   I. Since then it has undergone changes.
   II. It was incorporated in 1955 under the laws of the State of New York.
   III. Its primary purposes, a cleaner city, has, however, remained the same.
   IV. The Citizens Committee works in cooperation with the Mayor's Inter-departmental Committee for a Clean City. 3.____
   The order in which these sentences should be arranged to form a well-organized paragraph is:
   A. II, IV, I, III   B. III, IV, I, II   C. IV, II, I, III   D. IV, III, II, I

Questions 3-5.

DIRECTIONS: The sentences listed below are part of a meaningful paragraph but they are not given in their proper order. You are to decide what would be the BEST order in which to put the sentences so as to form a well-organized paragraph. Each sentence has a place in the paragraph; there are no extra sentences. You are then to answer Questions 3 through 5 inclusive on the basis of your rearrangements of these scrambled sentences into a properly organized paragraph.

In 1887 some insurance companies organized an Inspection Department to advise their clients on all phases of fire prevention and protection. Probably this has been due to the smaller annual fire losses in Great Britain than in the United States. It tests various fire prevention devices and appliances and determines manufacturing hazards and their safeguards. Fire research began earlier in the United States and is more advanced than in Great Britain. Later they established a laboratory specializing in electrical, mechanical, hydraulic, and chemical fields.

3. When the five sentences are arranged in proper order, the paragraph starts with the sentence which begins
   A. "In 1887..."   B. "Probably this..."   C. "It tests..."
   D. "Fire research..."   E. "Later they..."

3.____

4. In the last sentence listed above, "they" refers to
   A. the insurance companies
   B. the United States and Great Britain
   C. the Inspection Department
   D. clients
   E. technicians

4.____

5. When the above paragraph is properly arranged, it ends with the words
   A. "...and protection."
   B. "...the United States."
   C. "...their safeguards."
   D. "...in Great Britain."
   E. "...chemical fields."

5.____

KEY (CORRECT ANSWERS)

1. C
2. C
3. D
4. A
5. C

TEST 2

DIRECTIONS: In each of the questions numbered I through V, several sentences are given. For each question, choose as your answer the group of number that represents the MOST logical order of these sentences if they were arranged in paragraph form. *PRINT THE LETTER OF THE CORRECT ANSWER IN THE SPACE AT THE RIGHT.*

1.
   I. It is established when one shows that the landlord has prevented the tenant's enjoyment of his interest in the property leased.
   II. Constructive eviction is the result of a breach of the covenant of quiet enjoyment implied in all leases.
   III. In some parts of the United States, it is not complete until the tenant vacates within a reasonable time.
   IV. Generally, the acts must be of such serious and permanent character as to deny the tenant the enjoyment of his possessing rights.
   V. In this event, upon abandonment of the premises, the tenant's liability for that ceases.
   The CORRECT answer is:
   A. II, I, IV, III, V
   B. V, II, III, I, IV
   C. IV, III, I, II, V
   D. I, III, V, IV, II

1.____

2.
   I. The powerlessness before private and public authorities that is the typical experience of the slum tenant is reminiscent of the situation of blue-collar workers all through the nineteenth century.
   II. Similarly, in recent years, this chapter of history has been reopened by anti-poverty groups which have attempted to organize slum tenants to enable them to bargain collectively with their landlords about the conditions of their tenancies.
   III. It is familiar history that many of the worker remedied their condition by joining together and presenting their demands collectively.
   IV. Like the workers, tenants are forced by the conditions of modern life into substantial dependence on these who possess great political aid and economic power.
   V. What's more, the very fact of dependence coupled with an absence of education and self-confidence makes them hesitant and unable to stand up for what they need from those in power.
   The CORRECT answer is:
   A. V, IV, I, II, III
   B. II, III, I, V, IV
   C. III, I, V, IV, II
   D. I, IV, V, III, II

2.____

3.
   I. A railroad, for example, when not acting as a common carrier may contract away responsibility for its own negligence.
   II. As to a landlord, however, no decision has been found relating to the legal effect of a clause shifting the statutory duty of repair to the tenant.
   III. The courts have not passed on the validity of clauses relieving the landlord of this duty and liability.
   IV. They have, however, upheld the validity of exculpatory clauses in other types of contracts.

3.____

85

V. Housing regulations impose a duty upon the landlord to maintain leased premises in safe condition.
VI. As another example, a bailee may limit his liability except for gross negligence, willful acts, or fraud.

The CORRECT answer is:
- A. II, I, VI, IV, III, V
- B. I, III, IV, V, VI, II
- C. III, V, I, IV, II, VI
- D. V, III, IV, I, VI, II

4.
I. Since there are only samples in the building, retail or consumer sales are generally eschewed by mart occupants, and in some instances, rigid controls are maintained to limit entrance to the mart only to those persons engaged in retailing.
II. Since World War I, in many larger cities, there has developed a new type of property, called the mart building.
III. It can, therefore, be used by wholesalers and jobbers for the display of sample merchandise.
IV. This type of building is most frequently a multi-storied, finished interior property which is a cross between a retail arcade and a loft building.
V. This limitation enables the mart occupants to ship the orders from another location after the retailer or dealer makes his selection from the samples.

The CORRECT answer is:
- A. II, IV, III, I, V
- B. IV, III, V, I, II
- C. I, III, II, IV, V
- D. I, IV, II, III, V

5.
I. In general, staff-line friction reduces the distinctive contribution of staff personnel.
II. The conflicts, however, introduce an uncontrolled element into the managerial system.
III. On the other hand, the natural resistance of the line to staff innovations probably usefully restrains over-eager efforts to apply untested procedures on a large scale.
IV. Under such conditions, it is difficult to know when valuable ideas are being sacrificed.
V. The relatively weak position of staff, requiring accommodation to the line, tends to restrict their ability to engage in free, experimental innovation.

The CORRECT answer is:
- A. IV, II, III, I, V
- B. I, V, III, II, IV
- C. V, III, I, II, IV
- D. II, I, IV, V, III

KEY (CORRECT ANSWERS)

1. A
2. D
3. D
4. A
5. B

TEST 3

DIRECTIONS: Questions 1 through 4 consist of six sentences which can be arranged in a logical sequence. For each question, select the choice which places the numbered sentences in the MOST logical sequent. *PRINT THE LETTER OF THE CORRECT ANSWER IN THE SPACE AT THE RIGHT.*

1. I. The burden of proof as to each issue is determined before trial and remains upon the same party throughout the trial.
    II. The jury is at liberty to believe one witness' testimony as against a number of contradictory witnesses.
    III. In a civil case, the party bearing the burden of proof is required to prove his contention by a fair preponderance of the evidence.
    IV. However, it must be noted that a fair preponderance of evidence does not necessarily mean a greater number of witnesses.
    V. The burden of proof is the burden which rests upon one of the parties to an action to persuade the trier of the facts, generally the jury, that a proposition he asserts is true.
    VI. If the evidence is equally balanced, or if it leaves the jury in such doubt as to be unable to decide the controversy either way, judgment must be given against the party upon whom the burden of proof rests.
    The CORRECT answer is:
    A. III, II, V, IV, I, VI
    B. I, II, VI, V, III, IV
    C. III, IV, V, I, II, VI
    D. V, I, III, VI, IV, II

    1._____

2. I. If a parent is without assets and is unemployed, he cannot be convicted of the crime of non-support of a child.
    II. The term "sufficient ability" has been held to mean sufficient financial ability.
    III. It does not matter if his unemployment is by choice or unavoidable circumstances.
    IV. If he fails to take any steps at all, he may be liable to prosecution for endangering the welfare of a child.
    V. Under the penal law, a parent is responsible for the support of his minor child only if the parent is "of sufficient ability."
    VI. An indigent parent may meet his obligation by borrowing money or by seeking aid under the provisions of the Social Welfare Law.
    The CORRECT answer is:
    A. VI, I, V, III, II, IV
    B. I, III, V, II, IV, VI
    C. V, II, I, III, VI, IV
    D. I, VI, IV, V, II, III

    2._____

3. I. Consider, for example, the case of a rabble rouser who urges a group of twenty people to go out and break the windows of a nearby factory.
    II. Therefore, the law fills the indicated gap with the crime of inciting to riot.
    III. A person is considered guilty of inciting to riot when he urges ten or more persons to engage in tumultuous and violent conduct of a kind likely to create public alarm.
    IV. However, if he has not obtained the cooperation of at least four people, he cannot be charged with unlawful assembly.

    3._____

87

V. The charge of inciting to riot was added to the law to cover types of conduct which cannot be classified as either the crime of "riot" or the crime of "unlawful assembly."
VI. If he acquires the acquiescence of at least four of them, he is guilty of unlawful assembly even if the project does not materialize.

The CORRECT answer is:
- A. III, V, I, VI, IV, II
- B. V, I, IV, VI, II, III
- C. III, IV, I, V, II, VI
- D. V, I, IV, VI, III, II

4.
I. If, however, the rebuttal evidence presents an issue of credibility, it is for the jury to determine whether the presumption has, in fact, been destroyed.
II. Once sufficient evidence to the contrary is introduced, the presumption disappears from the trial.
III. The effect of a presumption is to place the burden upon the adversary to come forward with evidence to rebut the presumption.
IV. When a presumption is overcome and ceases to exist in the case, the fact or facts which gave rise to the presumption still remain.
V. Whether a presumption has been overcome is ordinarily a question for the court.
VI. Such information may furnish a basis for a logical inference.

The CORRECT answer is:
- A. IV, VI, II, V, I, III
- B. III, II, V, I, IV, VI
- C. V, III, VI, IV, II, I
- D. V, IV, I, II, VI, III

KEY (CORRECT ANSWERS)

1. D
2. C
3. A
4. B

PREPARING WRITTEN MATERIALS
EXAMINATION SECTION
TEST 1

DIRECTIONS: Each question or incomplete statement is followed by several suggested answers or completions. Select the one that BEST answers the question or completes the statement. *PRINT THE LETTER OF THE CORRECT ANSWER IN THE SPACE AT THE RIGHT.*

Questions 1-25.

DIRECTIONS: Questions 1 through 25 consist of sentences which may or may not be examples of good English usage. Consider grammar, punctuation, spelling, capitalization, awkwardness, etc. Examine each sentence and then choose the correct statement about it from the four choices below it. If the English usage in the sentence given is better than it would be with any of the changes suggested in options B, C, and D, choose option A. Do not choose an option that will change the meaning of the sentence.

1. According to Judge Frank, the grocer's sons found guilty of assault and sentenced last Thursday.
    A. This is an example of acceptable writing.
    B. A comma should be placed after the word *sentenced*.
    C. The word *were* should be placed after *sons*.
    D. The apostrophe in grocer's should be placed after the *s*.

1.____

2. The department heads assistant said that the stenographers should type duplicate copies of all contracts, leases, and bills.
    A. This is an example of acceptable writing,
    B. A comma should be placed before the word "*contracts*.
    C. An apostrophe should be placed before the *s* in *heads*.
    D. Quotation marks should be placed before the *stenographers* and after *bills*.

2.____

3. The lawyers questioned the men to determine who was the true property owner?
    A. This is an example of acceptable writing.
    B. The phrase *questioned the men* should be changed to *asked the men questions*.
    C. The word *was* should be changed to *were*.
    D. The question mark should be changed to a period.

3.____

4. The terms stated in the present contract are more specific than those stated in the previous contract.
   A. This is an example of acceptable writing,
   B. The word *are* should be changed to *is*.
   C. The word *than* should be changed to *then*.
   D. The word *specific* should be changed to *specified*.

   4.____

5. Of the few lawyers considered, the one who argued more skillful was chosen for the job.
   A. This is an example of acceptable writing.
   B. The word *more* should be replaced by the word *most*.
   C. The word *skillful* should be replaced by the word *skillfully*.
   D. The word *chosen* should be replaced by the word *selected*.

   5.____

6. Each of the states has a court of appeals; some states have circuit courts.
   A. This is an example of acceptable writing
   B. The semi-colon should be changed to a comma.
   C. The word *has* should be changed to *have*.
   D. The word *some* should be capitalized.

   6.____

7. The court trial has greatly effected the child's mental condition.
   A. This is an example of acceptable writing.
   B. The word *effected* should be changed to *affected*.
   C. The word *greatly* should be placed after *effected*.
   D. The apostrophe in *child's* should be placed after the *s*.

   7.____

8. Last week, the petition signed by all the officers was sent to the Better Business Bureau.
   A. This is an example of acceptable writing.
   B. The phrase *last week* should be placed after *officers*.
   C. A comma should be placed after *petition*.
   D. The word *was* should be changed to *were*.

   8.____

9. Mr. Farrell claims that he requested form A-12, and three booklets describing court procedures.
   A. This is an example of acceptable writing.
   B. The word *that* should be eliminated.
   C. A colon should be placed after *requested*.
   D. The comma after *A-12* should be eliminated.

   9.____

10. We attended a staff conference on Wednesday the new safety and fire rules were discussed.
    A. This is an example of acceptable writing.
    B. The words *safety*, *fire*, and *rules* should begin with capital letters.
    C. There should be a comma after the word *Wednesday*.
    D. There should be a period after the word *Wednesday*, and the word *the* should begin with a capital letter.

    10.____

11. Neither the dictionary or the telephone directory could be found in the office library. 11._____
    A. This is an example of acceptable writing.
    B. The word *or* should be changed to *nor*.
    C. The word *library* should be spelled *libery*.
    D. The word *neither* should be changed to *either*.

12. The report would have been typed correctly if the typist could read the draft. 12._____
    A. This is an example of acceptable writing.
    B. The word *would* should be removed.
    C. The word *have* should be inserted after the word *could*.
    D. The word *correctly* should be changed to *correct*.

13. The supervisor brought the reports and forms to an employees desk. 13._____
    A. This is an example of acceptable writing.
    B. The word *brought* should be changed to *took*.
    C. There should be a comma after the word *reports* and a comma after the word *forms*.
    D. The word *employees* should be spelled *employee's*.

14. It's important for all the office personnel to submit their vacation schedules on time. 14._____
    A. This is an example of acceptable writing.
    B. The word *It's* should be spelled *Its*.
    C. The word *their* should be spelled *they're*.
    D. The word *personnel* should be spelled *personal*.

15. The supervisor wants that all staff members report to the office at 9:00 A.M. 15._____
    A. This is an example of acceptable writing.
    B. The word *that* should be removed and the word *to* should be inserted after the word *members*.
    C. There should be a comma after the word *wants* and a comma after the word *office*.
    D. The word *wants* should be changed to *want* and the word *shall* should be inserted after the word *members*.

16. Every morning the clerk opens the office mail and distributes it. 16._____
    A. This is an example of acceptable writing.
    B. The word *opens* should be changed to *letters*.
    C. The word *mail* should be changed to *letters*.
    D. The word *it* should be changed to *them*.

17. The secretary typed more fast on a desktop computer than on a tablet. 17._____
    A. This is an example of acceptable writing.
    B. The words *more fast* should be changed to *faster*.
    C. There should be a comma after the words *desktop computer*.
    D. The word *than* should be changed to *then*.

18. The typist used an extention cord in order to connect her typewriter to the outlet nearest to her desks.
    A. This is an example of acceptable writing.
    B. A period should be placed after the word *cord*, and the word *in* should have a capital *I*.
    C. A comma should be placed after the word *typewriter*.
    D. The word *extention* should be spelled *extension*.

18.____

19. He would have went to the conference if he had received an invitation.
    A. This is an example of acceptable writing.
    B. The word *went* should be replaced by the word *gone*.
    C. The word *had* should be replaced by *would have*.
    D. The word *conference* should be spelled *conferance*.

19.____

20. In order to make the report neater, he spent many hours rewriting it.
    A. This is an example of acceptable writing.
    B. The word *more* should be inserted before the word *neater*.
    C. There should be a colon after the word *neater*.
    D. The word *spent* should be changed to *have spent*.

20.____

21. His supervisor told him that he should of read the memorandum more carefully.
    A. This is an example of acceptable writing.
    B. The word *memorandum* should be spelled *memorandom*.
    C. The word *of* should be replaced by the word *have*.
    D. The word *carefully* should be replaced by the word *careful*.

21.____

22. It was decided that two separate reports should be written.
    A. This is an example of acceptable writing.
    B. A comma should be inserted after the word *decided*.
    C. The word *be* should be replaced by the word *been*.
    D. A colon should be inserted after the word *that*.

22.____

23. She don't seem to understand that the work must be done as soon as possible.
    A. This is an example of acceptable writing.
    B. The word *doesn't* should replace the word *don't*.
    C. The word *why* should replace the word *that*.
    D. The word *as* before the word *soon* should be eliminated.

23.____

24. He excepted praise from his supervisor for a job well done.
    A. This is an example of acceptable writing.
    B. The word *excepted* should be spelled *accepted*.
    C. The order of the words *well done* should be changed to *done well*.
    D. There should be a comma after the word *supervisor*.

24.____

25. What appears to be intentional errors in grammar occur several times in the passage.   25.____
    A. This is an example of acceptable writing.
    B. The word *occur* should be spelled *occur*.
    C. The word *appears* should be changed to *appear*.
    D. The phrase *several times* should be changed to *from time to time*.

KEY (CORRECT ANSWERS)

1.	C	11.	B
2.	C	12.	C
3.	D	13.	D
4.	A	14.	A
5.	C	15.	B
6.	A	16.	A
7.	B	17.	B
8.	A	18.	D
9.	D	19.	B
10.	D	20.	A

21.	C
22.	A
23.	B
24.	B
25.	C

TEST 2

DIRECTIONS: Each question consists of a sentence which may or may not be an example of good formal English usage. Examine each sentence, considering grammar, punctuation, spelling, capitalization, and awkwardness. Then choose the CORRECT statement about it from the four options below it. If the English usage in the sentence given is better than any of the changes suggested in options B, C, or D, pick option A. Do not pick an option that will change the meaning of the sentence. *PRINT THE LETTER OF THE CORRECT ANSWER IN THE SPACE AT THE RIGHT.*

1. I don't know who could possibly of broken it.
   A. This is an example of acceptable writing.
   B. The word *who* should be replaced by the word *whom*.
   C. The word *of* should be replaced by the word *have*.
   D. The word *broken* should be replaced by the word *broke*.

2. Telephoning is easier than to write.
   A. This is an example of acceptable writing.
   B. The word *telephoning* should be spelled *telephoneing*.
   C. The word *than* should be replaced by the word *then*.
   D. The words *to write* should be replaced by the word *writing*.

3. The two operators who have been assigned to these consoles are on vacation.
   A. This is an example of acceptable writing.
   B. A comma should be placed after the word *operators*.
   C. The word *who* should be replaced by the word *whom*.
   D. The word *are* should be replaced by the word *is*.

4. You were suppose to teach me how to operate a plugboard.
   A. This is an example of acceptable writing,
   B. The word *were* should be replaced by the word *was*.
   C. The word *suppose* should be replaced by the word *supposed*.
   D. The word *teach* should be replaced by the word *team*.

5. If you had taken my advice; you would have spoken with him.
   A. This is an example of acceptable writing.
   B. The word *advice* should be spelled *advise*.
   C. The words *had taken* should be replaced by the word *take*.
   D. The semicolon should be changed to a comma.

6. The clerk could have completed the assignment on time if he knows where these materials were located.
   A. This is an example of acceptable writing.
   B. The word *knows* should be replaced by *had known*.
   C. The word "were" should be replaced by *had been*.
   D. The words *where these materials were located* should be replaced by *the location of these materials*.

94

7. All employees should be given safety training. Not just those who have accidents.
    A. This is an example of acceptable writing,
    B. The period after the word *training* should be changed to a colon.
    C. The period after the word *training* should be changed to a semicolon, and the first letter of the word *Not* should be changed to a small *n*.
    D. The period after the word *training* should be changed to a comma, and the first letter of the word *Not* should be changed to a small *n*,

7.____

8. This proposal is designed to promote employee awareness of the suggestion program, to encourage employee participation in the program, and to increase the number of suggestions submitted.
    A. This is an example of acceptable writing.
    B. The word *proposal* should be spelled *proposal*.
    C. The words *to increase the number of suggestions submitted* should be changed to *an increase in the number of suggestions is expected*.
    D. The word *promote* should be changed to *enhance*, and the word *increase* should be changed to *add to*.

8.____

9. The introduction of inovative managerial techniques should be preceded by careful analysis of the specific circumstances and conditions in each department.
    A. This is an example of acceptable writing.
    B. The word *techniques* should be spelled *techneques*.
    C. The word *inovative* should be spelled *innovative*.
    D. A comma should be placed after the word *circumstances* and after the word *conditions*.

9.____

10. This occurrence indicates that such criticism embarrasses him.
    A. This is an example of acceptable writing.
    B. The word *occurrence* should be spelled *occurrence*.
    C. The word *criticism* should be spelled *creticism*.
    D. The word *embarrasses* should be spelled *embarasses*.

10.____

11. He can recommend a mechanic whose work is reliable.
    A. This is an example of acceptable writing.
    B. the word *reliable* should be spelled *relyable*.
    C. The word *whose* should be spelled *who's*.
    D. The word *mechanic* should be spelled *mecanic*.

11.____

12. She typed quickly; like someone who had not a moment to lose.
    A. This is an example of acceptable writing.
    B. The word *not* should be removed.
    C. The semicolon should be changed to a comma.
    D. The word *quickly* should be placed before instead of after the word *typed*.

12.____

13. She insisted that she had to much work to do.
    A. This is an example of acceptable writing.
    B. The word *insisted* should be spelled *insisted*.
    C. The word *to* used in front of *much* should be spelled *too*.
    D. The word *do* should be changed to *be done*.

14. The report, along with the accompanying documents, were submitted for review.
    A. This is an example of acceptable writing.
    B. The words *were submitted* should be changed to *was submitted*.
    C. The word *accompanying* should be spelled *accompaning*.
    D. The comma after the word *report* should be taken out.

15. If others must use your files, be certain that they understand how the system works, but insist that you do all the filing and refiling.
    A. This is an example of acceptable writing.
    B. There should be a period after the word *works*, and the word *but* should start a new sentence.
    C. The words *filing* and *refiling* should be spelled *fileing* and *refileing*.
    D. There should be a comma after the word *but*.

16. The appeal was not considered because of its late arrival.
    A. This is an example of acceptable writing.
    B. The word *its* should be changed to *it's*.
    C. The word *its* should be changed to *the*.
    D. The words *late arrival* should be changed to *arrival late*.

17. The letter must be read carefully to determine under which subject it should be filed.
    A. This is an example of acceptable writing.
    B. The word *under* should be changed to *at*.
    C. The word *determine* should be spelled *determin*.
    D. The word *carefully* should be spelled *carefuly*.

18. He showed potential as an office manager, but he lacked skill in delegating work.
    A. This is an example of acceptable writing.
    B. The word *delegating* should be spelled *delagating*.
    C. The word *potential* should be spelled *potencial*.
    D. The words *he lacked* should be changed to *was lacking*.

19. His supervisor told him that it would be all right to receive personal mail at the office.
    A. This is an example of acceptable writing.
    B. The words *all right* should be changed to *alright*.
    C. The word *personal* should be spelled *personel*.
    D. The word *mail* should be changed to *letters*.

20. The report, along with the accompanying documents, were submitted for review. 20._____
    A. This is an example of acceptable writing.
    B. The words *were submitted* should be changed to *was submitted*.
    C. The word *accompanying* should be spelled *accompaning*.
    D. The comma after the word *report* should be taken out.

KEY (CORRECT ANSWERS)

1.	C	11.	A
2.	D	12.	C
3.	A	13.	C
4.	C	14.	B
5.	D	15.	A
6.	B	16.	A
7.	D	17.	D
8.	A	18.	A
9.	C	19.	A
10.	A	20.	B

WORK SCHEDULING

EXAMINATION SECTION
TEST 1

DIRECTIONS: Each question or incomplete statement is followed by several suggested answers or completions. Select the one that BEST answers the question or completes the statement. *PRINT THE LETTER OF THE CORRECT ANSWER IN THE SPACE AT THE RIGHT.*

Questions 1-6.

DIRECTIONS: Questions 1 through 6 are to be answered SOLELY on the basis of the information given in the ELEVATOR OPERATORS' WORK SCHEDULE shown below.

ELEVATOR OPERATORS' WORK SCHEDULE				
Operator	Hours of Work	A.M. Relief Period	Lunch Hour	P.M. Relief Period
Anderson	8:30-4:30	10:20-10:30	12:00-1:00	2:20-2:30
Carter	8:00-4:00	10:10-10:20	11:45-12:45	2:30-2:40
Daniels	9:00-5:00	10:20-10:30	12:30-1:30	3:15-3:25
Grand	9:30-5:30	11:30-11:40	1:00-2:00	4:05-4:15
Jones	7:45-3:45	9:45-9:55	11:30-12:30	2:05-2:15
Lewis	9:45-5:45	11:40-11:50	1:15-2:15	4:20-4:30
Nance	8:45-4:45	10:50-11:00	12:30-1:30	3:05-3:15
Perkins	8:00-4:00	10:00-10:10	12:00-1:00	2:40-2:50
Russo	7:45-3:45	9:30-9:40	11:30-12:30	2:10-2:20
Smith	9:45-5:45	11:45-11:55	1:15-2:15	4:05-4:15

1. The two operators who are on P.M. relief at the SAME time are

   A. Anderson and Daniels   B. Carter and Perkins
   C. Jones and Russo   D. Grand and Smith

   1.____

2. Of the following, the two operators who have the SAME lunch hour are

   A. Anderson and Perkins   B. Daniels and Russo
   C. Grand and Smith   D. Nance and Russo

   2.____

3. At 12:15, the number of operators on their lunch hour is

   A. 3   B. 4   C. 5   D. 6

   3.____

4. The operator who has an A.M. relief period right after Perkins and a P.M. relief period right before Perkins is

   A. Russo   B. Nance   C. Daniels D. Carter

   4.____

5. The number of operators who are scheduled to be working at 4:40 is

   A. 5   B. 6   C. 7   D. 8

   5.____

6. According to the schedule, it is MOST correct to say that
   A. no operator has a relief period during the time that another operator has a lunch hour
   B. each operator has to wait an identical amount of time between the end of lunch and the beginning of P.M. relief period
   C. no operator has a relief period before 9:45 or after 4:00
   D. each operator is allowed a total of 1 hour and 20 minutes for lunch hour and relief periods

KEY (CORRECT ANSWERS)

1. D
2. A
3. C
4. D
5. A
6. D

TEST 2

DIRECTIONS: Each question or incomplete statement is followed by several suggested answers or completions. Select the one that BEST answers the question or completes the statement. *PRINT THE LETTER OF THE CORRECT ANSWER IN THE SPACE AT THE RIGHT.*

Questions 1-7.

DIRECTIONS: Questions 1 through 7 are to be answered SOLELY on the basis of the time sheet and instructions given below.

The following time sheet indicates the times that seven laundry workers arrived and left each day for the week of August 23. The times they arrived for work are shown under the heading IN, and the times they left are shown under the heading OUT. The letter (P) indicates time which was used for personal business. Time used for this purpose is charged to annual leave. Lunch time is one-half hour from noon to 12:30 P.M. and is not accounted for on this time record.

The employees on this shift are scheduled to work from 8:00 A.M. to 4:00 P.M. Lateness is charged to annual leave. Reporting after 8:00 A.M. is considered late.

	MON.		TUES.		WED.		THURS.		FRI.	
	AM IN	PM OUT	AM IN	PM OUT	AM IN	PM OUT	AM IN	PM OUT	AM IN	PM OUT
Baxter	7:50	4:01	7:49	4:07	8:00	4:07	8:20	4:00	7:42	4:03
Gardner	8:02	4:00	8:20	4:00	8:05	3:30(P)	8:00	4:03	8:00	4:07
Clements	8:00	4:04	8:03	4:01	7:59	4:00	7:54	4:06	7:59	4:00
Tompkins	7:56	4:00	Annual leave		8:00	4:07	7:59	4:00	8:00	4:01
Wagner	8:04	4:03	7:40	4:00	7:53	4:04	8:00	4:09	7:53	4:00
Patterson	8:00	2:30(P)	8:15	4:04	Sick leave		7:45	4:00	7:59	4:04
Cunningham	7:43	4:02	7:50	4:00	7:59	4:02	8:00	4:10	8:00	4:00

1. Which one of the following laundry workers did NOT have any time charged to annual leave or sick leave during the week?

    A. Gardner   B. Clements   C. Tompkins   D. Cunningham

    1.____

2. On which day did ALL the laundry workers arrive on time?

    A. Monday   B. Wednesday   C. Thursday   D. Friday

    2.____

3. Which of the following laundry workers used time to take care of personal business?

    A. Baxter and Clements   B. Patterson and Cunningham
    C. Gardner and Patterson   D. Wagner and Tompkins

    3.____

4. How many laundry workers were late on Monday?

    A. 1   B. 2   C. 3   D. 4

    4.____

5. Which one of the following laundry workers arrived late on three of the five days?

    A. Baxter   B. Gardner   C. Wagner   D. Patterson

    5.____

101

6. The percentage of laundry workers reporting to work late on Tuesday is MOST NEARLY 6._____

   A. 15%   B. 25%   C. 45%   D. 50%

7. The percentage of laundry workers that were absent for an entire day during the week is MOST NEARLY 7._____

   A. 6%   B. 9%   C. 15%   D. 30%

KEY (CORRECT ANSWERS)

1. D
2. D
3. C
4. B
5. B
6. C
7. D

TEST 3

Questions 1-9.

DIRECTIONS: Questions 1 through 9 are to be answered SOLELY on the basis of the following information and timesheet given below.

The following is a foreman's timesheet for his crew for one week. The hours worked each day or the reason the man was off on that day are shown on the sheet. *R* means rest day. *A* means annual leave. *S* means sick leave. Where a man worked only part of a day, both the number of hours worked and the number of hours taken off are entered. The reason for absence is entered in parentheses next to the number of hours taken off.

Name	Saturday	Sunday	Monday	Tuesday	Wednesday	Thursday	Friday
Smith	R	R	7	7	7	3 4(A)	7
Jones	R	7	7	7	7	7	R
Green	R	R	7	7	S	S	S
White	R	R	7	7	A	7	7
Doe	7	7	7	7	7	R	R
Brown	R	R	A	7	7	7	7
Black	R	R	S	7	7	7	7
Reed	R	R	7	7	7	7	S
Roe	R	R	A	7	7	7	7
Lane	7	R	R	7	7	A	S

1. The caretaker who worked EXACTLY 21 hours during the week is

   A. Lane   B. Roe   C. Smith   D. White

2. The TOTAL number of hours worked by all caretakers during the week is

   A. 268   B. 276   C. 280   D. 288

3. The two days of the week on which MOST caretakers were off are

   A. Thursday and Friday
   B. Friday and Saturday
   C. Saturday and Sunday
   D. Sunday and Monday

4. The day on which three caretakers were off on sick leave is

   A. Monday   B. Friday   C. Saturday   D. Sunday

5. The two workers who took LEAST time off during the week are

   A. Doe and Reed
   B. Jones and Doe
   C. Reed and Smith
   D. Smith and Jones

6. The caretaker who worked the LEAST number of hours during the week is

   A. Brown   B. Green   C. Lane   D. Roe

7. The caretakers who did NOT work on Thursday are

   A. Doe, White, and Smith
   B. Green, Doe, and Lane
   C. Green, Doe, and Smith
   D. Green, Lane, and Smith

8. The day on which one caretaker worked ONLY 3 hours is   8.____
   A. Friday   B. Saturday   C. Thursday   D. Wednesday

9. The day on which ALL caretakers worked is   9.____
   A. Monday   B. Thursday   C. Tuesday   D. Wednesday

KEY (CORRECT ANSWERS)

1. A
2. B
3. C
4. B
5. B

6. B
7. B
8. C
9. C

TEST 4

Questions 1-6.

DIRECTIONS: Questions 1 through 6 are to be answered SOLELY on the basis of the table below which shows the initial requests made by staff for vacation. It is to be used with the RULES AND GUIDELINES to make the decisions and judgments called for in each of the questions.

VACATION REQUESTS FOR THE ONE YEAR PERIOD FROM MAY 1, YEAR X THROUGH APRIL 30, YEAR Y				
Name	Work Assignment	Date Appointed	Accumulated Annual Leave Days	Vacation Periods Requested
DeMarco	MVO	Mar. 2003	25	May 3-21; Oct. 25-Nov. 5
Moore	Dispatcher	Dec. 1997	32	May 24-June 4; July 12-16
Kingston	MVO	Apr. 2007	28	May 24-June 11; Feb. 7-25
Green	MVO	June 2006	26	June 7-18; Sept. 6-24
Robinson	MVO	July 2008	30	June 28-July 9; Nov. 15-26
Reilly	MVO	Oct. 2009	23	July 5-9; Jan. 31-Mar. 3
Stevens	MVO	Sept. 1996	31	July 5-23; Oct. 4-29
Costello	MVO	Sept. 1998	31	July 5-30; Oct. 4-22
Maloney	Dispatcher	Aug. 1992	35	July 5-Aug. 6; Nov. 1-5
Hughes	Director	Feb. 1990	38	July 26-Sept. 3
Lord	MVO	Jan. 2010	20	Aug. 9-27; Feb. 7-25
Diaz	MVO	Dec. 2009	28	Aug. 9-Sept. 10
Krimsky	MVO	May 2006	22	Oct. 18-22: Nov. 22-Dec. 10

RULES AND GUIDELINES

1. The two Dispatchers cannot be on vacation at the same time, nor can a Dispatcher be on vacation at the same time as the Director.

2. For the period June 1 through September 30, not more than three MVO's can be on vacation at the same time.

3. For the period October 1 through May 31, not more than two MVO's at a time can be on vacation.

4. In cases where the same vacation time is requested by too many employees for all of them to be given the time under the rules, the requests of those who have worked the longest will be granted.

5. No employee may take more leave days than the number of annual leave days accumulated and shown in the table.

6. All vacation periods shown in the table and described in the questions below begin on a Monday and end on a Friday.

7. Employees work a five-day week (Monday through Friday). They are off weekends and holidays with no charges to leave balances. When a holiday falls on a Saturday or Sunday, employees are given the following Monday off without charge to annual leave.

8. Holidays: May 31   October 25   January 1
               July 4   November 2   February 12
               September 6   November 25   February 21
               October 11   December 25   February 21

9. An employee shall be given any part of his initial requests that is permissible under the above rules and shall have first right to it despite any further adjustment of schedule.

---

1. Until adjustments in the vacation schedule can be made, the vacation dates that can be approved for Krimsky are

   A. Oct. 18-22; Nov. 22-Dec. 10
   B. Oct. 18-22; Nov. 29-Dec. 10
   C. Oct. 18-22 *only*
   D. Nov. 22-Dec. 10 *only*

2. Until adjustments in the vacation schedule can be made, the vacation dates that can be approved for Maloney are

   A. July 5-Aug. 6; Nov. 1-5
   B. July 5-23; Nov. 1-5
   C. July 5-9; Nov. 1-5
   D. Nov. 1-5 *only*

3. According to the table, Lord wants a vacation in August and another in February. Until adjustments in the vacation schedule can be made, he can be allowed to take _____ of the August vacation and _____ of the February vacation.

   A. all; none
   B. all; almost half
   C. almost all; almost half
   D. almost half; all

4. Costello cannot be given all the vacation he has requested because

   A. the MVO's who have more seniority than he has have requested time he wishes
   B. he does not have enough accumulated annual leave
   C. a dispatcher is applying for vacation at the same time as Costello
   D. there are five people who want vacation in July

5. According to the table, how many leave days will DeMarco be charged for his vacation from October 25 through November 5?

   A. 10   B. 9   C. 8   D. 7

6. How many leave days will Moore use if he uses the requested vacation allowable to him under the rules?

   A. 9   B. 10   C. 14   D. 15

KEY (CORRECT ANSWERS)

1. D
2. B
3. A
4. B
5. C
6. A

TEST 5

Questions 1-8.

DIRECTIONS: Questions 1 through 8 are to be answered SOLELY on the basis of Charts I, II, III, and IV. Assume that you are the supervisor of Operators R, S, T, U, V, W, and X, and it is your responsibility to schedule their lunch hours.

The charts each represent a possible scheduling of lunch hours during a lunch period from 11:30 - 2:00. An operator-hour is one hour of time spent by one operator. Each box on the chart represents one half-hour. The boxes marked L represent the time when each operator is scheduled to have her lunch hour. For example, in Chart I, next to Operator R, the boxes for 11:30 - 12:00 and 12:00 -12:30 are marked L. This means that Operator R is scheduled to have her lunch hour from 11:30 to 12:30.

I

	11:30-12:00	12:00-12:30	12:30-1:00	1:00-1:30	1:30-2:00
R	L	L			
S		L	L		
T		L	L		
U			L	L	
V			L	T	
W				L	L
X				L	L

II

	11:30-12:00	12:00-12:30	12:30-1:00	1:00-1:30	1:30-2:00
R				L	L
S		L	L		
T	L	L			
U			L	L	
V				L	L
W				L	L
X		L	L		

III

	11:30-12:00	12:00-12:30	12:30-1:00	1:00-1:30	1:30-2:00
R	L	L			
S				L	L
T	L	L			
U			L	L	
V	L	L			
W				L	L
X				L	L

IV

	11:30-12:00	12:00-12:30	12:30-1:00	1:00-1:30	1:30-2:00
R	L	L			
S	L	L			
T		L	L		
U			L	L	
V				L	L
W				L	L
X			L	L	

1. If, under the schedule represented in Chart II, Operator R has her lunch hour changed to 12:30-1:30, that leaves how many operator-hours of phone coverage from 1:00-2:00?

    A. 2   B. 2 1/2   C. 3   D. 4 1/2

2. If Operator S asks you whether she and Operator T may have the same lunch hour, you could accommodate her by using the schedule in Chart

    A. I   B. II   C. III   D. IV

3. From past experience you know that the part of the lunch period when the phones are busiest is from 12:30-1:30. Which chart shows the BEST phone coverage from 12:30 to 1:30?

    A. I   B. II   C. III   D. IV

4. At least three operators have the same lunch hour according to Chart(s)

    A. II and III
    B. II and IV
    C. III only
    D. IV only

108

5. Which chart would provide the POOREST phone coverage during the period 12:00-1:30, based on total number of operator-hours from 12:00 to 1:30?   5.____

   A. I B. II C. III D. IV

6. Which chart would make it possible for U, W, and X to have the same lunch hour?   6.____

   A. I B. II C. III D. IV

7. The portion of the lunch period during which the telephones are least busy is 11:30-12:30.   7.____
   Which chart is MOST likely to have been designed with that fact in mind?

   A. I B. II C. III D. IV

8. Assume that you have decided to use Chart IV to schedule your operators' lunch hours on a specific day. Operator T asks you if she can have her lunch hour changed to 1:00-2:00.   8.____
   If you grant her request, how many operators will be working during the period 12:00 to 12:30?

   A. 1 B. 2 C. 4 D. 5

KEY (CORRECT ANSWERS)

1. D
2. A
3. B
4. A
5. A
6. C
7. C
8. D

TEST 6

Questions 1-13.

DIRECTIONS: Questions 1 through 13 consist of a statement. You are to indicate whether the statement is TRUE (T) or FALSE (F). *PRINT THE LETTER OF THE CORRECT ANSWER IN THE SPACE AT THE RIGHT.* Questions 1 through 13 are to be answered SOLELY on the basis of the information given in the table below.

DEPARTMENT OF FERRIES
ATTENDANTS WORK ASSIGNMENT - JULY 2003

Name	Year Employed	Ferry Assigned	Hours of Work	Lunch Period	Days Off
Adams	1999	Hudson	7 AM - 3 PM	11-12	Fri. and Sat.
Baker	1992	Monroe	7 AM - 3 PM	11-12	Sun. and Mon.
Gunn	1995	Troy	8 AM - 4 PM	12-1	Fri. and Sat.
Hahn	1989	Erie	9 AM - 5 PM	1-2	Sat. and Sun.
King	1998	Albany	7 AM - 3 PM	11-12	Sun. and Mon.
Nash	1993	Hudson	11 AM - 7 PM	3-4	Sun. and Mon.
Olive	2003	Fulton	10 AM - 6 PM	2-3	Sat. and Sun.
Queen	2002	Albany	11 AM - 7 PM	3-4	Fri. and Sat.
Rose	1990	Troy	11 AM - 7 PM	3-4	Sun. and Mon.
Smith	1991	Monroe	10 AM - 6 PM	2-3	Fri. and Sat.

1. The chart shows that there are only five (5) ferries being used.   1.___

2. The attendant who has been working the LONGEST time is Rose.   2.___

3. The Troy has one more attendant assigned to it than the Erie.   3.___

4. Two (2) attendants are assigned to work from 10 P.M. to 6 A.M.   4.___

5. According to the chart, no more than one attendant was hired in any year.   5.___

6. The NEWEST employee is Olive.   6.___

7. There are as many attendants on the 7 to 3 shift as on the 11 to 7 shift.   7.___

8. MOST of the attendants have their lunch either between 12 and 1 or 2 and 3.   8.___

9. All the employees work four (4) hours before they go to lunch.   9.___

10. On the Hudson, Adams goes to lunch when Nash reports to work.   10.___

11. All the attendants who work on the 7 to 3 shift are off on Saturday and Sunday.   11.___

12. All the attendants have either a Saturday or Sunday as one of their days off.   12.___

13. At least two (2) attendants are assigned to each ferry.   13.___

KEY (CORRECT ANSWERS)

1. F
2. F
3. T
4. F
5. T
6. T
7. T
8. F
9. T
10. T
11. F
12. T
13. F

EXAMINATION SECTION
TEST 1

DIRECTIONS: Each question or incomplete statement is followed by several suggested answers or completions. Select the one that BEST answers the question or completes the statement. *PRINT THE LETTER OF THE CORRECT ANSWER IN THE SPACE AT THE RIGHT.*

1. A *basic* method of operation that a *good* supervisor should follow is to

    A. check the work of subordinates constantly to make sure they are not making exceptions to the rules
    B. train subordinates so they can handle problems that come up regularly themselves and come to him only with special cases
    C. delegate to subordinates only those duties which he cannot do himself
    D. issue directions to subordinates only on special matters

2. To do a *good* job of performance evaluation, it is BEST for a supervisor to

    A. compare the employee's performance to that of another employee doing similar work
    B. give greatest weight to instances of unusually good or unusually poor performance
    C. leave out any consideration of the employee's personal traits
    D. measure the employee's performance against standard performance requirements

3. Of the following, the MOST important reason for a supervisor to have private face to face discussions with subordinates about their performance is to

    A. help employees improve their work
    B. give special praise to employees who perform well
    C. encourage the employees to compete for higher performance ratings
    D. discipline employees who perform poorly

4. Of the following, the CHIEF purpose of a probationary period for a new employee is to allow time for

    A. finding out whether the selection processes are satisfactory
    B. the employee to make adjustments in his home circumstances made necessary by the job
    C. the employee to decide whether he wants a permanent appointment
    D. determining the fitness of the employee to continue in the job

5. When a subordinate resigns his job, it is MOST important to conduct an exit interview in order to

    A. try to get the employee to remain on the job
    B. learn the true reasons for the employee's resignation
    C. see that the employee leaves with a good opinion of the agency
    D. ask the employee if he would consider a transfer

6. Chronic lateness of employees is generally LEAST likely to be due to

    A. distance of job location from home   B. poor personnel administration
    C. unexpressed employee grievances   D. low morale

7. Of the following, the LEAST effective stimulus for motivating employees toward improved performance over a long-range period is

    A. their sense of achievement
    B. their feeling of recognition
    C. opportunity for their self-development
    D. an increase in salary

8. Suppose that NOT ONE of a group of employees has turned in an idea to the employees suggestion system during the past year.
   The *most probable* reason for this situation is that the

    A. money awards given for suggestions used are not high enough to make employees interested
    B. employees in this group are not able to develop any good ideas
    C. supervisor of these employees is not doing enough to encourage them to take part in the program
    D. methods and procedures of operation do not need improvement

9. A subordinate tells you that he is having trouble concentrating on his work due to a personal problem at home.
   Of the following, it would be BEST for you to

    A. refer him to a community service agency
    B. listen quietly to the story because he may just need a sympathetic ear
    C. tell him that you cannot help him because the problem is not job related
    D. ask him questions about the nature of the problem and tell him how you would handle it

10. For you as a supervisor to give each of your subordinates *exactly* the same type of supervision is

    A. *advisable,* because doing this insures fair and impartial treatment of each individual
    B. *not advisable,* because individuals like to think that they are receiving better treatment than others
    C. *advisable,* because once a supervisor learns how to deal with a subordinate who brings a problem to him, he can handle another subordinate with this problem in the same way
    D. *not advisable,* because each person is different and there is no one supervisory procedure for dealing with individuals that applies in every case

11. A senior employee under your supervision tells you that he is reluctant to speak to one of his subordinates about his poor work habits, because this worker is "strong-willed" and he does not want to antagonize him.
    For you to offer to speak to the subordinate about this matter yourself would be

    A. *advisable,* since you are in a position of greater authority
    B. *inadvisable,* since handling this problem is a basic supervisory responsibility of the senior employee
    C. *advisable,* since the senior employee must work more closely with the worker than you do
    D. *inadvisable,* since you should not risk antagonizing the employee yourself

12. Some of your subordinates have been coming to you with complaints you feel are unimportant. For you to hear their stories out is

    A. *poor practice,* you should spend your time on more important matters
    B. *good practice,* this will increase your popularity with your subordinates
    C. *poor practice,* subordinates should learn to come to you only with major grievances
    D. *good practice,* it may prevent minor complaints from developing into major grievances

13. Assume that an agency has an established procedure for handling employee grievances. An employee in this agency, comes to his immediate supervisor with a grievance. The supervisor investigates the matter and makes a decision.
    However, the employee is not satisfied with the decision made by the supervisor. The BEST action for the supervisor to take is to

    A. tell the employee he will review the matter further
    B. remind the employee that he is the supervisor and the employee must act in accordance with his decision
    C. explain to the employee how he can carry his complaint forward to the next step in the grievance procedure
    D. tell the employee he will consult with his own superiors on the matter

14. Subordinate employees and senior employees often must make quick decisions while in the field. The supervisor can BEST help subordinates meet such situations by

    A. training them in the appropriate action to take for every problem that may come up
    B. limiting the areas in which they are permitted to make decisions
    C. making certain they understand clearly the basic policies of the bureau and the department
    D. delegating authority to make such decisions to only a few subordinates on each level

15. Studies have shown that the CHIEF cause of failure to achieve success as a supervisor is

    A. an unwillingness to delegate authority to subordinates
    B. the establishment of high performance standards for subordinates
    C. the use of discipline that is too strict
    D. showing too much leniency to poor workers

16. When a supervisor delegates to a subordinate certain work that he normally does himself, it is MOST important that he give the subordinate

    A. responsibility for also setting the standards for the work to be done
    B. sufficient authority to be able to carry out the assignment
    C. written, step-by-step instructions for doing the work
    D. an explanation of one part of the task at a time

17. It is particularly important that disciplinary actions be equitable as between individuals. This statement *implies* that

    A. punishment applied in disciplinary actions should be lenient
    B. proposed disciplinary actions should be reviewed by higher authority
    C. subordinates should have an opportunity to present their stories before penalties are applied
    D. penalties for violations of the rules should be standardized and consistently applied

18. You discover that from time to time a number of false rumors circulate among your subordinates.
    Of the following, the BEST way for you to handle this situation is to

    A. ignore the rumors since rumors circulate in every office and can never be eliminated
    B. attempt to find those responsible for the rumors and reprimand them
    C. make sure that your employees are informed as soon as possible about all matters that affect them
    D. inform your superior about the rumors and let him deal with the matter

19. Supervisors who allow the "halo effect" to influence their evaluations of subordinates are *most likely* to

    A. give more lenient ratings to older employees who have longer service
    B. let one highly favorable or unfavorable trait unduly affect their judgment of an employee
    C. evaluate all employees on one trait before considering a second
    D. give high evaluations in order to avoid antagonizing their subordinates

20. For a supervisor to keep records of reprimands to subordinates about infractions of the rules is

    A. *good practice,* because these records are valuable to support disciplinary actions recommended or taken
    B. *poor practice,* because such records are evidence of the supervisor's inability to maintain discipline
    C. *good practice,* because such records indicate that the supervisor is doing a good job
    D. *poor practice,* because the best way to correct subordinates is to give them more training

21. When a new departmental policy has been established, it would be MOST advisable for you, as a supervisor, to

    A. distribute a memo which states the new policy and instruct your subordinates to read it
    B. explain specifically to your subordinates how the policy is going to affect them
    C. make sure your subordinates understand that you are not responsible for setting the policy
    D. tell your subordinates whether you agree or disagree with the policy

22. As a supervisor, you receive several complaints about the rude conduct of a subordinate. 22._____
The FIRST action you should take is to

   A. request his transfer to another office
   B. prepare a charge sheet for disciplinary action
   C. assign a senior employee to work with him for a week
   D. interview the employee to determine possible reason, and warn that correction is necessary

23. A supervisor is *most likely* to get subordinates to work cooperatively toward accomplishing bureau goals if he 23._____

   A. creates an atmosphere that contributes to their feeling of security
   B. backs up subordinates even when they occasionally disobey regulations
   C. shows interest in subordinates by helping them solve their personal problems
   D. uses an authoritarian or "bossy" approach to supervision

24. A supervisor is holding a staff meeting with his senior employees to try to find an acceptable solution to a problem that has come up. 24._____
Of the following, the CHIEF role of the supervisor at this meeting should be to

   A. see that every member of the group contributes at least one suggestions
   B. act as chairman of the meeting, but take no other active part to avoid influencing the senior employees
   C. keep the participants from wandering off into discussions of irrelevant matters
   D. make certain the participants hear his views on the matter at the beginning of the meeting

25. An employee shows you a certificate that he has just received for completing two years of study in conversational Spanish. As his supervisor, it would be BEST for you to 25._____

   A. put a note about this accomplishment in his personnel folder
   B. assign him to areas in which people of Spanish origin live
   C. congratulate him on this accomplishment, but tell him frankly that you doubt this is likely to have any direct bearing on his work
   D. encourage him to continue his studies and become thoroughly fluent in speaking the language

KEY (CORRECT ANSWERS)

1. B
2. D
3. A
4. D
5. B
6. A
7. D
8. C
9. B
10. D
11. B
12. D
13. C
14. C
15. A
16. B
17. D
18. C
19. B
20. A
21. B
22. D
23. A
24. C
25. A

TEST 2

DIRECTIONS: Each question or incomplete statement is followed by several suggested answers or completions. Select the one that BEST answers the question or completes the statement. *PRINT THE LETTER OF THE CORRECT ANSWER IN THE SPACE AT THE RIGHT.*

1. Of the following, the factor affecting employee morale which the immediate supervisor is LEAST able to control is

    A. handling of grievances
    B. fair and impartial treatment of subordinates
    C. general presonnel rules and regulations
    D. accident prevention

    1.____

2. When one of your workers does outstanding work, you should

    A. explain to your other employees that you expect the same kind of work of them
    B. praise him for his work so that he will know it is appreciated
    C. say nothing, because other employees may think you are showing favoritism
    D. show him how his work can be improved still more so that he will not sit back

    2.____

3. For you as a supervisor to consider a suggestion from a probationary worker for improving a procedure would be

    A. *poor practice,* because this employee is too new on the job to know much about it
    B. *good practice,* because you may be able to share credit for the suggestion
    C. *poor practice,* because it may hurt the morale of the older employees
    D. *good practice,* because the suggestion may be worthwhile

    3.____

4. If you find you must criticize the work of one of your workers, it would be BEST for you to

    A. mention the good points in his work as well as the faults
    B. caution him that he will receive an unsatisfactory performance report unless his work improves
    C. compare his work to that of the other agents you supervise
    D. apologize for making the criticism

    4.____

5. As a senior employee which one of the following matters would it be BEST for you to talk over with your supervisor before you take final action?

    A. One of the workers you supervise continues to disregard your instructions repeatedly in spite of repeated warnings
    B. One of your workers tells you he wants to discuss a personal problem
    C. A probationary employee tells you he does not understand a procedure
    D. One of your workers tells you he disagrees with the way you rate his work

    5.____

6. If one of your subordinates asks you a question about a department rule and you do not know the answer, you should tell him that

    A. he should try to get the information himself
    B. you do not have the answer, but you will get it for him as soon as you can
    C. he should ask you the question again a week from now
    D. he should put the question in writing

    6.____

7. If, as a supervisor, you realize that you have been unfair in criticizing one of your subordinates, the BEST action for you to take is to

   A. say nothing, but overlook some error made by this employee in the future
   B. be frank and tell the employee that you are sorry for the mistake you made
   C. let the employee know in some indirect way without admitting your mistake, that you realize he was not at fault
   D. say nothing, but be more careful about criticizing subordinates in the future

8. Of the following, the MOST important reason for a supervisor to write an accident report as soon as possible after an accident has happened is to

   A. make sure that important facts about the accident are not forgotten
   B. avoid delay in getting compensation for the injured person
   C. get adequate medical treatment for the injured person
   D. keep department accident statistics up to date

9. In any matter which may require disciplinary action, the FIRST responsibility of the supervisor is to

   A. decide what penalty should be applied for the offense
   B. refer the matter to a higher authority for complete investigation
   C. place the interests of the department above those of the employee
   D. investigate the matter fully to get all the facts

10. Suppose you find it necessary to criticize one of the subordinates you supervise. You should

    A. send an official letter to his home
    B. speak to him about the matter privately
    C. speak to him at a staff meeting
    D. ask another worker who is friendly with him to talk to him about the matter

11. Some of your subordinates have been coming to you with complaints you feel are unimportant. For you to hear their stories out is

    A. *poor practice,* you should spend your time on more important matters
    B. *good practice,* this will increase your popularity with your subordinates
    C. *poor practice,* subordinates should learn to come to you only with major grievances
    D. *good practice,* it may prevent minor complaints from developing into major grievances

12. Suppose that NOT ONE of a group of employees has turned in an idea to the employees' suggestion system during the past year. The *most probable* reason for this situation is that the

    A. supervisor of these employees is not doing enough to encourage them to take part in this program
    B. employees in this group are not able to develop any good ideas
    C. money awards given for suggestions used are not high enough to make employees interested
    D. methods and procedures of operation do not need improvement

13. For you as a supervisor to give each of your subordinates *exactly* the same type of supervision is

    A. *advisable*, because doing this insures fair and impartial treatment of each individual
    B. *not advisable*, because each person is different and there is no one supervisory procedure for dealing with individuals that applies in every case
    C. *advisable*, because once a supervisor learns how to deal with a subordinate who brings a problem to him, he can handle another subordinate with this problem in the same way
    D. *not advisable*, because individuals like to think that they are receiving better treatment than others

14. In evaluating personnel, a supervisor should keep in mind that the MOST important objective of performance evaluations is to

    A. encourage employees to compete for higher performance ratings
    B. give recognition to employees who perform well
    C. help employees improve their work
    D. discipline employees who perform poorly

15. A subordinate tells you that he is having trouble concentrating on his work due to a personal problem at home. Of the following, it would be BEST for you to

    A. refer him to a community service agency
    B. listen quietly to the story because he may just need a sympathetic ear
    C. tell him that you cannot help him because the problem is not job-related
    D. ask him some questions about the nature of the problem and tell him how you would handle it

16. To do a good job of performance evaluation, it is BEST for a supervisor to

    A. measure the employee's performance against standard performance requirements
    B. compare the employee's performance to that of another employee doing similar work
    C. leave out any consideration of the employee's personal traits
    D. give greatest weight to instances of unusually good or unusually poor performance

17. It is particularly important that disciplinary actions be equitable as between individuals. This statement *implies* that

    A. punishment applied in disciplinary actions should be lenient
    B. proposed disciplinary actions should be reviewed by higher authority
    C. subordinates should have an opportunity to present their stories before penalties are applied
    D. penalties for violations of the rules should be standardized and consistently applied

18. Assume that an agency has an established procedure for handling employee grievances. An employee in this agency comes to his immediate supervisor with a grievance. The supervisor investigates the matter and makes a decision. However, the employee is not satisfied with the decision made by the supervisor.
    The BEST action for the supervisor to take is to

A. tell the employee he will review the matter further
B. remind the employee that he is the supervisor and the employee must act in accordance with his decision
C. explain to the employee how he can carry his complaint forward to the next step in the grievance procedure
D. tell the employee he will consult with his own superiors on the matter

19. Of the following, the CHIEF purpose of a probationary period for a new employee is to allow time for

   A. finding out whether the selection processes are satisfactory
   B. determining the fitness of the employee to continue in the job
   C. the employee to decide whether he wants a permanent appointment
   D. the employee to make adjustments in his home circumstances made necessary by the job

20. Of the following, the subject that would be MOST important to include in a "break-in" program for new employees is

   A. explanation of rules, regulations and policies of the agency
   B. Instruction in the agency's history and programs
   C. explanation of the importance of the new employees' own particular job
   D. explanation of the duties and responsibilities of the employee

21. Suppose a new employee under your supervision seems slow to learn and is making mistakes in performing his duties. Your FIRST action should be to

   A. pass this information on to the bureau director
   B. reprimand the worker so he will not repeat these mistakes
   C. find out whether this worker understands your instructions
   D. note these facts for future reference when writing up the monthly performance evaluation

22. In training new employees to do a certain job it would be LEAST desirable for you to

   A. demonstrate how the job is done, step by step
   B. encourage the workers to ask questions if they aren't clear about any point
   C. tell them about the various mistakes other agents have made in doing this job
   D. have the workers do the job, explaining to you what they are doing and why

23. One of the workers under your supervision is resentful when you ask her to remove her jangling bracelets before she starts her tour of duty.
    Of the following, the BEST explanation you can give her for the rule against wearing such jewelry while on duty is that

   A. the jewelry may create a safety hazard
   B. employees must give up certain personal liberties if they want to keep their jobs
   C. workers cannot perform their duties as efficiently if they wear distracting jewelry
   D. citizens may receive an unfavorable impression of the department

24. Of the following, the LEAST important reason for having a department handbook and a bureau standard operating procedure is to

    A. help in training new employees
    B. provide a source of reference for department and bureau rules and procedures
    C. prevent errors in work by providing clear guidelines
    D. make the supervisor's job easy

25. On inspecting your squad prior to their tour of duty, you note an employee improperly and unacceptably dressed.
    The FIRST action you should take is to

    A. call the employee aside and insist on immediate correction if possible
    B. notify the district commander right away
    C. have the employee submit a memorandum explaining the reason for the improper uniform
    D. permit the employee to proceed on duty but warn him not to let this happen again

KEY (CORRECT ANSWERS)

1.	C	11.	D
2.	B	12.	A
3.	D	13.	B
4.	A	14.	C
5.	A	15.	B
6.	B	16.	A
7.	B	17.	D
8.	A	18.	C
9.	D	19.	B
10.	B	20.	D

21.	C
22.	C
23.	D
24.	D
25.	A

EXAMINATION SECTION
TEST 1

DIRECTIONS: Each question or incomplete statement is followed by several suggested answers or completions. Select the one that BEST answers the question or completes the statement. *PRINT THE LETTER OF THE CORRECT ANSWER IN THE SPACE AT THE RIGHT.*

1. When all of her employees are assigned to perform identical routine tasks, a supervisor would PROBABLY find it most difficult to differentiate among these employees as to the
    A. amount of work each completed
    B. initiative each one shows in doing the work
    C. number of errors in each one's work
    D. number of times each one is absent or late

1.____

2. The one of the following guiding principles to which a supervisor should give the GREATEST weight when it becomes necessary to discipline an employee is that the
    A. discipline should be of such a nature as to improve the future work of the employee
    B. main benefit gained in disciplining one employee is that all employees are kept from breaking the same rule
    C. morale of all the employees should be improved by the discipline of the one
    D. rules should be applied in a fixed and unchanging manner

2.____

3. In using praise to encourage employees to do better work, the supervisor should realize that praising an employee too often is not good MAINLY because the
    A. employee will be resented by her fellow employees
    B. employee will begin to think she's doing too much work
    C. praise will lose its value as an incentive
    D. supervisor doesn't have the time to praise an employee frequently

3.____

4. A supervisor notices that one of her best employees has apparently begun to loaf on the job.
   In this situation, the supervisor should FIRST
    A. allow the employee a period of grace in view of her excellent record
    B. change the employee's job assignment
    C. determine the reason for the change in the employee's behavior
    D. take disciplinary action immediately as she would with any other employee

4.____

5. A supervisor who wants to get a spirit of friendly cooperation from the employees in her unit is MOST likely to be successful if she
    A. makes no exceptions in strictly enforcing department procedures
    B. shows a cooperative spirit herself
    C. tells them they are the best in the department
    D. treats them to coffee once in a while

5.____

6. *Accidents do not just happen.*
   In view of this statement, it is important for the supervisor to realize that
   A. accidents are sometimes deliberate
   B. combinations of unavoidable circumstances cause accidents
   C. she must take the blame for each accident
   D. she should train her employees in accident prevention

7. Suppose your superior points out to you several jobs that were poorly done by the employees under your supervision.
   As the supervisor of these employees, you should
   A. accept responsibility for the poor work and take steps to improve the work in the future
   B. blame the employees for shirking on the job while you were busy on other work
   C. defend the employees since up to this time they were all good workers
   D. explain that the poor work was due to circumstances beyond your control

8. If a supervisor discovers a situation which is a possible source of grievance, it would be BEST for her to
   A. be ready to answer the employees when they make a direct complaint
   B. do nothing until the employees make a direct complaint
   C. tell the employees, in order to keep them from making a direct complaint, that nothing can be done
   D. try to remove the cause before the employees make a direct complaint

9. Suppose there is a departmental rule that requires supervisors to prepare reports of unusual incidents by the end of the tour of duty in which the incident occurs.
   The MAIN reason for requiring such prompt reporting is that
   A. a quick decision can be made whether the employee involved was neglectful of her duty
   B. other required reports cannot be made out until this one is turned in
   C. the facts are recorded before they are forgotten or confused by those involved in the incident
   D. the report is submitted before the supervisor required to make the report may possibly leave the department

10. A good practical method to use in determining whether an employee is doing his job properly is to
    A. assume that if he asks no questions, he knows the work
    B. question him directly on details of the job
    C. inspect and follow-up the work which is assigned to him
    D. ask other employees how this employee is making out

11. If an employee continually asks how he should do his work, you should
    A. dismiss him immediately
    B. pretend you do not hear him unless he persists
    C. explain the work carefully but encourage him to use his own judgment
    D. tell him not to ask so many questions

12. You have instructed an employee to complete a job in a certain area.
To be sure that the employee understands the instructions you have given him, you should
    A. ask him to repeat the instructions to you
    B. check with him after he has done the job
    C. watch him while he is doing the job
    D. repeat the instructions to the employee

13. One of your men disagrees with your evaluation of his work.
Of the following, the BEST way to handle this situation would be to
    A. explain that you are in a better position to evaluate his work than he is
    B. tell him that since other men are satisfied with your evaluation, he should accept their opinions
    C. explain the basis of your evaluation and discuss it with him
    D. refuse to discuss his complaint in order to maintain discipline

14. Of the following, the on which is NOT a quality of leadership desirable in a supervisor is
    A. intelligence   B. integrity   C. forcefulness   D. partiality

15. Of the following, the one which LEAST characterizes the grapevine is that it
    A. consists of a tremendous amount of rumor, conjecture, information, advice, prediction, and even orders.
    B. seems to rise spontaneously, is largely anonymous, spreads rapidly, and changes in unpredictable directions
    C. can be eliminated without any great effort
    D. commonly fills the gaps left by the regular organizational channels of communication

16. When a superintendent delegates authority to a foreman, of the following, it would be MOST advisable for the superintendent to
    A. set wide limits of such authority to allow the foreman considerable leeway
    B. define fairly closely the limits of the authority delegated to the foreman
    C. wait until the foreman has some experience in the assignment before setting limits to his authority
    D. inform him that it is the foreman's ultimate basic responsibility to get the work done

17. One of the hallmarks of a good supervisor is his ability to use many different methods of obtaining information about the status of work in progress.
Which one of the following would probably indicate that a supervisor does NOT have this ability?
    A. Holding specified staff meetings at specified intervals
    B. Circulating among his subordinates as often as possible
    C. Holding staff meetings only when absolutely necessary
    D. Asking subordinates to come in and discuss the progress of their work and their problems

4 (#1)

18. Of the following, the one which is the LEAST important factor in deciding that additional training is necessary for the men you supervise is that
    A. the quality of work is below standard
    B. supplies are being wasted
    C. too much time is required to do specific jobs
    D. the absentee rate has declined

19. To promote proper safety practices in the operation of power tools and equipment, you should emphasize in meetings with the staff that
    A. every accident can be prevented through proper safety regulations
    B. proper safety practices will probably make future safety meetings unnecessary
    C. when safety rules are followed, tools and equipment will work better
    D. safety rules are based on past experience with the best methods of preventing accidents

20. Employee morale is the way employees feel about each other and their job. To a supervisor, it should be a sign of good morale if the employees
    A. are late for work
    B. complain about their work
    C. willingly do difficult jobs
    D. take a long time to do simple jobs

21. A supervisor who encourages his workers to make suggestions about job improvement shows his workers that he
    A. is not smart enough to improve the job himself
    B. wants them to take part in making improvements
    C. does not take the job seriously
    D. is not a good supervisor

22. Suppose that your supervisor tells you that a procedure which has been followed for years is going to be changed. It is your job to make sure the workers you supervises understand and accept the new procedure.
    What would be the BEST thing for you to do in this situation?
    A. Give a copy of the new procedure to each worker with orders that it must be followed
    B. Explain the new procedure to one worker and have him explain it to the others
    C. Ask your supervisor to explain the new procedure since he has more authority
    D. call your workers together to explain and discuss the new procedure

23. One of the foundations of scientific management of an organization is the proper use of control measures.
    Of the following, the BEST way, in general, to implement control measures is to
    A. develop suitable procedures, systems, and guidelines for the organization
    B. evaluate the actual employees' job performance realistically and reasonably
    C. set standards which are designed to increase productivity
    D. publish a set of rules and insist upon strict compliance with these rules

24. A district superintendent would MOST likely be justified in taking up a matter with his borough superintendent when the problem involved
    A. a dispute among different factions in his district
    B. a section foreman's difficulties with his assistant foreman
    C. his own men and others not under his control
    D. methods of doing the work and the amount of production

25. The superintendent has the authority to recommend disciplinary action. He can BEST use this authority to
    A. demonstrate his authority as a superintendent
    B. improve a man's work
    C. make it less difficult for other superintendents to maintain order
    D. punish the men for wrong-doing

KEY (CORRECT ANSWERS)

1.	B	11.	C
2.	A	12.	A
3.	C	13.	C
4.	C	14.	D
5.	B	15.	C
6.	D	16.	B
7.	A	17.	C
8.	D	18.	D
9.	C	19.	D
10.	C	20.	C

21.	B
22.	D
23.	C
24.	B
25.	B

TEST 2

DIRECTIONS: Each question or incomplete statement is followed by several suggested answers or completions. Select the one that BEST answers the question or completes the statement. *PRINT THE LETTER OF THE CORRECT ANSWER IN THE SPACE AT THE RIGHT.*

1. From the standpoint of equal opportunity, the MOST critical item that a superintendent should focus on is
   A. assigning only minority workers to supervisory positions
   B. helping minority employees to upgrade their knowledge so they may qualify for higher positions
   C. placing minority workers in job categories above their present level of ability so that they can *sink or swim*
   D. disregarding merit system principles

   1.____

2. After careful deliberation, you have decided that one of your workers should be disciplined.
   It is MOST important that the
   A. discipline be severe for best results
   B. discipline be delayed as long as possible
   C. worker understands why he is being disciplined
   D. other workers be consulted before the discipline is administered

   2.____

3. Of the following, the MOST important qualities of an employee chosen for a supervisory position are
   A. education and intelligence
   B. interest in the objectives and activities of the agency
   C. skill in performing the type of work to be supervised
   D. knowledge of the work and leadership ability

   3.____

4. Of the following, the CHIEF characteristic which distinguishes a good supervisor from a poor supervisor is the good supervisor's
   A. ability to favorably impress others
   B. unwillingness to accept monotony or routine
   C. ability to deal constructively with problem situations
   D. strong drive to overcome opposition

   4.____

5. Of the following, the MAIN disadvantage of on-the-job training is that, generally,
   A. special equipment may be needed
   B. production may be slowed down
   C. the instructor must maintain an individual relationship with the trainee
   D. the on-the-job instructor must be better qualified than the classroom instructor

   5.____

6. If it becomes necessary for you, as a supervisor, to give a subordinate employee confidential information, the MOST effective of the following steps to take is to make sure the information is kept confidential by the employee is to

   6.____

130

A. tell the employee that the information is confidential and is not to be repeated
B. threaten the employee with disciplinary action if the information is repeated
C. offer the employee a merit increase as an incentive for keeping the information confidential
D. remind the employee at least twice a day that the information is confidential and is not to be repeated

7. Three new men have just been assigned to work under your supervision. Every time you give them an assignment, one of these men asks you several questions.
Of the following, the MOST desirable action for you to take is to
    A. assure him of your confidence in his ability to carry out the assignment correctly without asking so many questions
    B. have all three men listen to your answers to these questions
    C. point out that the other two men do the job without asking so many questions
    D. tell him to see if he can get the answers from other workers before coming to you

7.____

8. Two of your subordinates suggest that you recommend a third man for an above-standard service rating because of his superior work.
You should
    A. ask the two subordinates whether the third man knows that they intended to discuss this matter with you
    B. explain to the two subordinates that an above-standard service rating for one man would have a detrimental effect on many of the other men
    C. recommend the man for an above-standard service rating if there is sufficient justification for it
    D. tell the two subordinates that the matter of service ratings is not their concern

8.____

9. All of the following are indications of good employee morale EXCEPT
    A. the number of grievances are lowered
    B. labor turnover is decreased
    C. the amount of supervision required is lowered
    D. levels of production are lowered

9.____

10. All of the following statements regarding the issuance of direct orders are true EXCEPT
    A. use direct orders only when necessary
    B. make sure that the receiver of the direct order is qualified to carry out the order
    C. issue direct orders in clear, concise words
    D. give direct orders only in writing

10.____

11. In order to achieve the BEST results in on-the-job training, supervisors should   11.____
    A. allow frequent coffee breaks during the training period
    B. be in a higher salary range than that of the individuals they are training
    C. have had instructions or experience in conducting such training
    D. have had a minimum of five years' experience in the job

12. Of the following, the LEAST important quality of a good supervisor is   12.____
    A. technical competence
    B. teaching ability
    C. ability to communicate with others
    D. ability to socialize with subordinates

13. One of your usually very hard working, reliable employees brings in a bottle of whiskey to celebrate his birthday during the rest period.   13.____
    Which one of the following actions should you take?
    A. Offer to pay for the cost of the whiskey
    B. Confiscate the bottle
    C. Tell him to celebrate after working hours
    D. Pretend that you have not seen the bottle of whiskey

14. Assume that you find it necessary to discipline two subordinates, Mr. Tate and Mr. Sawyer, for coming to work late on several occasions. Their latenesses have had disruptive effects on the work schedule, and you have given both of them several verbal warnings. Mr. Tate has been in your work unit for many years, and his work has always been satisfactory. Mr. Sawyer is a probationary employee, who has had some problem in learning your procedures. You decide to give Mr. Tate one more warning, in private, for his latenesses.   14.____
    According to good supervisory practice, which one of the following disciplinary actions should you take with regard to Mr. Sawyer?
    A. Give him a reprimand in front of his co-workers, to make a lasting impression
    B. Recommend dismissal since he has not yet completed his probationary period
    C. Give him one more warning, in private, for his latenesses
    D. Recommend a short suspension or payroll deduction to impress upon him the importance of coming to work on time

15. Assume that you have delegated a very important work assignment to Johnson, one of your most experienced subordinates. Prior to completion of the assignment, your superior accidentally discovers that the assignment is being carried out incorrectly, and tells you about it.   15.____
    Which one of the following responses is MOST appropriate for you to give to your superior?
    A. *I take full responsibility, and I will see to it that the assignment is carried out correctly.*
    B. *Johnson has been with us for many years now and should know better.*

C. *It really isn't Johnson's fault, rather it is the fault of the ancient equipment we have to do the job.*
D. *I think you should inform Johnson since he is the one at fault, not I.*

16. Assume that you observe that one of your employees is talking excessively with other employees, quitting early, and taking unusually long rest periods. Despite these abuses, she is one of your most productive employees, and her work is usually of the highest quality.
    Of the following, the MOST appropriate action to take with regard to this employee is to
    A. ignore these infractions since she is one of your best workers
    B. ask your superior to reprimand her so that you can remain on the employee's good side
    C. reprimand her since not doing so would lower the morale of the other employees
    D. ask another of your subordinates to mention these infractions to the offending employee and suggest that she stop breaking rules

16.____

17. Assume that you have noticed that an employee whose attendance had been quite satisfactory is now showing marked evidence of a consistent pattern of absences.
    Of the following, the BEST way to cope with this problem is to
    A. wait several weeks to see whether this pattern continues
    B. meet with the employee to try to find out the reasons for this change
    C. call a staff meeting and discuss the need for good attendance
    D. write a carefully worded warning to the employee

17.____

18. It is generally agreed that the successful supervisor must know how to wisely delegate work to her subordinates since she cannot do everything herself.
    Which one of the following practices is MOST likely to result in ineffective delegation by a supervisor?
    A. Establishment of broad controls to assure feedback about any deviations from plans
    B. Willingness to let subordinates use their own ideas about how to get the job done, where appropriate
    C. Constant observance of employees to see if they are making any mistakes
    D. Granting of enough authority to make possible the accomplishment of the delegated work

18.____

19. Suppose that, in accordance with grievance procedures, an employee brings a complaint to you, his immediate supervisor.
    In dealing with his complaint, the one of the following which is MOST important for you to do is to
    A. talk to the employee's co-workers to learn whether the complaint is justified
    B. calm the employee by assuring him that you will look into the matter as soon as possible

19.____

C. tell your immediate superior about the employee's complaint
D. give the employee an opportunity to tell the full story

20. Holding staff meetings at regular intervals is generally considered to be a good supervisory practice.
    Which one of the following subjects is LEAST desirable for discussion at such a meeting?
    A. Revisions in agency personnel policies
    B. Violation of an agency rule by one of the employees present
    C. Problems of waste and breakage in the work area
    D. Complaints of employees about working conditions

21. Suppose that you are informed that your staff is soon to be reduced by one-third due to budget problems.
    Which one of the following steps would be LEAST advisable in your effort to maintain a quality service with the smaller number of employees?
    A. Directing employees to speed up operations
    B. Giving employees training or retraining
    C. Rearranging the work area
    D. Revising work methods

22. Of the following which action on the part of the supervisor LEAST likely to contribute to upgrading the skills of her subordinates?
    A. Providing appropriate training to subordinates
    B. Making periodic evaluations of subordinates and discussing the evaluations with the subordinates
    C. Consistently assigning subordinates to those tasks with which they are familiar
    D. Giving increased responsibility to appropriate subordinates

23. Suppose that a new employee on your staff has difficulty in performing his assigned tasks after having been given training.
    Of the following courses of action, the one which would be BEST for you, his supervisor, to take FIRST is to
    A. change his work assignment
    B. give him a poor evaluation since he is obviously unable to do the work
    C. give him the training again
    D. have him work with an employee who is more experienced in the tasks for a short while

24. Several times, an employee has reported to work unit for duty because he had been drinking. He refused to get counseling for his emotional problems when this was suggested by his superior. Last week, his supervisor warned him that he would face disciplinary action if he again reported to work unfit for duty because of drinking. Now, the employee has again reported to work in that condition.

Of the following, the BEST action for the supervisor to take now would be to
- A. arrange to have the employee transferred to another work location
- B. give the employee one more chance by pretending to not notice his condition this time
- C. start disciplinary action against the employee
- D. warn him that he will face disciplinary action if he reports for work in that condition again

25. An employee has been calling in sick repeatedly, and these absences have disrupted the work schedule.
To try to make sure that the employee use sick leave only on days when he is actually sick, which of the following actions would be the BEST for his supervisor to take?
- A. Telephone the employee's home on days when he is out on sick leave
- B. Require the employee to obtain a note from a physician explaining the reason for his absence whenever he uses sick leave in the future
- C. Require that he get a complete physical examination and have his doctor send a report to the supervisor
- D. Warn the employee that he will face disciplinary action the next time he stays out on sick leave

25.____

KEY (CORRECT ANSWERS)

1.	B	11.	C
2.	C	12.	D
3.	D	13.	C
4.	C	14.	C
5.	B	15.	A
6.	A	16.	C
7.	B	17.	B
8.	C	18.	C
9.	D	19.	D
10.	D	20.	B

21. A
22. C
23. D
24. C
25. B

TEST 3

DIRECTIONS: Each question or incomplete statement is followed by several suggested answers or completions. Select the one that BEST answers the question or completes the statement. *PRINT THE LETTER OF THE CORRECT ANSWER IN THE SPACE AT THE RIGHT.*

1. Suppose that, as a supervisor, you have an idea for changing the way a certain task is performed by your staff so that it will be less tedious and get done faster. Of the following, the MOST advisable action for you to take regarding this idea is to
    A. issue a written memorandum explaining the new method and giving reasons why it is to replace the old one
    B. discuss it with your staff to get their reactions and suggestions
    C. set up a training class in the new method for your staff
    D. try it out on an experimental basis on half the staff

    1.____

2. A troubled subordinate privately approaches his supervisor in order to talk about a problem on the job.
In this situation, the one of the following actions that is NOT desirable on the part of the supervisor is to
    A. ask the subordinate pertinent questions to help develop points further
    B. close his office door during the talk to block noisy distractions
    C. allow sufficient time to complete the discussion with the subordinate
    D. take over the conversation so the employee won't be embarrassed

    2.____

3. Suppose that one of your goals as a supervisor is to foster good working relationships between yourself and your employees, without undermining your supervisory effectiveness by being too friendly.
Of the following, the BEST way to achieve this goal when dealing with employees' work problems is to
    A. discourage individual personal conferences by using regularly scheduled staff meetings to discuss work problems
    B. try to resolve work problems within a relatively short period of time
    C. insist that employees put all work problems into writing before seeing you
    D. maintain an open-door policy, allowing employees complete freedom of access to you without making appointments to discuss work problems

    3.____

4. An employee under your supervision complains that he is assigned to work late more often than any of the other employees. You check the records and find that this isn't so.
You should
    A. advise this employee not to worry about what the other employees do but to see that he puts in a full day's work himself
    B. explain to this employee that you get the same complaint from all the other employees
    C. inform this employee that you have checked the records and the complaint is not justified
    D. not assign this employee to work late for a few days in order to keep him satisfied

    4.____

5. An employee has reported late for work several times. 5.____
His supervisor should
    A. give this employee less desirable assignments
    B. overlook the lateness if the employee's work is otherwise exceptional
    C. recommend disciplinary action for habitual lateness
    D. talk the matter over with the employee before doing anything further

6. In choosing a man to be in charge in his absence, the supervisor should select 6.____
FIRST the employee who
    A. has ability to supervise others
    B. has been longest with the organization
    C. has the nicest appearance and manner
    D. is most skilled in his assigned duties

7. An employee under your supervision comes to you to complain about a 7.____
decision you have made in assigning the men. He is excited and angry. You
think what he is complaining about is not important, but it seems very important
to him.
The BEST way for you to handle this is to
    A. let him talk until *he gets it off his chest* and then explain the reasons for
       your decision
    B. refuse to talk to him until he has cooled off
    C. show him at once how unimportant the matter is and how ridiculous his
       arguments are
    D. tell him to take it up with your superior if he disagrees with your decision

8. Suppose that a new employee has been appointed and assigned to your 8.____
supervision.
When this man reports for work, it would be BEST for you to
    A. ask him questions about different problems connected with his line of
       work and see if he answers them correctly
    B. check him carefully while he carries out some routine assignment that you
       give him
    C. explain to him the general nature of the work he will be required to do
    D. make a careful study of his previous work record before coming to your
       department

9. *The competent supervisor will be friendly with the employees under his* 9.____
supervision but will avoid close familiarity.
This statement is justified MAINLY because
    A. a friendly attitude on the part of the supervisor toward the employee is
       likely to cause suspicion on the part of the employee
    B. a supervisor can handle his employees better if he doesn't know their
       personal problems
    C. close familiarity may interfere with the discipline needed for good
       supervisor-subordinate relationships
    D. familiarity with the employees may be a sign of lack of ability on the part
       of the supervisor

10. An employee disagrees with the instructions that you, his supervisor, have given him for carrying out a certain assignment.
    The BEST action for you to take is to tell this employee that
    A. he can do what he wants but you will hold him responsible for failure
    B. orders must be carried out or morale will fall apart
    C. this job has been done in this way for many years with great success
    D. you will be glad to listen to his objections and to his suggestions for improvement

10.____

11. As a supervisor, it is LEAST important for you to use a new employee's probationary period for the purpose of
    A. carefully checking how he performs the work you assign him
    B. determining whether he can perform the duties of his job efficiently
    C. preparing him for promotion to a higher position
    D. showing him how to carry out his assigned duties properly

11.____

12. Suppose you have just given an employee under your supervision instructions on how to carry out a certain assignment.
    The BEST way to check that he has understood your instructions is to
    A. ask him to repeat your instructions word for word
    B. check the progress of his work the first chance you get
    C. invite him to ask questions if he has any doubts
    D. question him briefly about the main points of the assignment

12.____

13. Suppose you find it necessary to change a procedure that the men under your supervision have been following for a long time.
    A good way to get their cooperation for this change would be to
    A. bring them together to talk over the new procedure and explain the reasons for its adoption
    B. explain to the men that if most of them still don't approve of the change after giving it a fair try you will consider giving it up
    C. give them a few weeks' notice of the proposed change in procedure
    D. not enforce the new procedure strictly at the beginning

13.____

14. An order can be given by a supervisor in such a way as to make the employee want to obey it.
    According to this statement, it is MOST reasonable to suppose that
    A. a person will be glad to obey an order if he realizes that he must
    B. if an order is given properly, it will be obeyed more willingly
    C. it is easier to obey an order than to give one correctly
    D. supervisors should inspire confidence by their actions as well as by their words

14.____

15. If one of the men you supervise disagrees with how you rate his work, the BEST way for you to handle this is to
    A. advise him to appeal to your superior about it
    B. decline to discuss the matter with him in order to keep discipline
    C. explain why you rate him the way you do and talk it over with him
    D. tell him that you are better qualified to rate his work than he is

15.____

16. A supervisor should be familiar with the experience and abilities of the employees under his supervision MAINLY because
    A. each employee's work is highly important and requires a person of outstanding ability
    B. it will help him to know which employees are best fitted for certain assignments
    C. nearly all men have the same basic ability to do any job equally well
    D. superior background shortly shows itself in superior work quality, regardless of assignment

16.____

17. The competent supervisor will try to develop respect rather than fear in his subordinates.
    This statement is justified MAINLY because
    A. fear is always present and, for best results, respect must be developed to offset it
    B. it is generally easier to develop respect in the men than it is to develop fear
    C. men who respect their supervisor are more likely to give more than the required minimum amount and quality of work
    D. respect is based on the individual, and fear is based on the organization as a whole

17.____

18. If one of the employees you supervise does outstanding work, you should
    A. explain to him how his work can still be improved so that he will not become self-satisfied
    B. mildly criticize the other men for not doing as good a job as this man
    C. praise him for his work so that he will know it is appreciated
    D. say nothing or he might become conceited

18.____

19. A supervisor can BEST help establish good morale among his employees if he
    A. confides in them about his personal problems in order to encourage them to confide in him
    B. encourages them to become friendly with him but discourages social engagements with them
    C. points out to them the advantages of having a cooperative spirit in the department
    D. sticks to the same rules that he expects them to follow

19.____

20. The one of the following situations which would seem to indicate poor scheduling of work by the supervisor is
    A. everybody seeming to be very busy at the same time
    B. re-assignment of a man to other work because of breakdown of a piece of equipment
    C. two employees on vacation at the same time
    D. two operators waiting to use the same equipment at the same time

20.____

KEY (CORRECT ANSWERS)

1.	B	11.	C
2.	D	12.	D
3.	B	13.	A
4.	C	14.	B
5.	D	15.	C
6.	A	16.	B
7.	A	17.	C
8.	C	18.	C
9.	C	19.	D
10.	D	20.	D

EXAMINATION SECTION
TEST 1

DIRECTIONS: Each question or incomplete statement is followed by several suggested answers or completions. Select the one that BEST answers the question or completes the statement. *PRINT THE LETTER OF THE CORRECT ANSWER IN THE SPACE AT THE RIGHT.*

1. Public organizations usually share each of the following customer-service problems with private organizations EXCEPT
    A. aversion to risk
    B. staff-heaviness
    C. provision of reverse incentives
    D. control-apportionment functions

    1._____

2. A service representative demonstrates interpersonal skills by
    A. identifying a customer's expectations
    B. learning how to use a new office telephone system
    C. studying a competitor's approach to service
    D. anticipating how a customer will react to certain situations

    2._____

3. Of the following, _____ is NOT generally considered to be a common reason for flaws in an organization's customer focus.
    A. commissioned employee compensation
    B. full problem-solving authority for front-line personnel
    C. inadequate hiring practices
    D. specific, case-oriented policy and procedural statements

    3._____

4. According to MOST research, approximately _____ of dissatisfied customers will actually complain or make their dissatisfaction with a product known to the organization.
    A. 5%   B. 25%   C. 50%   D. 75%

    4._____

5. Which of the following is an example of an expected benefit associated with a product or service?
    A. Before buying a car, a customer believes she will not have to take the car in for repairs every few months.
    B. A customer in a sporting goods store tells a salesperson exactly what kind of trolling motor will meet the requirements of the lakes the customer wanted to fish.
    C. A supermarket shopper buys a loaf of bread, believing that the bread will remain fresh for a few days.
    D. An airline passenger discover that the meals served on board are good.

    5._____

6. During a meeting with a service representative, a customer makes an apparently reasonable request. However, the representative knows that satisfying the customer's request will violate a rule that is part of the organization's policy. Although the representative feels that an exception to the rule should be made in this case, she is not sure whether an exception can or should be made.

    6._____

The BEST course of action for the representative would be to
A. deny the request and apologize, explaining the company policy
B. rely on good judgment and allow the request
C. try to steer the customer toward a similar but clearly permissible request
D. contact a manager or more experienced peer to handle the request

7. While organizing an effective customer service department, it would be LEAST effective to
A. create procedures for relaying reasons for complaints to other departments
B. set up a clear chain-of-command for handling specific customer complaints
C. continually monitor performance of front-line personnel
D. give front-line people full authority to resolve all customer dissatisfaction

7.____

8. Of the following, _____ is an example of *tangible* service.
A. an interior decorator telling his/her ideas to a potential client
B. a salesclerk giving a written cost estimate to a potential buyer
C. an automobile salesman telling a showroom customer about a car's performance
D. a stockbroker offering investment advice over the telephone

8.____

9. As a rule, a customer service representative who handles telephones should always answer a call within no more than _____ ring(s).
A. 1   B. 3   C. 5   D. 8

9.____

10. In order to be as useful as possible to an organization, feedback received from customers should NOT be
A. portrayed on a line graph or similar device
B. used to provide a general overview
C. focused on end-use customers
D. available upon demand

10.____

11. Of all the customers who switch to competing organizations approximately _____ percent do so because of poor service.
A. 25   B. 40   C. 75   D. 95

11.____

12. When customers offer information that is incorrect in their complaints, a service representative should do each of the following EXCEPT
A. assume that the customer is making an innocent mistake
B. look for opportunities to educate the customer
C. calmly state a reasonable argument that will correct the customer's mistake
D. believe the customer until he/she is able to find proof of his/her error

12.____

13. In order to insure that a customer feels comfortable in a face-to-face meeting, a service representative should
    A. avoid discussing controversial issues
    B. use personal terms such as *dear* or *friend*
    C. address the customer by his/her first name
    D. tell a few jokes

13.____

14. Customer satisfaction is MOST effectively measured in terms of
    A. cost   B. benefit   C. convenience   D. value

14.____

15. Making a sale is NOT considered good service when
    A. there are no alternatives to the subject of the customer's complaint
    B. when the original product or service is outdated
    C. an add-in feature will forestall other problems
    D. the product or service the customer has been using is the wrong product

15.____

16. When dealing with an indecisive customer, the service representative should
    A. expand available possibilities
    B. offer a way out of unsatisfying decisions
    C. ask probing questions for understanding
    D. steer the customer toward one particular decision

16.____

17. Of the following, _____ would NOT be a source of direct organizational service promises.
    A. advertising materials
    B. published organizational policies
    C. contracts
    D. the customer's past experience with the organization

17.____

18. Generally, the only kind of organization that can validly circumvent the requirements of customer service is one that
    A. cannot afford to staff an entire service department
    B. relies solely on the sale of ten or fewer items per year
    C. has little or no competition
    D. serves clients that are separated from consumers

18.____

19. When using the problem-solving approach to solve the problem of an upset customer, the service representative should FIRST
    A. express respect for the customer
    B. identify the customer's expectations
    C. outline a solution or alternatives
    D. listen to understand the problem

19.____

20. During face-to-face meetings with strangers such as service personnel, most North Americans consider a comfortable proximity to be
    A. 6 inches - 1 foot   B. 8 inches - 1½ feet
    C. 1½ - 2 feet   D. 2-4 feet

20.____

21. When answering phone calls, a service representative should ALWAYS do each 21._____
    of the following EXCEPT
    A. state his/her name
    B. give the name of the organization or department
    C. ask probing questions
    D. offer assistance

22. If a customer appears to be emotionally neutral when lodging a complaint, it 22._____
    would be MOST appropriate for a service representative to demonstrate _____
    in reaction to the complaint.
    A. urgency   B. empathy   C. nonchalance   D. surprise

23. When soliciting customer feedback, standard practice is to limit the number 23._____
    of questions asked to APPROXIMATELY
    A. 3-5   B. 5-10   C. 10-20   D. 15-40

24. A customer has purchased an item from a company and has been told that 24._____
    the item will be delivered in two weeks. However, a customer service
    representative later discovers that deliveries are running about three days
    behind schedule.
    The MOST appropriate course of action for the representative would be to
    A. call the customer immediately, apologize for the delay, and await the
       customer's response
    B. call the customer a few days before delivery is due and explain that the
       delay is the fault of the delivery company
    C. immediately sent out a *loaner* of the ordered item to the customer
    D. wait for the customer to note the delay and contact the organization

25. Most research show that _____% of what is communicated between people 25._____
    during face-to-face meetings is conveyed through words alone.
    A. 10   B. 30   C. 50   D. 80

5 (#1)

KEY (CORRECT ANSWERS)

1.	D		11.	B
2.	D		12.	C
3.	B		13.	A
4.	A		14.	D
5.	B		15.	A
6.	D		16.	B
7.	B		17.	D
8.	B		18.	C
9.	B		19.	A
10.	B		20.	C

21. C
22. D
23. B
24. A
25. A

TEST 2

DIRECTIONS: Each question or incomplete statement is followed by several suggested answers or completions. Select the one that BEST answers the question or completes the statement. *PRINT THE LETTER OF THE CORRECT ANSWER IN THE SPACE AT THE RIGHT.*

1. When working cooperatively to identify specific internal service targets, personnel typically encounter each of the following obstacles EXCEPT 1.____
   A. rapidly-changing work environment
   B. philosophical differences about the nature of service
   C. specialized knowledge of certain personnel exceeds that of others
   D. a chain-of-command that isolates the end user

2. Which of the following is an example of an external customer relationship? 2.____
   A. Baggage clerks to travelers
   B. Catering staff to flight attendants
   C. Managers to ticketing agents
   D. Maintenance workers to ground crew

3. When a service representative puts a customer's complaint in writing, results will be produced more quickly than if the representative had merely told someone. 3.____
   Which of the following is NOT generally considered to be a reason for this?
   A. The complaint can be more easily routed to parties capable of solving the problem.
   B. Management will understand the problem more clearly.
   C. The representative can more clearly see the main aspects of the complaint.
   D. The complaint and response will become a part of a public record.

4. A customer service representative creates a client file, which contains notes about what particular clients want, need, and expect. 4.____
   Which of the following basic areas of learning is the representative exercising?
   A. Interpersonal skills   B. Product and service knowledge
   C. Customer knowledge   D. Technical skills

5. A customer complains that a desired product, which is currently on sale, is needed in at least two weeks, but the company is out of stock and the product will not be available for another four weeks. 5.____
   Of the following, the BEST example of a service *recovery* on the part of a representative would be to
   A. apologize for the company's inability to serve the customer while expressing a wish to deal with the customer in the future
   B. attempt to steer the customer's interest toward an unrelated product
   C. offer a comparable model at the same sale price

146

6. Of the following, _____ is NOT generally considered to be a function of closed questioning when dealing with a customer.
   A. understanding requests
   B. getting the customer to agree
   C. clarifying what has been said
   D. summarizing a conversation

7. When dealing with a customer who speaks with a heavy foreign accent, a service representative should NOT
   A. speak loudly
   B. speak slowly
   C. avoid humor or witticism
   D. repeat what has been said

8. If a customer service representative is aware that time will be a factor in the delivery of service to a customer, the representative should FIRST
   A. warn the customer that the organization is under time constraints
   B. suggest that the customer return another time
   C. ask the customer to suggest a service deadline
   D. tell the customer when service can reasonably be expected

9. In relation to a customer service representative's view of an organization, the customer's view of the company tends to be
   A. more negative
   B. more objective
   C. broader in scope
   D. less forgiving

10. When asked to define the factors that determine whether they will do business with an organization, most customers maintain that _____ is the MOST important.
    A. friendly employees
    B. having their needs met
    C. convenience
    D. product pricing

11. While a customer is stating her service requirements, a service representative should do each of the following EXCEPT
    A. ask questions about complex or unclear information
    B. formulate a response to the customer's remarks
    C. repeat critical information
    D. attempt to roughly outline the customer's main points

12. If a customer service representative must deal with other member of a service team in order to resolve a problem, the representative should avoid
    A. conveying every single detail of a problem to others
    B. suggesting deadlines for problem resolution
    C. offering opinions about the source of the problem
    D. explaining the specifics concerning the need for resolution

13. Of the following, the LAST step in the resolution of a service problem should be
    A. the offer of an apology for the problem
    B. asking probing questions to understand and conform the nature of the problem
    C. listening to the customer's description of the problem
    D. determining and implementing a solution to the problem

14. _____ is a poor scheduling strategy for a customer service representative. 14.____
    A. Performing the easiest tasks first
    B. Varying work routines
    C. Setting deadlines that will allow some restful work periods
    D. Doing similar jobs at the same time

15. The MOST defensible reason for the avoidance of customer satisfaction guarantees is 15.____
    A. buyer remorse
    B. repeated customer contact
    C. high costs
    D. ability of buyers to take advantage of guarantees

16. A customer service representative demonstrates knowledge and courtesy to customers and is able to convey trust, competence, and confidence. 16.____
    Of the following service factors, the representative is demonstrating
    A. assurance   B. responsiveness
    C. empathy   D. reliability

17. If a service representative is involved in sales, _____ is NOT one of the primary pieces of information he/she will need to supply the customer. 17.____
    A. cost of product or service   B. how the product works
    C. how to repair the product   D. available payment plans

18. A customer appears to be experiencing extreme feelings of anger and frustration when loading a complaint. 18.____
    The MOST appropriate reaction for a service representative to demonstrate is
    A. urgency   B. empathy   C. nonchalance   D. surprise

19. Of the following obstacles to customer service, _____ is NOT generally considered to be unique to public organizations. 19.____
    A. ambivalence toward clients   B. limited competition
    C. a rule-based mission   D. clients who are not really customers

20. Most customers report that the MOST frustrating aspect of waiting in line for service is 20.____
    A. not knowing how long they will have to wait for service
    B. rudeness on the part of the service representatives
    C. being expected to wait for service at all
    D. unfair prioritizing on the part of service representatives

21. Which of the following is an example of an *assumed benefit* associated with a product or service? 21.____
    A customer
    A buys a sporty sedan and finds that its tight turning ratio makes it easy to park
    B. visits a fast-food restaurant because she is in a hurry to get dinner over with

C. buys a videotape and believes it will not cause damage to her VCR
D. tells a salesman that he wants to purchase a high-status automobile

22. On an average, for every complaint received by an organization, there are actually about _____ customers who have legitimate problems. 22._____
    A. 3   B. 5   C. 15   D. 25

23. Once a customer problem is identified, each of the following should become a part of the service recovery process EXCEPT 23._____
    A. apologizing   B. an offer of compensation
    C. empathetic listening D. sympathy

24. As a rule, customers who telephone organizations should not be put on hold for any longer than 24._____
    A. 10 seconds   B. 60 seconds
    C. 5 minutes   D. 10 minutes

25. The LEAST effective way to make customers feel as if they are a part of a service team would be to ask them for 25._____
    A. information about similar products/services they have used
    B. opinions about how to solve problems
    C. personally contact the department that can best help them
    D. opinions about particular products and services

KEY (CORRECT ANSWERS)

1.	B		11.	B
2.	A		12.	C
3.	D		13.	A
4.	C		14.	A
5.	D		15.	B
6.	A		16.	A
7.	A		17.	C
8.	C		18.	B
9.	C		19.	B
10.	B		20.	A

21. C
22. D
23. D
24. B
25. C

EXAMINATION SECTION
TEST 1

DIRECTIONS: Each question or incomplete statement is followed by several suggested answers or completions. Select the one that BEST answers the question or completes the statement. *PRINT THE LETTER OF THE CORRECT ANSWER IN THE SPACE AT THE RIGHT.*

1. Good procedure in handling complaints from the public may be divided into the following four principal stages:
   I. Investigation of the complaint
   II. Receipt of the complaint
   III. Assignment of responsibility for investigation and correction
   IV. Notification of correction

   The ORDER in which these stages ordinarily come is:
   A. III, II, I, IV
   B. II, III, I, IV
   C. II, III, IV, I
   D. II, IV, III, I

   1.____

2. The department may expect the MOST severe public criticism if
   A. it asks for an increase in its annual budget
   B. it purchases new and costly street cleaning equipment
   C. sanitation officers and men are reclassified to higher salary grades
   D. there is delay in cleaning streets of snow

   2.____

3. The MOST important function of public relations in the department should be to
   A. develop cooperation on the part of the public in keeping streets clean
   B. get stricter penalties enacted for health code violations
   C. recruit candidates for entrance positions who ca be developed into supervisors
   D. train career personnel so that they can advance in the department

   3.____

4. The one of the following which has MOST frequently elicited unfavorable public comment has been
   A. dirty sidewalks or streets
   B. dumping on lot
   C. failure to curb dogs
   D. overflowing garbage cans

   4.____

5. It has been suggested that, as a public relations measure, sections hold *open house* for the public.
   The MOST effective time for this would be
   A. during the summer when children are not in school and can accompany their parents
   B. during the winter when show is likely to fall and the public can see snow removal preparations
   C. immediately after a heavy snow storm when department snow removal operations are in full progress
   D. when street sanitation is receiving general attention as during *Keep City Clean* week

   5.____

6. When a public agency conducts a public relations program, it is MOST likely to find that each recipient of its message will
   A. disagree with the basic purpose of the message if the officials are not well known to him
   B. accept the message if it is presented by someone perceived as having a definite intention to persuade
   C. ignore the message unless it is presented in a literate and clever manner
   D. give greater attention to certain portions of the message as a result of his individual and cultural differences

7. Following are three statements about public relations and communications:
   I. A person who seeks to influence public opinion can speed up a trend
   II. Mass communications is the exposure of a mass audience to an idea
   III. All media are equally effective in reaching opinion leaders
   Which of the following choices CORRECTLY classifies the above statements into those which are correct and those which are not?
   A. I and II are correct, but III is not.
   B. II and III are correct, but I is not.
   C. I and III are correct, but II is not.
   D. III is correct, but I and II are not.

8. Public relations experts say that MAXIMUM effect for a message results from
   A. concentrating in one medium
   B. ignoring mass media and concentrating on *opinion makers*
   C. presenting only those factors which support a given position
   D. using a combination of two or more of the available media

9. To assure credibility and avoid hostility, the public relations man MUST
   A. make certain his message is truthful, not evasive or exaggerated
   B. make sure his message contains some dire consequence if ignored
   C. repeat the message often enough so that it cannot be ignored
   D. try to reach as many people and groups as possible

10. The public relations man MUST be prepared to assume that members of his audience
    A. may have developed attitudes toward his proposals—favorable, neutral, or unfavorable
    B. will be immediately hostile
    C. will consider his proposals with an open mind
    D. will invariably need an introduction to his subject

11. The one of the following statements that is CORRECT is:
    A. When a stupid question is asked of you by the public, it should be disregarded
    B. If you insist on formality between you and the public, the public will not be able to ask stupid questions that cannot be answered
    C. The public should be treated courteously, regardless of how stupid their questions may be
    D. You should explain to the public how stupid their questions are

12. With regard to public relations, the MOST important item which should be emphasized in an employee training program is that
    A. each inspector is a public relations agent
    B. an inspector should give the public all the information it asks for
    C. it is better to make mistakes and give erroneous information than to tell the public that you do not know the correct answer to their problem
    D. public relations is so specialized a field that only persons specially trained in it should consider it

12.____

13. Members of the public frequently ask about departmental procedures.
    Of the following, it is BEST to
    A. advise the public to put the question in writing so that he can get a proper formal reply
    B. refuse to answer because this is a confidential matter
    C. explain the procedure as briefly as possible
    D. attempt to avoid the issue by discussing other matters

13.____

14. The effectiveness of a public relations program in a public agency such as the authority is BEST indicated by the
    A. amount of mass media publicity favorable to the policies of the authority
    B. morale of those employees who directly serve the patrons of the authority
    C. public's understanding and support of the authority's program and policies
    D. number of complaint received by the authority from patrons using its facilities

14.____

15. In an attempt to improve public opinion about a certain idea, the BEST course of action for an agency to take would be to present the
    A. clearest statements of the idea even though the language is somewhat technical
    B. idea as the result of long-term studies
    C. idea in association with something familiar to most people
    D. idea as the viewpoint of the majority leaders

15.____

16. The fundamental factor in any agency's community relations program is
    A. an outline of the objectives
    B. relations with the media
    C. the everyday actions of the employees
    D. a well-planned supervisory program

16.____

17. The FUNDAMENTAL factor in the success of a community relations program is
    A. true commitment by the community
    B. true commitment by the administration
    C. a well-planned, systematic approach
    D. the actions of individuals in their contacts with the public

17.____

18. The statement below which is LEAST correct is:
    A. Because of selection standards, the supervisor frequently encounters problems resulting from subordinates' inability to express themselves in the language of the profession.
    B. Distortion of the meaning of a communication is usually brought about by a failure to use language that has a precise meaning to others.
    C. The term *filtering* is the distortion or dilution of content of a communication that occurs as information is passed from individual to individual.
    D. The complexity of the *communications net* will directly affect.

19. Consider the following three statements that may or may not be CORRECT:
    I. In order to prevent the stifling of communications flow, supervisors should insist that employees use the formal communications network.
    II. Two-way communications are faster and more accurate than one-way communications.
    III. There is a direct correlation between the effectiveness of communications and the total setting in which they occur.
    The choice below which MOST accurately describes the above statement is:
    A. All three are correct.
    B. All three are incorrect.
    C. More than one statement is correct.
    D. Only one of the statements is correct.

20. The statement below which is MOST inaccurate is:
    A. The supervisor's most important tool in learning whether or not he is communicating well is feedback.
    B. Follow-up is essential if useful feedback is to be obtained.
    C. Subordinates are entitled, as a matter of right, to explanations from management concerning the reasons for orders or directives.
    D. A skilled supervisor is often able to use the grapevine to good advantage.

21. *Since concurrence by those affected is not sought, this kind of communication can be issued with relative ease.*
    The kind of communication being referred to in this quotation is
    A. autocratic   B. democratic   C. directive   D. free-rein

22. The statement below which is LEAST correct is:
    A. Clarity is more important in oral communicating than in written since the readers of a written communication can read it over again.
    B. Excessive use of abbreviations in written communications should be avoided.
    C. Short sentences with simple words are preferred over complex sentences and difficult words in a written communication.
    D. The *newspaper* style of writing ordinarily simplifies expression and facilitates understanding.

23. Which one of the following is the MOST important factor for the department to consider in building a good public image?
    A. A good working relationship with the news media
    B. An efficient community relations program
    C. An efficient system for handling citizen complaints
    D. The proper maintenance of facilities and equipment
    E. The behavior of individuals in their contacts with the public.

24. It has been said that the ability to communicate clearly and concisely is the MOST important single skill of the supervisor.
    Consider the following statements:
    I. The adage, *Actions speak louder than words*, has NO application in superior/subordinate communications since good communications are accomplished with words.
    II. The environment in which a communication takes place will *rarely* determine its effect.
    III. Words are symbolic representations which must be associated with past experience or else they are meaningless.
    The choice below which MOST accurately describes the above statements is:
    A. I, II, and III are correct.
    B. I and II are correct, but III is not.
    C. I and III are correct, but II is not.
    D. III is correct, but I and II are not.
    E. I, II, and III are incorrect.

25. According to expert opinion, the effectiveness of an organization is very dependent upon good upward, downward, and lateral communications. Lateral communications are most important to the activity of coordinating the efforts of organizational units. Before real communication can take place at any level, barriers to communication must be recognized, understood, and removed.
    Consider the following three statements:
    I. The *principal* barrier to good communications is a failure to establish empathy between sender and receiver.
    II. The difference in status or rank between the sender and receiver of a communication may be a communications barrier.
    III. Communications are easier if they travel upward from subordinate to superior
    The choice below which MOST accurately describes the above statements is:
    A. I, II and III are incorrect.   B. I and II are incorrect.
    C. I, II, and III are correct.   D. I and II are correct.
    E. I and III are incorrect.

KEY (CORRECT ANSWERS)

1.	B		11.	C
2.	D		12.	A
3.	A		13.	C
4.	A		14.	C
5.	D		15.	C
6.	D		16.	C
7.	A		17.	D
8.	D		18.	A
9.	D		19.	D
10.	A		20.	C

21. A
22. A
23. E
24. D
25. E

PHILOSOPHY, PRINCIPLES, PRACTICES, AND TECHNICS OF SUPERVISION, ADMINISTRATION, MANAGEMENT, AND ORGANIZATION

TABLE OF CONTENTS

	Page
MEANING OF SUPERVISION	1
THE OLD AND THE NEW SUPERVISION	1
THE EIGHT (8) BASIC PRINCIPLES OF THE NEW SUPERVISION	1
I. Principle of Responsibility	1
II. Principle of Authority	2
III. Principle of Self-Growth	2
IV. Principle of Individual Worth	2
V. Principle of Creative Leadership	2
VI. Principle of Success and Failure	2
VII. Principle of Science	3
VIII. Principle of Cooperation	3
WHAT IS ADMINISTRATION?	3
I. Practices Commonly Classed as "Supervisory"	3
II. Practices Commonly Classed as "Administrative"	3
III. Practices Commonly Classed as Both "Supervisory" and "Administrative"	4
RESPONSIBILITIES OF THE SUPERVISOR	4
COMPETENCIES OF THE SUPERVISOR	4
THE PROFESSIONAL SUPERVISOR-EMPLOYEE RELATIONSHIP	4
MINI-TEXT IN SUPERVISION, ADMINISTRATION, MANAGEMENT, AND ORGANIZATION	5
I. Brief Highlights	5
A. Levels of Management	6
B. What the Supervisor Must Learn	6
C. A Definition of Supervision	6
D. Elements of the Team Concept	6
E. Principles of Organization	6
F. The Four Important Parts of Every Job	7
G. Principles of Delegation	7
H. Principles of Effective Communications	7
I. Principles of Work Improvement	7
J. Areas of Job Improvement	7
K. Seven Key Points in Making Improvements	8

	L.	Corrective Techniques for Job Improvement	8
	M.	A Planning Checklist	8
	N.	Five Characteristics of Good Directions	9
	O.	Types of Directions	9
	P.	Controls	9
	Q.	Orienting the New Employee	9
	R.	Checklist for Orienting New Employees	9
	S.	Principles of Learning	10
	T.	Causes of Poor Performance	10
	U.	Four Major Steps in On-the-Job Instructions	10
	V.	Employees Want Five Things	10
	W.	Some Don'ts in Regard to Praise	11
	X.	How to Gain Your Workers' Confidence	11
	Y.	Sources of Employee Problems	11
	Z.	The Supervisor's Key to Discipline	11
	AA.	Five Important Processes of Management	12
	BB.	When the Supervisor Fails to Plan	12
	CC.	Fourteen General Principles of Management	12
	DD.	Change	12
II.	Brief Topical Summaries		13
	A.	Who/What is the Supervisor?	13
	B.	The Sociology of Work	13
	C.	Principles and Practices of Supervision	14
	D.	Dynamic Leadership	14
	E.	Processes for Solving Problems	15
	F.	Training for Results	15
	G.	Health, Safety, and Accident Prevention	16
	H.	Equal Employment Opportunity	16
	I.	Improving Communications	16
	J.	Self-Development	17
	K.	Teaching and Training	17
		1. The Teaching Process	17
		a. Preparation	17
		b. Presentation	18
		c. Summary	18
		d. Application	18
		e. Evaluation	18
		2. Teaching Methods	18
		a. Lecture	18
		b. Discussion	18
		c. Demonstration	19
		d. Performance	19
		e. Which Method to Use	19

PHILOSOPHY, PRINCIPLES, PRACTICES, AND TECHNICS OF SUPERVISION, ADMINISTRATION, MANAGEMENT, AND ORGANIZATION

MEANING OF SUPERVISION

The extension of the democratic philosophy has been accompanied by an extension in the scope of supervision. Modern leaders and supervisors no longer think of supervision in the narrow sense of being confined chiefly to visiting employees, supplying materials, or rating the staff. They regard supervision as being intimately related to all the concerned agencies of society, they speak of the supervisor's function in terms of "growth," rather than the "improvement" of employees.

This modern concept of supervision may be defined as follows: Supervision is leadership and the development of leadership within groups which are cooperatively engaged in inspection, research, training, guidance, and evaluation.

THE OLD AND THE NEW SUPERVISION

TRADITIONAL
1. Inspection
2. Focused on the employee
3. Visitation
4. Random and haphazard
5. Imposed and authoritarian
6. One person usually

MODERN
1. Study and analysis
2. Focused on aims, materials, methods, supervisors, employees, environment
3. Demonstrations, intervisitation, workshops, directed reading, bulletins, etc.
4. Definitely organized and planned (scientific)
5. Cooperative and democratic
6. Many persons involved (creative)

THE EIGHT (8) BASIC PRINCIPLES OF THE NEW SUPERVISION

I. Principle of Responsibility
   Authority to act and responsibility for acting must be joined.
   A. If you give responsibility, give authority.
   B. Define employee duties clearly.
   C. Protect employees from criticism by others.
   D. Recognize the rights as well as obligations of employees.
   E. Achieve the aims of a democratic society insofar as it is possible within the area of your work.
   F. Establish a situation favorable to training and learning.
   G. Accept ultimate responsibility for everything done in your section, unit, office, division, department.
   H. Good administration and good supervision are inseparable.

II. Principle of Authority
The success of the supervisor is measured by the extent to which the power of authority is not used.
   A. Exercise simplicity and informality in supervision
   B. Use the simplest machinery of supervision
   C. If it is good for the organization as a whole, it is probably justified.
   D. Seldom be arbitrary or authoritative.
   E. Do not base your work on the power of position or of personality.
   F. Permit and encourage the free expression of opinions.

III. Principle of Self-Growth
The success of the supervisor is measured by the extent to which, and the speed with which, he is no longer needed.
   A. Base criticism on principles, not on specifics.
   B. Point out higher activities to employees.
   C. Train for self-thinking by employees to meet new situations.
   D. Stimulate initiative, self-reliance, and individual responsibility
   E. Concentrate on stimulating the growth of employees rather than on removing defects.

IV. Principle of Individual Worth
Respect for the individual is a paramount consideration in supervision.
   A. Be human and sympathetic in dealing with employees.
   B. Don't nag about things to be done.
   C. Recognize the individual differences among employees and seek opportunities to permit best expression of each personality.

V. Principle of Creative Leadership
The best supervision is that which is not apparent to the employee.
   A. Stimulate, don't drive employees to creative action.
   B. Emphasize doing good things.
   C. Encourage employees to do what they do best.
   D. Do not be too greatly concerned with details of subject or method.
   E. Do not be concerned exclusively with immediate problems and activities.
   F. Reveal higher activities and make them both desired and maximally possible.
   G. Determine procedures in the light of each situation but see that these are derived from a sound basic philosophy.
   H. Aid, inspire, and lead so as to liberate the creative spirit latent in all good employees.

VI. Principle of Success and Failure
There are no unsuccessful employees, only unsuccessful supervisors who have failed to give proper leadership.
   A. Adapt suggestions to the capacities, attitudes, and prejudices of employees.
   B. Be gradual, be progressive, be persistent.
   C. Help the employee find the general principle; have the employee apply his own problem to the general principle.
   D. Give adequate appreciation for good work and honest effort.
   E. Anticipate employee difficulties and help to prevent them.
   F. Encourage employees to do the desirable things they will do anyway.
   G. Judge your supervision by the results it secures.

VII. Principle of Science
Successful supervision is scientific, objective, and experimental. It is based on facts, not on prejudices.
- A. Be cumulative in results.
- B. Never divorce your suggestions from the goals of training.
- C. Don't be impatient of results.
- D. Keep all matters on a professional, not a personal, level.
- E. Do not be concerned exclusively with immediate problems and activities.
- F. Use objective means of determining achievement and rating where possible.

VIII. Principle of Cooperation
Supervision is a cooperative enterprise between supervisor and employee.
- A. Begin with conditions as they are.
- B. Ask opinions of all involved when formulating policies.
- C. Organization is as good as its weakest link.
- D. Let employees help to determine policies and department programs.
- E. Be approachable and accessible—physically and mentally.
- F. Develop pleasant social relationships.

WHAT IS ADMINISTRATION

Administration is concerned with providing the environment, the material facilities, and the operational procedures that will promote the maximum growth and development of supervisors and employees. (Organization is an aspect and a concomitant of administration.)

There is no sharp line of demarcation between supervision and administration; these functions are intimately interrelated and, often, overlapping. They are complementary activities.

I. Practices Commonly Classed as "Supervisory"
- A. Conducting employees' conferences
- B. Visiting sections, units, offices, divisions, departments
- C. Arranging for demonstrations
- D. Examining plans
- E. Suggesting professional reading
- F. Interpreting bulletins
- G. Recommending in-service training courses
- H. Encouraging experimentation
- I. Appraising employee morale
- J. Providing for intervisitation

II. Practices Commonly Classified as "Administrative"
- A. Management of the office
- B. Arrangement of schedules for extra duties
- C. Assignment of rooms or areas
- D. Distribution of supplies
- E. Keeping records and reports
- F. Care of audio-visual materials
- G. Keeping inventory records
- H. Checking record cards and books

I. Programming special activities
J. Checking on the attendance and punctuality of employees

III. Practices Commonly Classified as Both "Supervisory" and "Administrative"
A. Program construction
B. Testing or evaluating outcomes
C. Personnel accounting
D. Ordering instructional materials

RESPONSIBILITIES OF THE SUPERVISOR

A person employed in a supervisory capacity must constantly be able to improve his own efficiency and ability. He represent the employer to the employees and only continuous self-examination can make him a capable supervisor.

Leadership and training are the supervisor's responsibility. An efficient working unit is one in which the employees work with the supervisor. It is his job to bring out the best in his employees. He must always be relaxed, courteous, and calm in his association with his employees. Their feelings are important, and a harsh attitude does not develop the most efficient employees.

COMPETENCES OF THE SUPERVISOR

I. Complete knowledge of the duties and responsibilities of his position.
II. To be able to organize a job, plan ahead, and carry through.
III. To have self-confidence and initiative.
IV. To be able to handle the unexpected situation and make quick decisions.
V. To be able to properly train subordinates in the positions they are best suited for.
VI. To be able to keep good human relations among his subordinates.
VII. To be able to keep good human relations between his subordinates and himself and to earn their respect and trust.

THE PROFESSIONAL SUPERVISOR-EMPLOYEE RELATIONSHIP

There are two kinds of efficiency: one kind is only apparent and is produced in organizations through the exercise of mere discipline; this is but a simulation of the second, or true, efficiency which springs from spontaneous cooperation. If you are a manager, no matter how great or small your responsibility, it is your job, in the final analysis, to create and develop this involuntary cooperation among the people whom you supervise. For, no matter how powerful a combination of money, machines, and materials a company may have, this is a dead and sterile thing without a team of willing, thinking, and articulate people to guide it.

The following 21 points are presented as indicative of the exemplary basic relationship that should exist between supervisor and employee:

1. Each person wants to be liked and respected by his fellow employee and wants to be treated with consideration and respect by his superior.
2. The most competent employee will make an error. However, in a unit where good relations exist between the supervisor and his employees, tenseness and fear do not exist. Thus, errors are not hidden or covered up, and the efficiency of a unit is not impaired.

3. Subordinates resent rules, regulations, or orders that are unreasonable or unexplained.
4. Subordinates are quick to resent unfairness, harshness, injustices, and favoritism.
5. An employee will accept responsibility if he knows that he will be complimented for a job well done, and not too harshly chastised for failure; that his supervisor will check the cause of the failure, and, if it was the supervisor's fault, he will assume the blame therefore. If it was the employee's fault, his supervisor will explain the correct method or means of handling the responsibility.
6. An employee wants to receive credit for a suggestion he has made, that is used. If a suggestion cannot be used, the employee is entitled to an explanation. The supervisor should not say "no" and close the subject.
7. Fear and worry slow up a worker's ability. Poor working environment can impair his physical and mental health. A good supervisor avoids forceful methods, threats, and arguments to get a job done.
8. A forceful supervisor is able to train his employees individually and as a team, and is able to motivate them in the proper channels.
9. A mature supervisor is able to properly evaluate his subordinates and to keep them happy and satisfied.
10. A sensitive supervisor will never patronize his subordinates.
11. A worthy supervisor will respect his employees' confidences.
12. Definite and clear-cut responsibilities should be assigned to each executive.
13. Responsibility should always be coupled with corresponding authority.
14. No change should be made in the scope or responsibilities of a position without a definite understanding to that effect on the part of all persons concerned.
15. No executive or employee, occupying a single position in the organization, should be subject to definite orders from more than one source.
16. Orders should never be given to subordinates over the head of a responsible executive. Rather than do this, the officer in question should be supplanted.
17. Criticisms of subordinates should, whoever possible, be made privately, and in no case should a subordinate be criticized in the presence of executives or employees of equal or lower rank.
18. No dispute or difference between executives or employees as to authority or responsibilities should be considered too trivial for prompt and careful adjudication.
19. Promotions, wage changes, and disciplinary action should always be approved by the executive immediately superior to the one directly responsible.
20. No executive or employee should ever be required, or expected, to be at the same time an assistant to, and critic of, another.
21. Any executive whose work is subject to regular inspection should, wherever practicable, be given the assistance and facilities necessary to enable him to maintain an independent check of the quality of his work.

MINI-TEXT IN SUPERVISION, ADMINISTRATION, MANAGEMENT, AND ORGANIZATION

I. Brief Highlights

Listed concisely and sequentially are major headings and important data in the field for quick recall and review.

A. Levels of Management
Any organization of some size has several levels of management. In terms of a ladder, the levels are:

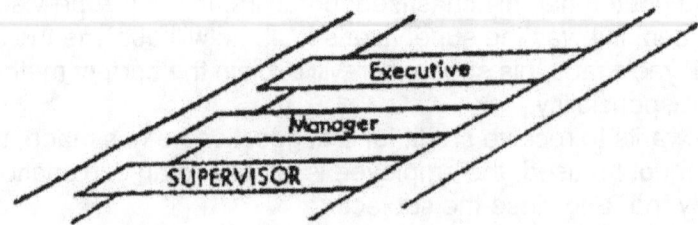

The first level is very important because it is the beginning point of management leadership.

B. What the Supervisor Must Learn
A supervisor must learn to:
1. Deal with people and their differences
2. Get the job done through people
3. Recognize the problems when they exist
4. Overcome obstacles to good performance
5. Evaluate the performance of people
6. Check his own performance in terms of accomplishment

C. A Definition of Supervisor
The term supervisor means any individual having authority, in the interests of the employer, to hire, transfer, suspend, lay-off, recall, promote, discharge, assign, reward, or discipline other employees or responsibility to direct them, or to adjust their grievances, or effectively to recommend such action, if, in connection with the foregoing, exercise of such authority is not of a merely routine or clerical nature but requires the use of independent judgment.

D. Elements of the Team Concept
What is involved in teamwork? The component parts are:
1. Members
2. A leader
3. Goals
4. Plans
5. Cooperation
6. Spirit

E. Principles of Organization
1. A team member must know what his job is.
2. Be sure that the nature and scope of a job are understood.
3. Authority and responsibility should be carefully spelled out.
4. A supervisor should be permitted to make the maximum number of decisions affecting his employees.
5. Employees should report to only one supervisor.
6. A supervisor should direct only as many employees as he can handle effectively.
7. An organization plan should be flexible.

8. Inspection and performance of work should be separate.
9. Organizational problems should receive immediate attention.
10. Assign work in line with ability and experience.

F. The Four Important Parts of Every Job
1. Inherent in every job is the *accountability* for results.
2. A second set of factors in every job is *responsibilities*.
3. Along with duties and responsibilities one must have the *authority* to act within certain limits without obtaining permission to proceed.
4. No job exists in a vacuum. The supervisor is surrounded by key *relationships*.

G. Principles of Delegation
Where work is delegated for the first time, the supervisor should think in terms of these questions:
1. Who is best qualified to do this?
2. Can an employee improve his abilities by doing this?
3. How long should an employee spend on this?
4. Are there any special problems for which he will need guidance?
5. How broad a delegation can I make?

H. Principles of Effective Communications
1. Determine the media.
2. To whom directed?
3. Identification and source authority.
4. Is communication understood?

I. Principles of Work Improvement
1. Most people usually do only the work which is assigned to them.
2. Workers are likely to fit assigned work into the time available to perform it.
3. A good workload usually stimulates output.
4. People usually do their best work when they know that results will be reviewed or inspected.
5. Employees usually feel that someone else is responsible for conditions of work, workplace layout, job methods, type of tools/equipment, and other such factors.
6. Employees are usually defensive about their job security.
7. Employees have natural resistance to change.
8. Employees can support or destroy a supervisor.
9. A supervisor usually earns the respect of his people through his personal example of diligence and efficiency.

J. Areas of Job Improvement
The areas of job improvement are quite numerous, but the most common ones which a supervisor can identify and utilize are:
1. Departmental layout
2. Flow of work
3. Workplace layout
4. Utilization of manpower
5. Work methods
6. Materials handling

7. Utilization
8. Motion economy

K. Seven Key Points in Making Improvements
1. Select the job to be improved
2. Study how it is being done now
3. Question the present method
4. Determine actions to be taken
5. Chart proposed method
6. Get approval and apply
7. Solicit worker participation

L. Corrective Techniques of Job Improvement
Specific Problems
1. Size of workload
2. Inability to meet schedules
3. Strain and fatigue
4. Improper use of men and skills
5. Waste, poor quality, unsafe conditions
6. Bottleneck conditions that hinder output
7. Poor utilization of equipment and machine
8. Efficiency and productivity of labor

General Improvement
1. Departmental layout
2. Flow of work
3. Work plan layout
4. Utilization of manpower
5. Work methods
6. Materials handling
7. Utilization of equipment
8. Motion economy

Corrective Techniques
1. Study with scale model
2. Flow chart study
3. Motion analysis
4. Comparison of units produced to standard allowance
5. Methods analysis
6. Flow chart and equipment study
7. Down time vs. running time
8. Motion analysis

M. A Planning Checklist
1. Objectives
2. Controls
3. Delegations
4. Communications
5. Resources
6. Manpower

7. Equipment
8. Supplies and materials
9. Utilization of time
10. Safety
11. Money
12. Work
13. Timing of improvements

N. Five Characteristics of Good Directions
In order to get results, directions must be:
1. Possible of accomplishment
2. Agreeable with worker interests
3. Related to mission
4. Planned and complete
5. Unmistakably clear

O. Types of Directions
1. Demands or direct orders
2. Requests
3. Suggestion or implication
4. volunteering

P. Controls
A typical listing of the overall areas in which the supervisor should establish controls might be:
1. Manpower
2. Materials
3. Quality of work
4. Quantity of work
5. Time
6. Space
7. Money
8. Methods

Q. Orienting the New Employee
1. Prepare for him
2. Welcome the new employee
3. Orientation for the job
4. Follow-up

R. Checklist for Orienting New Employees   Yes   No
1. Do you appreciate the feelings of new employees when they first report for work? ___ ___
2. Are you aware of the fact that the new employee must make a big adjustment to his job? ___ ___
3. Have you given him good reasons for liking the job and the organization? ___ ___
4. Have you prepared for his first day on the job? ___ ___
5. Did you welcome him cordially and make him feel needed? ___ ___

	Yes	No

6. Did you establish rapport with him so that he feels free to talk and discuss matters with you? ___ ___
7. Did you explain his job to him and his relationship to you? ___ ___
8. Does he know that his work will be evaluated periodically on a basis that is fair and objective? ___ ___
9. Did you introduce him to his fellow workers in such a way that they are likely to accept him? ___ ___
10. Does he know what employee benefits he will receive? ___ ___
11. Does he understand the importance of being on the job and what to do if he must leave his duty station? ___ ___
12. Has he been impressed with the importance of accident prevention and safe practice? ___ ___
13. Does he generally know his way around the department? ___ ___
14. Is he under the guidance of a sponsor who will teach the right way of doing things? ___ ___
15. Do you plan to follow-up so that he will continue to adjust successfully to his job? ___ ___

S. Principles of Learning
1. Motivation
2. Demonstration or explanation
3. Practice

T. Causes of Poor Performance
1. Improper training for job
2. Wrong tools
3. Inadequate directions
4. Lack of supervisory follow-up
5. Poor communications
6. Lack of standards of performance
7. Wrong work habits
8. Low morale
9. Other

U. Four Major Steps in On-The-Job Instruction
1. Prepare the worker
2. Present the operation
3. Tryout performance
4. Follow-up

V. Employees Want Five Things
1. Security
2. Opportunity
3. Recognition
4. Inclusion
5. Expression

W. Some Don'ts in Regard to Praise
1. Don't praise a person for something he hasn't done.
2. Don't praise a person unless you can be sincere.
3. Don't be sparing in praise just because your superior withholds it from you.
4. Don't let too much time elapse between good performance and recognition of it

X. How to Gain Your Workers' Confidence
Methods of developing confidence include such things as:
1. Knowing the interests, habits, hobbies of employees
2. Admitting your own inadequacies
3. Sharing and telling of confidence in others
4. Supporting people when they are in trouble
5. Delegating matters that can be well handled
6. Being frank and straightforward about problems and working conditions
7. Encouraging others to bring their problems to you
8. Taking action on problems which impede worker progress

Y. Sources of Employee Problems
On-the-job causes might be such things as:
1. A feeling that favoritism is exercised in assignments
2. Assignment of overtime
3. An undue amount of supervision
4. Changing methods or systems
5. Stealing of ideas or trade secrets
6. Lack of interest in job
7. Threat of reduction in force
8. Ignorance or lack of communications
9. Poor equipment
10. Lack of knowing how supervisor feels toward employee
11. Shift assignments

Off-the-job problems might have to do with:
1. Health
2. Finances
3. Housing
4. Family

Z. The Supervisor's Key to Discipline
There are several key points about discipline which the supervisor should keep in mind:
1. Job discipline is one of the disciplines of life and is directed by the supervisor.
2. It is more important to correct an employee fault than to fix blame for it.
3. Employee performance is affected by problems both on the job and off.
4. Sudden or abrupt changes in behavior can be indications of important employee problems.
5. Problems should be dealt with as soon as possible after they are identified.
6. The attitude of the supervisor may have more to do with solving problems than the techniques of problem solving.
7. Correction of employee behavior should be resorted to only after the supervisor is sure that training or counseling will not be helpful.

12

      8. Be sure to document your disciplinary actions.
      9. Make sure that you are disciplining on the basis of facts rather than personal feelings.
     10. Take each disciplinary step in order, being careful not to make snap judgments, or decisions based on impatience.

AA. Five Important Processes of Management
   1. Planning
   2. Organizing
   3. Scheduling
   4. Controlling
   5. Motivating

BB. When the Supervisor Fails to Plan
   1. Supervisor creates impression of not knowing his job
   2. May lead to excessive overtime
   3. Job runs itself—supervisor lacks control
   4. Deadlines and appointments missed
   5. Parts of the work go undone
   6. Work interrupted by emergencies
   7. Sets a bad example
   8. Uneven workload creates peaks and valleys
   9. Too much time on minor details at expense of more important tasks

CC. Fourteen General Principles of Management
   1. Division of work
   2. Authority and responsibility
   3. Discipline
   4. Unity of command
   5. Unity of direction
   6. Subordination of individual interest to general interest
   7. Remuneration of personnel
   8. Centralization
   9. Scalar chain
  10. Order
  11. Equity
  12. Stability of tenure of personnel
  13. Initiative
  14. Esprit de corps

DD. Change

Bringing about change is perhaps attempted more often, and yet less well understood, than anything else the supervisor does. How do people generally react to change? (People tend to resist change that is imposed upon them by other individuals or circumstances.

Change is characteristic of every situation. It is a part of every real endeavor where the efforts of people are concerned.

1. Why do people resist change?
   People may resist change because of:
   a. Fear of the unknown
   b. Implied criticism
   c. Unpleasant experiences in the past
   d. Fear of loss of status
   e. Threat to the ego
   f. Fear of loss of economic stability

2. How can we best overcome the resistance to change?
   In initiating change, take these steps:
   a. Get ready to sell
   b. Identify sources of help
   c. Anticipate objections
   d. Sell benefits
   e. Listen in depth
   f. Follow up

II. Brief Topical Summaries

   A. Who/What is the Supervisor?
      1. The supervisor is often called the "highest level employee and the lowest level manager."
      2. A supervisor is a member of both management and the work group. He acts as a bridge between the two.
      3. Most problems in supervision are in the area of human relations, or people problems.
      4. Employees expect: Respect, opportunity to learn and to advance, and a sense of belonging, and so forth.
      5. Supervisors are responsible for directing people and organizing work. Planning is of paramount importance.
      6. A position description is a set of duties and responsibilities inherent to a given position.
      7. It is important to keep the position description up-to-date and to provide each employee with his own copy.

   B. The Sociology of Work
      1. People are alike in many ways; however, each individual is unique.
      2. The supervisor is challenged in getting to know employee differences. Acquiring skills in evaluating individuals is an asset.
      3. Maintaining meaningful working relationships in the organization is of great importance.
      4. The supervisor has an obligation to help individuals to develop to their fullest potential.
      5. Job rotation on a planned basis helps to build versatility and to maintain interest and enthusiasm in work groups.
      6. Cross training (job rotation) provides backup skills.

7. The supervisor can help reduce tension by maintaining a sense of humor, providing guidance to employees, and by making reasonable and timely decisions. Employees respond favorably to working under reasonably predictable circumstances.
8. Change is characteristic of all managerial behavior. The supervisor must adjust to changes in procedures, new methods, technological changes, and to a number of new and sometimes challenging situations.
9. To overcome the natural tendency for people to resist change, the supervisor should become more skillful in initiating change.

C. Principles and Practices of Supervision
1. Employees should be required to answer to only one superior.
2. A supervisor can effectively direct only a limited number of employees, depending upon the complexity, variety, and proximity of the jobs involved.
3. The organizational chart presents the organization in graphic form. It reflects lines of authority and responsibility as well as interrelationships of units within the organization.
4. Distribution of work can be improved through an analysis using the "Work Distribution Chart."
5. The "Work Distribution Chart" reflects the division of work within a unit in understandable form.
6. When related tasks are given to an employee, he has a better chance of increasing his skills through training.
7. The individual who is given the responsibility for tasks must also be given the appropriate authority to insure adequate results.
8. The supervisor should delegate repetitive, routine work. Preparation of recurring reports, maintaining leave and attendance records are some examples.
9. Good discipline is essential to good task performance. Discipline is reflected in the actions of employees on the job in the absence of supervision.
10. Disciplinary action may have to be taken when the positive aspects of discipline have failed. Reprimand, warning, and suspension are examples of disciplinary action.
11. If a situation calls for a reprimand, be sure it is deserved and remember it is to be done in private.

D. Dynamic Leadership
1. A style is a personal method or manner of exerting influence.
2. Authoritarian leaders often see themselves as the source of power and authority.
3. The democratic leader often perceives the group as the source of authority and power.
4. Supervisors tend to do better when using the pattern of leadership that is most natural for them.
5. Social scientists suggest that the effective supervisor use the leadership style that best fits the problem or circumstances involved.
6. All four styles—telling, selling, consulting, joining—have their place. Using one does not preclude using the other at another time.

7. The theory X point of view assumes that the average person dislikes work, will avoid it whenever possible, and must be coerced to achieve organizational objectives.
8. The theory Y point of view assumes that the average person considers work to be a natural as play, and, when the individual is committed, he requires little supervision or direction to accomplish desired objectives.
9. The leader's basic assumptions concerning human behavior and human nature affect his actions, decisions, and other managerial practices.
10. Dissatisfaction among employees is often present, but difficult to isolate. The supervisor should seek to weaken dissatisfaction by keeping promises, being sincere and considerate, keeping employees informed, and so forth.
11. Constructive suggestions should be encouraged during the natural progress of the work.

E. Processes for Solving Problems
1. People find their daily tasks more meaningful and satisfying when they can improve them.
2. The causes of problems, or the key factors, are often hidden in the background. Ability to solve problems often involves the ability to isolate them from their backgrounds. There is some substance to the cliché that some persons "can't see the forest for the trees."
3. New procedures are often developed from old ones. Problems should be broken down into manageable parts. New ideas can be adapted from old one.
4. People think differently in problem-solving situations. Using a logical, patterned approach is often useful. One approach found to be useful includes these steps:
    a. Define the problem
    b. Establish objectives
    c. Get the facts
    d. Weigh and decide
    e. Take action
    f. Evaluate action

F. Training for Results
1. Participants respond best when they feel training is important to them.
2. The supervisor has responsibility for the training and development of those who report to him.
3. When training is delegated to others, great care must be exercised to insure the trainer has knowledge, aptitude, and interest for his work as a trainer.
4. Training (learning) of some type goes on continually. The most successful supervisor makes certain the learning contributes in a productive manner to operational goals.
5. New employees are particularly susceptible to training. Older employees facing new job situations require specific training, as well as having need for development and growth opportunities.
6. Training needs require continuous monitoring.
7. The training officer of an agency is a professional with a responsibility to assist supervisors in solving training problems.

8. Many of the self-development steps important to the supervisor's own growth are equally important to the development of peers and subordinates. Knowledge of these is important when the supervisor consults with others on development and growth opportunities.

G. Health, Safety, and Accident Prevention
1. Management-minded supervisors take appropriate measures to assist employees in maintaining health and in assuring safe practices in the work environment.
2. Effective safety training and practices help to avoid injury and accidents.
3. Safety should be a management goal. All infractions of safety which are observed should be corrected without exception.
4. Employees' safety attitude, training and instruction, provision of safe tools and equipment, supervision, and leadership are considered highly important factors which contribute to safety and which can be influenced directly by supervisors.
5. When accidents do occur, they should be investigated promptly for very important reasons, including the fact that information which is gained can be used to prevent accidents in the future.

H. Equal Employment Opportunity
1. The supervisor should endeavor to treat all employees fairly, without regard to religion, race, sex, or national origin.
2. Groups tend to reflect the attitude of the leader. Prejudice can be detected even in very subtle form. Supervisors must strive to create a feeling of mutual respect and confidence in every employee.
3. Complete utilization of all human resources is a national goal. Equitable consideration should be accorded women in the work force, minority-group members, the physically and mentally handicapped, and the older employee. The important question is: "Who can do the job?"
4. Training opportunities, recognition for performance, overtime assignments, promotional opportunities, and all other personnel actions are to be handled on an equitable basis.

I. Improving Communications
1. Communications is achieving understanding between the sender and the receiver of a message. It also means sharing information—the creation of understanding.
2. Communication is basic to all human activity. Words are means of conveying meanings; however, real meanings are in people.
3. There are very practical differences in the effectiveness of one-way, impersonal, and two-way communications. Words spoken face-to-face are better understood. Telephone conversations are effective, but lack the rapport of person-to-person exchanges. The whole person communicates.
4. Cooperation and communication in an organization go hand in hand. When there is a mutual respect between people, spelling out rules and procedures for communicating is unnecessary.
5. There are several barriers to effective communications. These include failure to listen with respect and understanding, lack of skill in feedback, and misinterpreting the meanings of words used by the speaker. It is also common

practice to listen to what we want to hear, and tune out things we do not want to hear.
6. Communication is management's chief problem. The supervisor should accept the challenge to communicate more effectively and to improve interagency and intra-agency communications.
7. The supervisor may often plan for and conduct meetings. The planning phase is critical and may determine the success or the failure of a meeting.
8. Speaking before groups usually requires extra effort. Stage fright may never disappear completely, but it can be controlled.

J. Self-Development
1. Every employee is responsible for his own self-development.
2. Toastmaster and toastmistress clubs offer opportunities to improve skills in oral communications.
3. Planning for one's own self-development is of vital importance. Supervisors know their own strengths and limitations better than anyone else.
4. Many opportunities are open to aid the supervisor in his developmental efforts, including job assignments; training opportunities, both governmental and non-governmental—to include universities and professional conferences and seminars.
5. Programmed instruction offers a means of studying at one's own rate.
6. Where difficulties may arise from a supervisor's being away from his work for training, he may participate in televised home study or correspondence courses to meet his self-development needs.

K. Teaching and Training
1. The Teaching Process
Teaching is encouraging and guiding the learning activities of students toward established goals. In most cases this process consists of five steps: preparation, presentation, summarization, evaluation, and application.

   a. Preparation
   Preparation is two-fold in nature; that of the supervisor and the employee. Preparation by the supervisor is absolutely essential to success. He must know what, when, where, how, and whom he will teach. Some of the factors that should be considered are:
   1) The objectives
   2) The materials needed
   3) The methods to be used
   4) Employee participation
   5) Employee interest
   6) Training aids
   7) Evaluation
   8) Summarization

   Employee preparation consists in preparing the employee to receive the material. Probably the most important single factor in the preparation of the employee is arousing and maintaining his interest. He must know the objectives of the training, why he is there, how the material can be used, and its importance to him.

b. Presentation
In presentation, have a carefully designed plan and follow it. The plan should be accurate and complete, yet flexible enough to meet situations as they arise. The method of presentation will be determined by the particular situation and objectives.

c. Summary
A summary should be made at the end of every training unit and program. In addition, there may be internal summaries depending on the nature of the material being taught. The important thing is that the trainee must always be able to understand how each part of the new material relates to the whole.

d. Application
The supervisor must arrange work so the employee will be given a chance to apply new knowledge or skills while the material is still clear in his mind and interest is high. The trainee does not really know whether he has learned the material until he has been given a chance to apply it. If the material is not applied, it loses most of its value.

e. Evaluation
The purpose of all training is to promote learning. To determine whether the training has been a success or failure, the supervisor must evaluate this learning.
In the broadest sense, evaluation includes all the devices, methods, skills, and techniques used by the supervisor to keep himself and the employees informed as to their progress toward the objectives they are pursuing. The extent to which the employee has mastered the knowledge, skills, and abilities, or changed his attitudes, as determined by the program objectives, is the extent to which instruction has succeeded or failed.
Evaluation should not be confined to the end of the lesson, day, or program but should be used continuously. We shall note later the way this relates to the rest of the teaching process.

2. Teaching Methods
A teaching method is a pattern of identifiable student and instructor activity used in presenting training material.
All supervisors are faced with the problem of deciding which method should be used at a given time.

a. Lecture
The lecture is direct oral presentation of material by the supervisor. The present trend is to place less emphasis on the trainer's activity and more on that of the trainee.

b. Discussion
Teaching by discussion or conference involves using questions and other techniques to arouse interest and focus attention upon certain areas, and by doing so creating a learning situation. This can be one of the most

valuable methods because it gives the employees an opportunity to express their ideas and pool their knowledge.

c. Demonstration
The demonstration is used to teach how something works or how to do something. It can be used to show a principle or what the results of a series of actions will be. A well-staged demonstration is particularly effective because it shows proper methods of performance in a realistic manner.

d. Performance
Performance is one of the most fundamental of all learning techniques or teaching methods. The trainee may be able to tell how a specific operation should be performed but he cannot be sure he knows how to perform the operation until he has done so.
As with all methods, there are certain advantages and disadvantages to each method.

e. Which Method to Use
Moreover, there are other methods and techniques of teaching. It is difficult to use any method without other methods entering into it. In any learning situation, a combination of methods is usually more effective than any one method alone.

Finally, evaluation must be integrated into the other aspects of the teaching-learning process.

It must be used in the motivation of the trainees; it must be used to assist in developing understanding during the training; and it must be related to employee application of the results of training.

This is distinctly the role of the supervisor.

BASIC FUNDAMENTALS OF DRIVING

TABLE OF CONTENTS

PART ONE - Information for Drivers and Vehicle Owners

Chapter 1 - Driver Licenses 8
Types of License 8
Applying for Your First License 10
Non-Resident and New Resident Drivers 16
License Renewal 16
License Renewal Fees 17
Change of Address 17
Junior Operator Restrictions 17

Chapter 2 - Keeping Your License 20
Probation Period 20
If You Receive A Traffic Ticket 21
Traffic Tickets Received Out of State 21
Mandatory Suspension or Revocation 22
The Point System 24
Traffic Crashes 25
Fees and Civil Penalties 25
Driving While Suspended or Revoked 26

Chapter 3 - Owning a Vehicle 27
Registration and Title 27
Registration Renewal 30
Resident and Non-Resident Responsibility 32
Inspection 32
Complaints Against Businesses 33

PART TWO - Rules of the Road

Chapter 4 - Traffic Control 36
Signs 36
Traffic Signals 38
Pavement Markings 40
Traffic Officers 42

Chapter 5 - Intersections and Turns 44
Right-of-Way 44
Emergency Vehicles 46
Blue, Green and Amber Lights 46
Turns 46
U-Turns 50

Chapter 6 - Passing 52
Passing on the Left 52
Passing on the Right 53
Being Passed 53
School Buses 54

Chapter 7 - Parking 56
How to Park 56
Parking on a Hill 57
Pulling Out 57

TABLE OF CONTENTS

Parking Regulations 57
Reserved Parking for the Disabled 58

PART THREE - Safe Driving Tips

Chapter 8 - Defensive Driving 62
Be Prepared and Look Ahead 62
Aggressive Drivers 63
Speed 64
Allowing Yourself Space 65
Seat Belts, Child Safety Seats, and Air Bags 65
Drowsy and Fatigued Driving .67
Vehicle Condition 69

Chapter 9 - Alcohol and Other Drugs 71
What Alcohol Does 71
Other Drugs 72
Alcohol, Drugs and the Law 72
Your BAC 73
Chemical Tests 74
The Consequences 75
A Few Important Words 76
Avoiding Trouble 77

Chapter 10 - Special Driving Conditions 79
Expressway Driving 79
Night Driving 80
Driving in Rain or Fog 81
Winter Driving 82
Avoiding Collisions With Deer .83
Driving Emergencies 84

Chapter 11 - Sharing the Road 87
Pedestrians 87
Bicyclists and In-Line Skaters .88
Motorcyclists 89
Moped Operators 90
Large Vehicles 91
Slow Moving Vehicles 94
Horseback Riders 94

Chapter 12 - If You Are in a Traffic Crash 96
At the Scene 96
Emergency First-Aid 97
Reports to DMV 97

BASIC FUNDAMENTALS OF DRIVING

CHAPTER 1 — Driver Licenses

You must have a valid driver license to drive legally in New York State. If you reside in and hold another license from another state or nation, you probably can drive legally in New York State. However, even if you are licensed elsewhere, you may not drive in New York State if you are under age 16.

If you have moved here, you must turn in your out-of-state driver license and obtain a New York State license within 30 days after you become a permanent resident. With few exceptions, it is illegal to hold both a New York State driver license and a license from another state. It is also a violation of Federal law to hold more than one commercial driver license (CDL).

TYPES OF LICENSES

It is a crime to alter or forge any motor vehicle document, including a driver license. This may result in suspension or revocation of the driver license and criminal prosecution leading to a fine or imprisonment.

New York State issues six types of non-commercial licenses. The information in this chapter applies primarily to passenger car and motorcycle licenses. To drive most other types of vehicles, you need a commercial driver license (CDL). For information about commercial driver licenses, refer to the *Commercial Driver's Manual* (CDL-10) available from the DMV Internet Office, by request from a DMV Call Center, or at any motor vehicle office. You must have a CDL if you drive any vehicle that:

- Has a manufacturer's gross vehicle weight rating (GVWR) or gross combination weight rating (GCWR) of more than 26,000 lbs. (*11,794 kg*); **or,**
- Pulls a trailer that has a GVWR of more than 10,000 lbs. (*4,536 kg*) and the GCWR of the hauling vehicle plus the trailer is more than 26,000 lbs. (*11,794 kg*); **or,**

- Is designed or used to carry 15 or more persons, not counting the driver; **or,**
- Regardless of seating capacity, is defined as a bus by Article 19-A of the Vehicle and Traffic Law (including vehicles carrying school children or disabled people); **or,**
- Carries hazardous materials required by federal law to be placarded.

The non-commercial licenses reviewed in this manual are:

Operator, Class D - Minimum age is 18, or age 17 with driver education (see Driver Education). Allows you to drive a vehicle with a manufacturer's gross vehicle weight rating (GVWR) of 18,000 lbs. (*8,165 kg*) or less, and a tow vehicle with a GVWR of 10,000 lbs. (*4,536 kg*) or less, if the gross combination weight rating (GCWR) of the two vehicles together is no more than 26,000 lbs. (*11,794 kg*). You may also operate Class B and C mopeds with this license.

Junior Operator, Class DJ - Minimum age is 16. Allows you to drive the same vehicles as Class D license with certain restrictions (see Junior Operator Restrictions).

Non-CDL Class C - Minimum age is 18. Allows you to drive a vehicle with a GVWR of more than 18,000 lbs. (*8,165 kg*) up to 26,000 lbs. (*11,794 kg*) that does not require a CDL endorsement. You may tow a vehicle with a GVWR of 10,000 lbs. (*4,536 kg*) or less.

Taxi/Livery, Class E - Minimum age is 18. Allows you to drive the same vehicles as a Class D license, plus transport passengers for hire in a vehicle designed or used to carry 14 or fewer passengers. However, if the vehicle is defined as a bus under Article 19-A of the Vehicle and Traffic Law (e.g., a school car or a van used to transport physically or mentally disabled people), regardless of seating capacity, you must have a CDL.

Motorcycle, Class M - Minimum age is 18, or age 17 with driver education (see Driver Education). Allows you to drive motorcycles and mopeds.

Junior Motorcycle, Class MJ - Minimum age is 16. Allows you to drive the same vehicles as a Class M license with certain restrictions (see Junior Operator Restrictions).

Note: If you have a motorcycle license and another type of license, both classes will be listed on one document (e.g., "Class DM")

Driver Education (To Change Your Class DJ or MJ License to Class D or M) - You may apply to change your junior license to a full license at age 17 if you have received a Student Certificate of Completion (MV-285) from an approved driver education course. Apply at any motor vehicle office. Otherwise, your junior license will automatically become a full license when you become 18 years old and you do not need to apply for a license change.

Recreational Vehicle or "R" endorsement. Recreational vehicles, with or without air brakes, are not defined as commercial vehicles. You may apply for an "R" endorsement for your Class D, Class E, or non-CDL Class C driver license to allow you to operate a recreational vehicle (RV) with a Gross Vehicle Weight Rating of over 26,000 lbs. (*11,794 kg*).

To obtain an "R" endorsement, you must: submit a completed Application for Driver License or ID Card (MV-44), indicating a license amendment, to any state or county motor vehicle office; pay a $10.00 permit fee, which is valid for up to two road tests; and pass a road test in the size and type of vehicle you will be driving. No written test is required. To take the road test, you must be accompanied by a licensed driver at least 18 years old who has a license valid for the type of vehicle you will be driving during the test (e.g., a driver license with an "R" endorsement or the appropriate Commercial Driver License). The road test will be about 15 minutes in length and will include turns, intersections and backing the vehicle to the curb. Upon passing the road test, you must go to a motor vehicle office and pay the required $8.00 fee to complete the license amendment process.

APPLYING FOR YOUR FIRST LICENSE

All information and required application forms you need to apply for a driver license are available at any state or county motor vehicle office. Information and application forms, including this driver's manual, are also available from a DMV Call Center and the DMV Internet Office (www.nysdmv.com). To apply for a learner permit or driver license, you must complete an *Application For Driver License or ID Card* (MV-44). As part of the application, state law requires that you provide your social security number. You also must pass a vision and written test, and pay application and license fees. Most drivers also must complete an approved 5-hour classroom training course and pass a road test. For more information about how to apply for and receive a license to drive a motorcycle or a commercial vehicle that requires a CDL, refer to the *Motorcycle Operator's Manual* (MV-21MC) or the *Commercial Driver's Manual* (CDL-10).

The addresses of motor vehicle offices may be obtained from the DMV Internet Office or by request from a DMV Call Center. You must bring your completed application to any motor vehicle office, show the required proof of name and date of birth, and pay the appropriate fee.

Your first New York State driver license will expire in about 4½ to 5 years, on your month and day of birth. Depending on your age and whether you are applying for a junior operator or full-license permit, your fee for a non-commercial license will be $38.50 to $47.00. Your fee will be $28.00 to $38.00 if you are over 21 years old, are turning in an out-of-state license for a non-commercial New York State license, and no road test is required.

The fee for a Class-E or non-CDL Class-C license will be no more than $69.

Proof of Name and Age

For your own protection, we must be sure who you are. You must present documents that prove your name and age. These required documents are listed on the *License/Permit/ID Instructions* (MV-44.1). All proofs must be in English or accompanied by a certified English translation. If you do not have the proofs on the instruction list, a supervisor may be authorized to examine and approve other documents.

Proof of Name

Documents that prove your name are assigned a point value. You must present proofs that total six points or more. At least one of the proofs must have your signature. A few examples of common proofs and their point values are listed below. The *License/Permit/ID Instructions* (MV-44.1) presents a more complete list.

Each document below has a value of 6 points:

- New York State Photo Driver License/Permit/Non-Driver ID Card
- If Under Age 21 — must be accompanied by an affidavit by parent or legal guardian (see special instructions and requirements on DMV form MV-45). Proof of date of birth is required for the applicant.

The document below has a value of 4 points:

- U.S. Passport, valid or expired within the past two years

Each document below has a value of 3 points:

- Photo Driver License issued by another U.S. State, jurisdiction, territory or possession, or Canadian province or territory (must be in effect at least 6 months and not expired for more than 12 months)
- U.S. Military Photo ID Card
- N.Y.S. Medicaid/Benefit/Food Stamp Card, with photo (or, 2 points without photo)
- Foreign passport - in English and with a U.S. Visa and valid I-94 or unexpired I-155 stamp attached. If not in English, a certified translation by the embassy or consulate of the issuing country is required.
- Canadian Immigration Record and Visa or Record of Landing (IMM-1000)
- U.S. Re-entry Permit (I-327)
- Refugee Travel Document (I-571)
- Certificate of Citizenship (N-560, N-561 or N-645)
- Certificate of Naturalization (N-550, N-570 or N-578)
- Valid Resident Alien Card (INS I-551, with photo)
- Valid Employment Authorization Card (INS I-688B or I-766, with photo)

Each documents below has a value of 2 points:

- N.Y.S. DMV Non-Photo Interim License or Computer Generated Learner Permit

- N.Y.S. Vehicle Title Certificate
- N.Y.S. Vehicle Registration Receipt
- U.S. Social Security Card (must have your signature)
- U.S. High School ID With Report Card
- U.S. College ID With Photo and Transcript
- U.S. Marriage or Divorce Record
- N.Y.S. Professional License
- N.Y.S. or New York City Pistol Permit

Each document below has a value of 1 point:

- Valid U.S. Major Credit Card
- Supermarket Check Cashing Card (must have your signature)
- U.S. Parole Papers (issued in arrest name)
- Cash Card or ATM Card (must have your pre-printed name and signature)
- U.S. Insurance Policy (in effect at least two years)
- Canceled Check (with your pre-printed name)
- U.S. Health Insurance Card/Prescription Card
- Employee Identification Card
- Bank Statement/Record
- Computerized Pay Stub (must include Social Security Number)
- Utility Bill (must have your name and address)
- General Equivalency Diploma (GED)
- W-2 Form (must include Social Security Number)
- Union Card

Proof of Age

You also must prove your date of birth. Your document must be the original or a certified photocopy from the issuing agency. DMV will accept ANY ONE of these documents:

- Birth Certificate issued and certified by a Board of Health or Bureau of Vital Statistics in the U.S., its territories or possessions. *Foreign birth certificates are not acceptable.*
- Photo Driver License/Permit/Non-Driver Identification Card, Photo Driver License (U.S. or Canada)
- Military Separation Papers (DD-214) or Photo Identification Card
- U.S. Passport
- Foreign Passport (with INS documentation)
- Immigration Documents

Vision & Written Tests

To pass the vision test, you must have 20/40 vision in at least one eye with or without corrective lenses. If you cannot pass this test or if you wear telescopic lenses, contact a DMV Call Center for further guidance.

The written test for a Class D, M, DJ, MJ or E license examines your knowledge of the rules of the road, safe driving techniques, road signs and their meanings, and the laws about the use of alcohol and drugs while driving. To pass the written test, you must correctly answer at least 14 of the 20 questions asked. All the information you need to pass the written test is contained in this Driver's Manual.

If you are applying for a Non-CDL Class C license, also study the *Supplement To Driver's Manual For Class 1, 2, and 3 Driver's Licenses* (MV-21.IX). If you want a motorcycle license, study the *Motorcycle Operator's Manual* (MV-21MC). There is a separate commercial driver license written test for a CDL Class A, B, or C. If you are applying for a commercial driver's license, study the *Commercial Driver's Manual* (CDL-10).

The Learner Permit

When you pass the vision and written tests and pay your fees, your permit will be issued and you may begin learning to drive. Every time you practice driving, you must be accompanied by a licensed driver at least 18 years old who has a license valid for the type of vehicle you are driving.

There are special restrictions for a learner under 18 years old (see publication, Learner Permits & Junior Licenses (C-41). Depending on your age when you apply, your permit will be valid for three to five years. When you pass the road test, your new license will expire on the same date as your permit would have expired.

However, if you have an existing license or permit and are applying for a permit for a different class of license, the new permit will be valid for one year only. In this case, when you submit your permit application, be sure to ask about special procedures you must follow.

Preparing for the Road Test

Safe drivers, confident in today's traffic situations, often find their amount of practice driving before the road test had made a positive difference when they took the road test. Before you take the test, it is very important that you have had at least 30 hours of driving practice, with **at least 10 hours in moderately heavy traffic.** Road tests are given on city streets, but you also should practice driving on expressways and other types of highways. We suggest you take a high school or college driver education course, or lessons from a DMV-licensed driving school. If you cannot take a course or lessons, have the person who teaches you "brush up" by reading Parts Two and Three of this manual.

You may not practice driving in a DMV road test area or on any restricted roads. In New York City, these include the Bronx River Parkway, the Sprain Brook Parkway, and any street within a park, all bridges and tunnels under the jurisdiction of the Triborough Bridge and Tunnel Authority. In Westchester County, the streets and roadways you are prohibited from practice driving on include these parkways: Cross County, Hutchinson River, Saw Mill River, and Taconic State.

Safe Driving Course Requirement

Before you can make a road test appointment, you must first complete an approved pre-licensing safe driving course and pass a 25-question multiple-choice test. This requirement is automatically fulfilled as part of every high school or college driver education course. All other drivers must complete this requirement by taking a special five-hour course available at most professional driving schools. To locate where this course is offered, look in the yellow pages of your local telephone directory under "Driving Instruction." After you take the course and pass the written test, you will receive a certificate to present when you make your road test appointment. The certificate is valid for one year.

Note: A defensive driving course taught through the DMV-certified Point/Insurance Reduction Program does NOT qualify as the required 5-hour classroom pre-licensing course.

The Road Test

In most areas of the state, you must make your road test appointment by telephone at: 1-(800) 801-3614. To schedule an appointment, you must already have your five-hour *Pre-licensing Course Completion Certificate* (MV-278) or your driver education course *Student Certificate Of Completion* (MV-285) before you schedule your appointment. During your phone call, you will be informed whether or not your local motor vehicle office participates in the road test telephone-appointment program. A non-participating office may schedule your appointment in person or by postal mail. In that case, bring or mail your permit and safe driving course certificate to your local motor vehicle office in accordance with their instructions.

If you cannot be at the road test site at the appointed time, you may request to reschedule your road test appointment for a non-commercial driver license. You must make this request at least 24 hours before the scheduled test date – call the road test appointment telephone number, 1-(800) 801-3614, or contact the local non-participating office, wherever you made the original appointment. A CDL test will be rescheduled at your request only if you notify the office at least three business days before the test date.

The DMV may cancel road tests due to bad weather. You may call the road test appointment telephone number or contact your local motor vehicle office, wherever you made your original appointment, for announcements of road test cancellations.

A DMV motor vehicle license examiner will conduct the road test. Before the test begins, the license examiner will explain the test procedures. The road test will last about 15 minutes a non-commercial license test. During the test, the examiner must assess a "negative" score for important safe driving mistakes. To pass, you must not accumulate 30 or more points. Automatic disqualification can result from making a dangerous driving action or a serious violation of traffic law, or becoming involved in a traffic crash.

When you qualify for a non-commercial license (Class Non-CDL C, D, DJ, E, M, MJ) the license examiner will validate your Road Test Evaluation Form (MV-501) as a temporary license (CDL-200, for CDL licenses). The valid periods are:

90 days Class Non-CDL C, D, DJ, E; and M or MJ original licenses. Your new photo-license will arrive in the postal mail within four to six weeks. All photo licenses are mailed from Albany. You cannot get one more quickly by going to a local motor vehicle office.

10 days Class CDL A, B, or C licenses, and M or MJ amendments to a different class license. To amend your original license, you must go <u>in person</u> to a state or county motor vehicle office after five business days following your passing of the road test.

If you do not pass the road test, the license examiner will return your permit immediately after the test is over. The examiner will explain why you did not pass and give you a copy of the road test evaluation. You should ask questions if you do not understand. Review the road test evaluation sheet and discuss this information with your driving teacher. As you practice for your next road test, concentrate on correcting the mistakes you had made. When your driving teacher feels you are ready, make an appointment for your next road test.

If you hold a Class D, DJ permit or other permit for a non-commercial license and do not pass your second road test, you may continue practice driving until the date the permit expires. However, you must pay a $10 fee at any motor vehicle office to purchase two more road tests. If you hold a Class CDL permit and did not pass your road test, you may continue practice driving until the date the permit expires. However, the CDL permit holder must pay a $40 fee for each additional road test.

To take a road test for an M or MJ license (motorcycle), you must bring a car or truck and a driver who is licensed to drive both this vehicle and the motorcycle you will drive during the test. A DMV motor vehicle license examiner will conduct the road test from the passenger seat in this accompanying vehicle by observing your driving.

Even after you qualify for a license, remember that you are still learning to drive. You must continue to show caution, concentration and obedience to the rules of the road to become a truly experienced, capable driver. For additional training, many motorists enroll in a DMV-certified Point & Insurance Reduction Program (PIRP). The PIRP is available through private companies or corporations throughout New York State. This program reviews time-tested safe driving tips and provides an overview of today's vehicle and traffic laws. If you are eligible for point reduction, as many as four (4) points may be reduced from your driving record. You may complete this course every 18 months for the purpose of point reduction. All participants who complete the program will receive a minimum 10% reduction in the base rate of their automobile and motorcycle liability and collision insurance premiums each year for three years. For more information, see our publication *Point & Insurance Reduction Program* (C-32A), available from the DMV Internet Office, by request from a DMV Call Center, or at any motor vehicle office.

NON-RESIDENT AND NEW RESIDENT DRIVERS

If you are a resident of another state or country and hold a valid driver license there, you may legally drive in New York State. You **should not** apply for a New York license. Apply for a New York license **only** after you become a resident of this state. Then, to remain legally licensed, you must apply for a New York State driver license within 30 days after establishing residency.

If you are a new resident with a valid license issued by a U.S. state, territory or possession, or a Canadian province or territory, you must turn in your out-of-state license, show additional proof of name worth three points (see ID proofs), and pass only the vision test to get a New York license. However, if your out-of-state license expired more than one year ago, you must also pass the written and road tests and complete the safe driving course.

If you are a new resident licensed in a country other than Canada, you must pass the vision, written and road tests, complete the safe driving course, and turn in your foreign license. When you pass the road test, you must give your foreign license to the DMV motor vehicle license examiner who conducted the test. If you are from Canada, you must only surrender your license at time of application for the New York State license. Your foreign driver license will be destroyed unless you provide the examiner a written request to hold your foreign license on file at a New York State office of the Department of Motor Vehicles. The license examiner will tell you which DMV District Office will hold your foreign license. Your foreign license will be returned at your request, but only after you surrender your New York State license.

LICENSE RENEWAL

You are responsible for knowing when your driver license expires and for making sure you renew it on time. In most cases, if the DMV has your current address, you should receive a renewal notice and instructions in the mail about 45 days before your license is due to expire. If you do not receive the notice, you may apply for renewal at any motor vehicle office. You also may renew your license up to one year before its printed expiration date.

You must pass a vision test before you renew your driver license. If your license renewal notice allows you to renew by mail, you must return to the DMV your renewal application and a completed *Visual Acuity Report* (MV-619) from a licensed eye-care provider, which documents that you have passed the vision test. Other drivers must renew their licenses in person at a state or county motor vehicle office. The Visual Acuity test must be done <u>within six months</u> before the date you renew your license. You also may bring the renewal form and the Visual Acuity Report to any state or county motor vehicle office and renew in person. If you apply for renewal in person, you can take the vision test at the motor vehicle office.

When renewing in person, you must present your current license and one other proof of identity (see Proof of Name). You may renew your license up to one year before your current license expires. It is especially important to renew early if your license will expire while you are out of state.

If you cannot renew early or a serious illness prevents you from renewing, contact the DMV License Production Bureau at (518) 474-2068.

If you enter military service, your license is automatically extended throughout your active service and for six months afterward. To ensure you will be able to renew your license after you leave the service, notify DMV within 60 days of your induction. You may notify the DMV by letter or use notification form MV-75, available at any motor vehicle office and at the DMV Internet Office.

LICENSE RENEWAL FEES

Class D, M, and DM driver licenses are renewed for 8 years. The fee is $43 to renew a Class D or Class M license, and $51 for a Class DM license. All other license classes are renewed for 5 years – the renewal fee is $53 for a Class E or Non-CDL C license; and $78 to renew a license in Class CDL A, CDL B, or CDL C. Add $5 to the renewal fee for a five-year license that has a motorcycle (Class M) endorsement.

CHANGE OF ADDRESS

If you change your address you must notify DMV within ten days by letter or on a *Change-of-Address Form* (MV-232). You also must write the new address in the space provided on the back of your photo license.

JUNIOR OPERATOR RESTRICTIONS

The restrictions on drivers holding junior learner permits and licenses are also presented in the publication *Learner Permits & Junior Licenses* (C-41), available from the DMV Internet Office. The definitions and restrictions for junior drivers are summarized below. These restrictions also apply to out-of-state drivers under 18 years old.

Definitions

"PROPERLY LICENSED" means the supervising driver has a license valid for driving the type of vehicle the learner is driving.

"GUARDIAN" means a person who, on a regular and extended basis, has assumed the character of a parent and is discharging parental duties as the result of the death, disability or absence of the natural parent. In legal terminology, the guardian is described as being in *loco parentis* to the junior learner or driver.

"SCHOOL" means instruction, education or training that is licensed or approved by a state agency or department, or training conducted by the U.S. armed forces. The term "school" **does not include** extra-curricular activities, such as attending a sporting event or school social event for which no scholastic credits are given.

"WORK" means a place of business at which the driver is employed on a regularly scheduled basis. You may not drive during work or as part of your job, such as for deliveries.

"WORK STUDY PROGRAM" means a state-approved cooperative work-study program. For example, a Board of Cooperative Educational Services (BOCES) course for which academic credit is granted for work experience qualifies as an approved work-study program.

Restrictions

With a JUNIOR LEARNER PERMIT:

- In the five boroughs of **New York City**, you may drive between the hours of 5 a.m. and 9 p.m. only when operating a vehicle that is equipped with dual controls (instructor's brake), <u>and</u> you must be accompanied by a driver education teacher or driving school instructor. You may **not** drive between *9 p.m. and 5 a.m.* under any circumstances.

- In **Nassau and Suffolk Counties,** you may drive between *5 a.m. and 9 p.m.* <u>only</u> when accompanied by your properly licensed parent, guardian, a driver education teacher or driving school instructor. You may **not** drive between *9 p.m. and 5 a.m.* under any circumstances.

- **Upstate** (in all other counties) you may drive between *5 a.m. and 9 p.m.* **only** when accompanied by a properly licensed driver age 18 or older. From *9 p.m. to 5 a.m.,* you must be accompanied by your properly licensed parent or guardian, a driver education teacher or driving school instructor.

With a JUNIOR LICENSE:

- In the five boroughs of **New York City,** you may **not** drive under any circumstances.

- In **Nassau and Suffolk Counties,** you may drive between *5 a.m. and 9 p.m.* <u>only</u> when accompanied by your licensed parent or guardian, a driver education teacher or driving school instructor; or, not accompanied, when traveling directly between home and work.

- Between *9 p.m. and 5 a.m.*, you may not drive except when traveling directly between home and a state approved work-study program; a credit-bearing course at a college, university or registered evening high school; or a driver education course (*only on days you have a driver education class*); or while you are engaged in farm employment. Each time you drive, you must carry a completed Certificate of Employment (MV-58A) from your employer or a letter from the appropriate school or program official. The letter, on the school or program's official letterhead, should list the hours, location and nature of your credit bearing school activity, your motorist identification number, and the address and telephone number of the employer or school or program official.

- **In all other counties,** you may drive between *5 a.m. and 9 p.m.* without being accompanied. Between *9 p.m. and 5 a.m.*, you may drive only when accompanied by a parent or guardian, or when not accompanied while going to work or a credit-bearing course at school. Each time you drive, you must carry a letter or a completed Certificate of Employment (MV-58A) from your employer or a letter from the appropriate school official. The letter, on the business or school official letterhead, should list your hours of employment, the hours, location and nature of your job or credit bearing school activity, your motorist identification number, and the address and telephone number of the employer or school official.

Motorcycles and Mopeds

Learner permit and junior operator restrictions also apply when operating motorcycles and mopeds (limited use motorcycles). In addition, a motorcycle or moped learner may not carry a passenger other than a properly licensed motorcycle or moped operator who is serving as the accompanying driver.

An accompanying driver for a learner or junior operator using a motorcycle or moped must exercise "general supervision." This means he or she must remain within one-quarter mile of the learner or junior operator at all times. The DMV recommends that the junior operator remain in sight of the accompanying driver at all times.

If you already have a motorcycle learner permit and already have a driver license, the DMV will waive your motorcycle road test if you complete the Motorcycle Safety Foundation's Motorcycle Rider Course®: Riding and Street Skills. To qualify for the road test waiver option, the course must have been given by a provider that is certified by the Motorcycle Association of New York State, Inc. (MANYS). For information about the nearest course, call the Foundation at 1-800-446-9227 or the MANYS at 1-888-4NY-RIDE.

CHAPTER 2   Keeping Your License

If you commit a serious traffic violation or several violations that are less serious, you may lose your driving privilege through license suspension or revocation.

"Suspension" means your license is taken away from you for a certain period of time and then returned.

"Revocation" means your license is canceled completely. The Department of Motor Vehicles then determines when you are eligible to apply for a new license. The law provides minimum revocation periods. A poor driving record or failure to comply with the DMV's requirements may result in a longer revocation period.

"Driving privilege" means the courtesy extended to out-of-state drivers which allows them to drive a motor vehicle in New York State. It also refers to permission from New York State for an unlicensed person to obtain a New York State license. A driving privilege can be suspended or revoked for the same reasons as are New York State driver licenses. Driving with a suspended or revoked privilege carries the same penalties as driving with a suspended or revoked license.

PROBATION PERIOD

After you pass your road test or get a new license following revocation, your new driver license will be automatically on probation for six months. An exception: you will not serve probation if you have turned in an out-of-state license to get your New York State license and were not required to pass a road test.

During the probation period, your license will be suspended for 60 days if you are found guilty of even just one violation of speeding, reckless driving or tailgating. It will be suspended for 60 days if you are found guilty of committing any two other moving traffic violations during the probation period, and for 90 days if you are convicted of driving while ability impaired by alcohol or drugs (DWAI).

When the suspension ends, you will be placed on probation for another six months. During the second probationary period, your license will be revoked for at least six months if you are found guilty of any one of the single violations listed above or any two other moving violations.

IF YOU RECEIVE A TRAFFIC TICKET

If you receive a traffic ticket, <u>do not delay</u> – follow the instructions on the ticket for the plea you wish to make. Your driver license will be suspended if you do not answer the ticket in the time allowed. If you do not respond to receiving the ticket, you could be found guilty by default conviction. If you are convicted by default, your license will then be suspended for not paying the fine and a judgment will be entered against you.

The New York State Department of Motor Vehicles Traffic Violations Bureau (TVB) processes the tickets for non-criminal moving traffic violations issued in the five boroughs of New York City, Buffalo, Rochester, and the Suffolk County towns of Babylon, Brookhaven, Huntington, Islip and Smithtown. By processing these traffic tickets, the TVB system allows the other courts in these areas to concentrate on criminal cases, including driving offenses such as Driving While Intoxicated (DWI) and driving while suspended or revoked (Aggravated Unlicensed Operation – AUO). <u>The TVB does NOT handle parking violations and cannot answer questions about parking tickets.</u> Elsewhere in New York State, traffic violations are processed in the criminal and traffic court of the city, county, town or village where the alleged offense took place. Whichever court system is involved, every motorist who receives a traffic ticket may present a defense and be represented by an attorney.

TRAFFIC TICKETS RECEIVED OUT OF STATE

The New York State Department of Motor Vehicles does **not record convictions of moving traffic violations by NYS non-commercial licensed drivers in other jurisdictions, except traffic offenses committed in the provinces of Ontario and Quebec, in Canada.** Therefore, except for traffic convictions in Ontario and Quebec, out-of-state traffic convictions are not added to your New York State "violation point" driving record.

However, your New York State license will be suspended **if you fail to answer a ticket** for a moving violation in any state except Alaska, California, Michigan, Montana, Oregon or Wisconsin. Your license will remain suspended until you answer the ticket. Likewise, drivers from any state, except those from the six states listed above, will have their driver licenses suspended in their own state for failure to answer a moving violation summons in New York State.

If you are **over 21 years old, and are convicted of an alcohol-related driving violation (e.g., DUI) in any other state or the provinces of Ontario and Quebec**, in

Canada, your New York State driver license will be suspended for 90 days. If you are convicted of a drug-related driving violation in any of these jurisdictions, your New York State license will be revoked for at least six months. Out-of-state drivers ticketed in New York State should contact the motor vehicle department of their own state or province about the effect of a conviction.

If you are under 21 years old and convicted of any alcohol or drug-related violation that occurred out of state on or after November 1, 2000, your New York State driver license will be revoked for at least one year. If you have a prior conviction, even if the violation occurred before November 1, 2000, your license will be revoked for at least one year or until the age of 21, whichever is longer.

In addition to the above, the New York State Department of Motor Vehicles records the conviction of any driver, and revokes the driver's license and vehicle registrations, of criminal negligence which results in death, or of homicide or assault, that arise out of the operation of a motor vehicle, whether the condition occurred in this state or elsewhere.

MANDATORY SUSPENSION OR REVOCATION

Your driver license or driving privilege can be suspended or revoked for many reasons. The following suspensions and revocations are *required by law:*

Alcohol and Drug Violations

- Driving while ability impaired by alcohol (DWAI): *90-day suspension.*
- Driving while ability impaired by drugs (DWAI-drug): *six-month suspension*
- Driving while intoxicated (DWI), with .10 of one percent blood alcohol content (.10 BAC): *minimum six-month revocation.*
- Driving under the influence of alcohol or drugs out-of-state (DUI): *minimum 90-day revocation.*
- DWAI violation within five years of any prior alcohol or drug-related violation: *minimum six-month revocation.*
- DWI, .10 BAC, or DWAI-drug violation committed within ten years of any prior DWI, .10 BAC, or DWAI-drug violation: *minimum one-year revocation.*

Younger Drivers

If you are under 21 when arrested, conviction for any of the alcohol or drug related violations listed above will result in a minimum one-year revocation. A second violation while under 21 requires a revocation for one year or until you reach age 21, whichever is longer. These penalties apply even if you are adjudicated as a youthful offender, or if you were arrested or convicted out of state (see Traffic Tickets Received Out Of State).

Under the state's "Zero Tolerance Law," a driver under 21 will have his or her license suspended for six months if found to have a BAC from .02 to .07.

A .02 BAC could occur with as little as one drink. For a second Zero Tolerance violation, the driver's license will be revoked for one year or until the driver turns 21, whichever is longer.

NOTE: Motorboat and snowmobile operators under 21 years old who drink alcohol are subject to similar penalties and sanctions against their privileges to operate a motorboat or snowmobile.

Commercial Drivers

Because of their extra responsibility to traffic safety, drivers of tractor-trailers, heavy trucks and vehicles carrying hazardous materials face stiffer penalties than non-commercial drivers if convicted of certain violations. For information about the commercial driver penalties, read Section 1 of the *Commercial Driver's Manual* (CDL-10).

It is a felony to drive a school bus carrying one or more students while you are impaired or intoxicated. If you are found guilty of an alcohol or drug-related violation while driving a school bus, taxi, or livery vehicle while carrying a passenger, your license will be revoked for at least one year. If found guilty of a second violation within ten years, you could be *permanently prohibited* from holding a Class CDL license.

NOTE: See Chapter 9 for more information about alcohol and drug-related violations.

Chemical Test Refusals (Also see Chapter 9)

- Chemical test refusal, drivers over age 21: *minimum six-month revocation.*
- Chemical test refusal, drivers over age 21, within five years of a prior refusal revocation or any alcohol or drug-related violation: *minimum one-year revocation.*
- Chemical test refusal, drivers under age 21, first time: *minimum one-year revocation.*
- Chemical test refusal, drivers under age 21, second time: *minimum revocation until age 21 or one year, whichever is longer.*
- Zero Tolerance test refusal: *minimum one-year revocation.*

Speeding and Other Violations

Your license will be **revoked for at least six months** if you are found guilty of:

- Three speeding and/or misdemeanor traffic violations within 18 months (based on date of violation, not date of conviction).
- Three "passing a stopped school bus" violations within three years.
- One violation of "leaving the scene of a personal injury or fatal accident."
- One "participating in a speed contest" violation. Conviction of a second speed contest violation within 12 months results in a revocation of at least one year.

No Insurance

Operating or permitting operation of an uninsured vehicle or involvement in an accident without insurance: *minimum one-year revocation*. (See also "Insurance" in Chapter 3.)

Indefinite Suspensions/Revocations

If you do not answer a traffic summons or pay a fine and/or surcharge (except those for parking violations), your license will be suspended until you answer the summons or pay the fine and/or surcharge. If you do not answer a ticket, a guilty judgment may be ordered and a fine imposed. If you fail to file an accident report with DMV (see Chapter 12) your license may be suspended until you file the report.

THE POINT SYSTEM

The DMV point system identifies "persistent violators"; that is, drivers who commit a series of violations in a relatively short time period. The table in this chapter lists the point values assigned to various moving traffic violations. Please note that traffic laws that must be obeyed on public highways, roads, and streets, also apply to parking lots open to the public.

While each violation listed, by itself, may not be serious enough to require license suspension or revocation, the accumulation of several violations on your driving record may indicate that action should be taken.

The point values charged against your record are based on the date you commit the violation, not the date you are convicted in court. If you acquire 11 or more points within 18 months,

Violation	Points
Speeding MPH not specified	3
Speeding MPH over posted limit: 1 to 10	3
11 to 20	4
21 to 30	6
31 to 40	8
More than 40	11
Reckless driving	5
Failing to stop for school bus	5
Inadequate brakes	4

Violation	Points
Following too closely (tailgating)	4
Improper passing, unsafe lane change, drove left of center, or drove wrong direction	3
Violation involving a traffic signal, stop sign or yield sign	3
Failing to yield right-of-way	3
Railroad crossing violation	3
Leaving scene of incident involving property damage or injury to domestic animal	3
Safety restraint violation involving person under 16	3
Inadequate brakes (while driving employer's vehicle)	2
Any other moving violation	2

you will be notified by mail that your license will be suspended. You may request a DMV hearing only to show that the convictions in question were not yours. You may not re-argue the convictions or request the suspension be waived based upon special or mitigating circumstances.

You can reduce your point total by up to four points and save up to ten percent on your auto liability insurance premiums by taking a DMV-approved accident prevention course. However, completion of a point reduction course cannot prevent a mandatory suspension or revocation or be applied as a "credit" against future points. For more information, see the publication *Point & Insurance Reduction* (C-32A), available from the DMV Internet Office, by request from a DMV Call Center, and at any motor vehicle office.

Please note that insurance companies may also have point systems of their own. These have no relationship to, and should not be confused with, the DMV point system.

TRAFFIC CRASHES

Today, except where required by law, the term "accident" is frequently being replaced by "crash." This is because a "crash" can usually be avoided. If you are involved in a traffic crash in which another person is killed, your license may be suspended or revoked after a DMV hearing even if you were not charged with a violation at the time of the incident.

FEES AND CIVIL PENALTIES

If your driver license has been suspended for a definite period, such as 30 days, 90 days, etc., your license will not be returned until you pay a non-refundable $25 suspension termination fee.

In most cases, if your license has been revoked, you may not apply for a new license until you pay a non-refundable $50 re-application fee. This fee is not required if your license was revoked due to operating without insurance or if you had been issued a conditional or restricted use license.

After the following revocations, you must pay a civil penalty to DMV before your application for a new license can be accepted:

- Operating without insurance or uninsured accident: *$500 civil penalty.*
- Chemical test refusal: *$300 civil penalty ($350 if while operating commercial motor vehicle).*
- Chemical test refusal within five years of a prior alcohol, drug or refusal-related revocation: *$750 civil penalty.*
- Zero Tolerance Law suspension: *$125 civil penalty and $100 suspension termination fee.*

DRIVING WHILE SUSPENDED OR REVOKED

It is a criminal violation to drive while your license is suspended or revoked, and there are mandatory fines from $200 to $5,000. You also may face mandatory imprisonment or probation, and seizure and possible forfeiture of the vehicle being driven. More severe penalties apply to drivers who are caught driving while intoxicated or impaired by alcohol or drugs while their licenses or privileges are already under suspension or revocation for a previous alcohol or drug-related incident, and to drivers caught driving with 10 or more suspensions for failure to answer traffic tickets or pay fines. In addition, drivers with 20 or more suspensions for failure to answer tickets or pay fines face a criminal charge, even if not driving when caught. The penalties for driving while suspended or revoked are described in detail in the publication *Suppose Your License Were Taken Away* (C-12) available from the DMV Internet Office, by request from a DMV Call Center, and at any motor vehicle office.

CHAPTER 3 — Owning a Vehicle

Whether you are a vehicle owner or registrant, or a driver of a vehicle owned or registered by someone else, you are responsible for making sure it is properly registered, insured and inspected before the vehicle is used on a public roadway.

REGISTRATION AND TITLE

A registration allows a vehicle to be driven on public roads and highways. A title certificate proves who owns the vehicle. In New York, only 1973 and newer model vehicles receive titles. For 1972 and older models, the registration is proof of ownership.

You must be at least 16 years old to register a vehicle. A new resident of the state must obtain a New York registration within 30 days of establishing residence.

To register a vehicle, you must prove you own the vehicle or that the owner authorizes you to register it, that the vehicle is insured, and that state and county sales taxes have been paid.

To Register a Vehicle

<u>Before you apply to register a vehicle</u>, make sure you have proper proofs of ownership, insurance, and sales tax payment, and any required mileage and/or damage disclosure statement. If the ownership proofs listed below are not available from the seller, contact any motor vehicle office or a DMV Call Center before you buy the vehicle.

To apply for registration, you must complete a *Vehicle Registration/Title Application* (MV-82). You must also present proof of identity worth six points. For additional information about these requirements, please refer to the information guide *Registering A Vehicle In New York State* (MV-82.1), available from the DMV Internet Office, by request from a DMV Call Center, and at any motor vehicle office. When your vehicle is registered, you will receive license plates, a registration receipt, and a sticker for the windshield or license plate. If you bought the vehicle from someone other than a dealership, you will also receive a ten-day inspection extension sticker. You must then have the vehicle inspected within 10 days from the date of registration. It should already have a valid inspection sticker if you bought the vehicle from a dealer.

When you buy a new or used vehicle from a dealer registered with the DMV, the dealer may register the vehicle for you and give you a temporary registration and, if you need them, new license plates. The dealer may charge $20 for this service in addition to registration, plate and title fees.

If your vehicle is a 1973 or newer model, your title certificate will be mailed to you from Albany several weeks after the vehicle is registered.

Proof of Ownership

If you purchase your vehicle from a dealership, the proof of ownership for a new vehicle will be a Manufacturer's Certificate of Origin (MCO) and a dealer's *Certificate of Sale* (MV-50). For a used 1973 or newer vehicle, proof of ownership is the previous owner's *Certificate of Title* (MV-999), the appropriate odometer and salvage disclosure statement, and the dealer's *Certificate of Sale* (MV-50). For a used 1972 or older vehicle, proof of ownership is the dealer's *Certificate of Sale* (MV-50) and the previous owner's transferable registration signed over to the dealer.

If the dealer does not register the vehicle for you, make sure you receive the ownership documents listed above. In any case, *examine the ownership documents carefully before closing the deal.*

When you buy a vehicle from someone who is <u>not</u> a dealership, you should receive the following proof of ownership:

- 1973 or newer model: the title certificate signed over to you and the appropriate mileage and/or damage disclosure statement.

- 1972 or older model: the transferable registration signed over to you.

<u>Disclosure Statements</u> —

- If you buy a vehicle eight model years old or newer, **the DMV will NOT register your vehicle or issue you a new title certificate unless the seller has completed, and you have signed, both the odometer and the damage disclosure statements on the reverse of the vehicle's** *Certificate of Title* (MV-999) or have attached a completed odometer and damage disclosure on an *Odometer And Damage Disclosure Statement* (MV-103). This statement indicates whether or not the vehicle's new title certificate should be branded "Rebuilt Salvage." Title branding is explained in detail in the publications *Let The Buyer Be Aware* (C-18) and *Q & A About Your Vehicle Title* (C-19). An *Odometer*

And Damage Disclosure Statement (MV-103) is available at any motor vehicle office, by request from a DMV Call Center, or from the DMV Internet Office.

- If you buy a vehicle 10 model years old or newer, **be sure the private seller has completed the odometer statement portion on the back of the vehicle's** *Certificate of Title* **(MV-999) or has attached to the title certificate a completed mileage disclosure on an** *Odometer And Damage Disclosure Statement* **(MV-103)**. The damage disclosure is not required for vehicles nine model years old or older. As buyer, you must confirm the odometer statement as indicated on the title certificate, either by initialing next to the odometer box on the title certificate or by signing the form. You should compare the odometer statement on the title certificate with the actual odometer reading in the vehicle.

IMPORTANT: THE DMV MUST EXAMINE EVERY VEHICLE IDENTIFIED "REBUILT SALVAGE" FOR STOLEN PARTS BEFORE THE VEHICLE CAN BE REGISTERED OR TITLED. For more information, or if you are going to buy a vehicle registered or titled out-of-state, contact a DMV Call Center.

Proof of Insurance

When you buy auto liability insurance, the insurance agent or broker gives you two insurance identification cards. The name(s) on these cards must exactly match the name(s) on the registration application. You must present one card when registering your vehicle. Keep the second card with the vehicle.

"No-fault" auto insurance is issued in New York State. For more information on no-fault insurance contact the NYS Department of Insurance, Agency Building 1, Empire State Plaza, Albany, NY 12257.

Proof of Sales Tax Payment

When you buy a vehicle from a dealer, the dealer collects the sales tax.

If you are buying a vehicle from someone other than a dealer, obtain a *Statement of Transaction - Sale or Gift of Motor Vehicle* (DTF-802), available at any motor vehicle office, by request from a DMV Call Center, and from the DMV Internet Office. One side of the form must be completed and signed by the seller, the other by the buyer. This form certifies the purchase price and determines the sales tax you must pay when registering the vehicle. Bring the completed form to a state or county motor vehicle office when you register your vehicle. If the form is not filled out by the seller, you will be charged sales tax based on the vehicle's current fair market value.

Fees

Registrations for most vehicles under 18,000 pounds (*8,165 kg*) maximum gross weight are valid for two years, and registration fees are based on vehicle weight. There are also plate and title fees.

By law, registration fees cannot be refunded, if you use the license plates or registration sticker on your vehicle even for only one day. However, if your license plates and registration sticker are returned <u>completely unused</u> within 60 days after registering your vehicle, you may receive a full refund, minus a one dollar processing fee. You may receive a refund of the fee for the second year of a two-year registration, minus a one dollar processing fee, if you use the plates and registration only during the first year. Be sure to obtain a DMV Universal Receipt (FS6T) for turning in your plates.

If you transfer a registration from one vehicle to a replacement vehicle, you will receive credit for the remaining portion of your current registration. This credit cannot be applied to other vehicles already registered to you.

REGISTRATION RENEWAL

Most registrations are renewed every two years. About 45 to 60 days before your registration will expire, you should receive a renewal reminder in the mail unless you have changed your address and did not notify DMV, or if you have failed to answer three or more parking tickets, or if your registration is suspended or revoked. Allow up to two weeks for processing and delivery. *Whether or not you receive a reminder, you are responsible for knowing when your registration expires, and for renewing it on time.*

If the expiration date falls on a weekend or legal state holiday, your registration is automatically extended to midnight of the next business day. Be sure you maintain liability insurance on your vehicle during the extension period.

If you have not received a renewal notice, you may be able to renew your registration –

By mail: Complete a *Vehicle Registration/Title Application* (MV-82), available at any motor vehicle office, by request from a DMV Call Center, and from the DMV Internet Office. If your registration should be sent to an address other than the mailing address you entered on the application form (MV-82), enclose a separate note requesting the DMV to mail your registration to the other address. Do not put this mailing address on form MV-82 unless you want it to appear on the registration and your DMV registration record. **Reminder – if you indicate a change of address on your registration, it will affect ONLY that registration. Use a *Change of Address Form* (MV-232) to change all your DMV records. This form is available at any motor vehicle office, by request from a DMV Call Center, and from the DMV Internet Office.**

Enclose a check or money order for the appropriate fee, payable to the "Commissioner of Motor Vehicles." If you do not know the exact fee you should pay, you may determine the fee through a work-sheet at the DMV Internet Office or contact a DMV Call Center. Be sure to include your insurance card with your renewal application if your registration has been expired for more than 30 days, or if your insurance company has changed and you have not responded to a DMV Insurance Inquiry Letter.

Mail your completed Vehicle Registration/Title Application and other documents to:

>Port Jefferson Office, NYS DMV
>3 Roads Plaza
>1055 Route 112
>Port Jefferson Station, NY 11776

Allow two weeks to receive your registration renewal. If you do not receive it after two weeks, contact a DMV Call Center or visit any state or county motor vehicle office. Allow more time for overseas mail.

If your name has changed and you have not yet notified the DMV, you must visit a DMV office and show proofs of your identity. For more information, contact a DMV Call Center.

On-line at the DMV Internet Office: www.nysdmv.com. On-line registration renewal requires that you have <u>not</u> changed your address or insurance company, that your registration has not been expired more than 30 days, and that the registration is for a passenger car, small commercial truck, or a motorcycle that has not been taken off the road. Your registration fee, including any other related fees, will be displayed on the computer screen. In just three quick steps, you may renew your registration on-line and use your credit card for fee payment. Your renewal will be automatically processed and mailed to you. Allow two weeks for delivery.

In person at a state or county motor vehicle office: You must complete and submit an *Vehicle Registration/Title Application* (MV-82). Please note: an application brought into an office by a 2nd party (someone other than the registrant) must be accompanied by the <u>original</u> New York State license/permit/non-driver identification card for <u>both</u> the applicant <u>and</u> the 2nd party. This includes spouses (husbands and wives). The application must be signed by the registrant, not the person bringing the form into the office.

Insurance

Your vehicle must be covered by liability insurance as long as it is registered, even if you do not drive it.

Minimum liability coverage is required of $50,000 against the death of one person and $100,000 against the death of two or more persons, $25,000 against injury to one person and $50,000 against injury to two or more persons, and $10,000 against property damage. Coverage limits refer to death, injury or damage related to any one incident.

Before your liability insurance lapses or is canceled, turn in your plates at any state or county motor vehicle office. <u>Be sure to obtain a *DMV Universal Receipt* (FS6T) for turning in your plates</u>. Otherwise, you may have to pay a civil penalty for each day the vehicle was not insured, or your vehicle registration may be suspended. If your vehicle remains uninsured for 90 days, unless you have already turned in your license plates, your driver license will also be suspended.

If you receive a letter from DMV inquiring about your auto insurance, read it carefully and respond within seven days.

Motorcycles must be insured, but you are not required to turn in the plate when your insurance for a motorcycle is canceled or lapses.

RESIDENT AND NON-RESIDENT RESPONSIBILITY

Anyone who drives or permits his or her vehicle to be driven in New York State, even a non-resident, must be able to prove the vehicle has adequate liability insurance. (See "Insurance," above, for minimum coverage required.) If you are convicted of operating an uninsured vehicle or permitting another person to operate your uninsured vehicle, your license or privilege to drive in New York State will be revoked for at least one year. The same penalty applies if the DMV receives evidence that you were involved in an a traffic crash without being insured.

INSPECTION

A motor vehicle dealership is required to have each vehicle pass inspection within 30 days before the vehicle is delivered to a customer. If you buy a vehicle from someone other than a dealer, you must register it and have it inspected within ten days.

After your vehicle's first inspection, it must be inspected at an official state-licensed inspection station at least once every 12 months and whenever ownership changes. These stations are identified by yellow and black "Official Motor Vehicle Inspection Station" signs. Heavy trucks, buses, tractors and semi-trailers must be inspected at special "Heavy Vehicle" inspection stations, and motorcycles at special motorcycle inspection stations.

When you sign a registration renewal form, you are certifying under penalty of law that the vehicle was inspected as required by law. Keep track of when your yearly inspection is due. Schedule a new inspection early, so you will have time to repair your vehicle if it does not pass.

After inspection, the vehicle inspector will issue a sticker for the vehicle to prove it has passed inspection. If your vehicle did not pass, the inspector will give you a rejection notice. Then, your vehicle must be repaired to meet inspection standards and be re-inspected. In certain areas of the state, your gasoline-powered vehicle (except a motorcycle) must also be inspected for exhaust emissions at the time of the safety inspection. More information about safety inspections and emissions inspections is detailed in the publications *Vehicle Inspection Program, Facts for Consumers* (MV-50) and *What You Should Know About The New York State Emissions Test* (C-61), available from the DMV Internet Office, by request from a DMV Call Center, or at any motor vehicle office.

COMPLAINTS AGAINST BUSINESSES

The DMV regulates dealers, inspection stations and auto repair shops. These businesses should be identified by outdoor signs and registration or license certificates. Make sure you are dealing with a registered or licensed business.

If you have a complaint against one of these businesses, first try to resolve it with the management. If that fails, call (518) 474-8943 between 9 a.m. and 3 p.m. weekdays. You may also write to Vehicle Safety Services, DMV, 6 Empire State Plaza, Albany, NY 12228. Please note that, by law, DMV can handle complaints only made within 90 days or 3,000 miles (*1,864 km*) of the repairs, whichever comes first.

For more information about your rights in dealing with auto repair shops and car dealers, ask for our publications *Know Your Rights in Auto Repairs* (C-17) and *Let the Buyer Be Aware* (C-18), available from the DMV Internet Office, by request from a DMV Call Center, or at any motor vehicle office.

CHAPTER 4 Traffic Control

SIGNS

Traffic signs tell you about traffic rules, special hazards, where you are, how to get where you are going and where services are available.

The shape and color of traffic signs give clues to the type of information they provide:

REGULATION SIGNS usually are white rectangles with black lettering or symbols, but some are different shapes, and some may use red letters or symbols

WARNING SIGNS usually are yellow and diamond-shaped, with black lettering or symbols.

DESTINATION SIGNS are green with white letters and symbols.

SERVICE SIGNS are blue with white letters and symbols.

Know the signs shown below and what they mean. You will be asked about them on your written test.

Here are descriptions of the most common traffic signs and what they mean:

STOP Sign

COLOR: Red, with white letters.

MEANING: Come to a full stop, yield the right-of-way to vehicles and pedestrians in or approaching the intersection. Go when it is safe. You must come to a stop before the stop line, if there is one. If not, you must stop before entering the crosswalk. (See "Stop and Crosswalk Lines" under the "Pavement

Markings" section of this chapter.) If there is no stop line or crosswalk, you must stop before entering the intersection, at the point nearest the intersection that gives you a view of traffic on the intersecting roadway.

YIELD Sign

COLOR: Red and white, with red letters.

MEANING: Slow down as you approach the intersection. Prepare to stop and yield the right-of-way to vehicles and pedestrians in or approaching the intersection. You must come to a full stop at a YIELD sign if traffic conditions require it. When you approach a YIELD sign, check carefully for traffic, and be prepared to stop.

REGULATION Signs

COLOR: White, with black and/or red letters or symbols.

MEANING: These signs give information about rules for traffic direction, lane use, turning, speed, parking, and other special requirements.

Some regulation signs have a red circle with a slash over a symbol indicating that an action, such as a right turn, is not allowed, or that certain vehicles are restricted from the road. Rectangular white signs with black or red letters or symbols are clues to be alert for special rules.

WARNING Signs

COLOR: Yellow, with black letters or symbols.

MEANING: You are approaching an especially hazardous location or a place where there is a special rule, as shown in the sample signs. Sometimes a warning sign is combined with a rectangular yellow and black "recommended speed" sign. This means reduced speed is advised in that area.

RAILROAD CROSSING WARNING Sign

COLOR: Yellow with black letters "RR" and "X" symbol.

MEANING: There is a railroad crossing ahead. Use caution, and be prepared to stop. If you are following a bus or truck toward a railroad crossing, be careful. Most buses and some trucks must stop at railroad crossings. (See "Railroad Crossing Signals" later in this chapter.)

WORK AREA Signs

COLOR: Orange, with black letters or symbols.

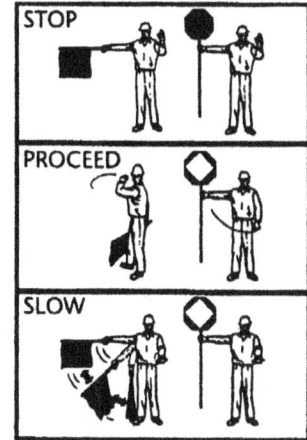

MEANING: People are working on or near the roadway, and traffic may be controlled by a flag person. A work area speed limit as low as 25 MPH (40 km/h) may be posted. Even if no speed limit is posted, you must drive at a reduced speed through the work zone, and you must always obey flag persons. These illustrations show some of the signals a flag person will use. Know and obey them.

DESTINATION Signs

COLOR: Green, with white lettering.

MEANING: Show direction and distance to various locations.

ROUTE Signs

COLOR: Varied.

MEANING: Indicate interstate, U.S., state or county routes. The shape tells you what type of route you are on. The sample signs, left to right, are for interstate U.S., and state routes. When planning a trip, use a highway map to decide which routes to take. During the trip, watch for destination signs so you will not get lost, or have to turn or stop suddenly.

SERVICE Signs

COLOR: Blue, with white letters or symbols.

MEANING: Show the location of services, such as rest areas, gas stations, hospitals and campgrounds.

TRAFFIC SIGNALS

Traffic Lights

Traffic lights are usually red, yellow and green from top to bottom, or left to right. At some intersections, there are single red, yellow or green lights. Some traffic lights are steady, others flash. Some are circular, and some are arrows.

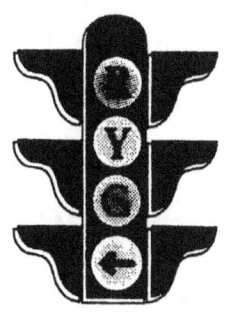

Here is what various traffic lights mean:

STEADY RED: Stop. Do not go until the light is green. If a green arrow is shown with the red light, you may go only in the direction of the arrow and only if the way is clear.

You may make a right turn at a steady red light after coming to a full stop and yielding the right-of-way to oncoming traffic and pedestrians. You may make a left turn at a steady red light when turning from a one-way road into another one-way road after coming to a full stop and yielding the right-of-way to oncoming traffic and pedestrians.

You may not make a turn at a red light if there is a NO TURN ON RED sign posted, or another sign, signal or pavement marking prohibits the turn. Also, turning on a red light is not allowed in New York City unless a sign is posted permitting it.

The driver of a school bus carrying pupils may not turn right on any red light.

FLASHING RED: Means the same as a STOP sign: Stop, yield the right-of-way, and go when it is safe.

RED ARROW: Do not go in the direction of the arrow until the red arrow light goes out and a green light or arrow light goes on. A right or left turn on red is not permitted at a red arrow.

STEADY YELLOW: The light is changing from green to red. Be ready to stop for the red light.

FLASHING YELLOW: Drive with caution.

YELLOW ARROW: The protection of a green arrow is ending. If you intend to turn in the direction of the arrow, be prepared to stop.

STEADY GREEN: Go, but yield the right-of-way to other traffic at the intersection as required by law (see Chapter 5).

GREEN ARROW: You may go in the direction of the arrow, but you must yield the right-of-way to other traffic at the intersection as required by law (see Chapter 5.)

Lane Use Control Lights

Special overhead lights are sometimes used to indicate which lanes of a highway may be used at certain times:

STEADY RED "X": Do not drive in this lane.

STEADY YELLOW "X": Move out of this lane.

FLASHING YELLOW "X": This lane may only be used for a left turn.

GREEN ARROW: You may use this lane. Railroad Crossing Signals

Railroad Crossing Signals

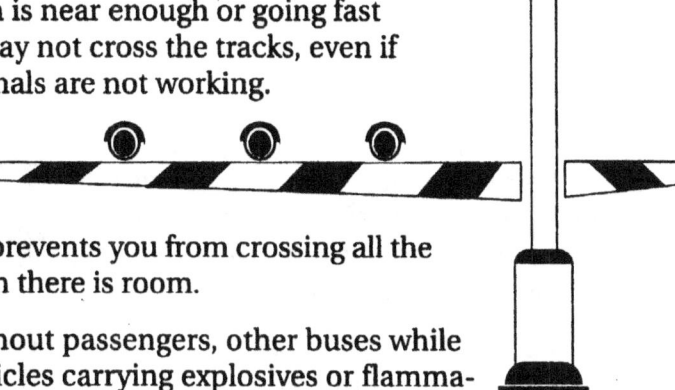

Flashing red lights, lowered crossing gates and/or a ringing bell at a railroad crossing mean that you must stop, at least 15 feet (5 m) from the tracks. Do not cross the tracks until the lights and bell have stopped and the crossing gates are all the way up. Do not drive around or under a gate that is being lowered or raised.

Look and listen for trains before crossing any railroad tracks. If an approaching train is near enough or going fast enough to be a danger, you may not cross the tracks, even if there are no signals or the signals are not working.

You may not cross any railroad tracks unless there is room for your vehicle on the other side. If other traffic prevents you from crossing all the way, wait, and cross only when there is room.

School buses with or without passengers, other buses while carrying passengers, and vehicles carrying explosives or flammable cargo must stop at all railroad crossings. Keep this in mind if you are following one of these vehicles.

PAVEMENT MARKINGS

Lines and symbols on the roadway divide lanes and tell you when you may pass other vehicles or change lanes, which lanes to use for turns, and where you must stop for signs or traffic signals. The arrows on these illustrations show the direction of traffic.

Edge and Lane Lines

Solid lines along the side of the road tell you where its edge is – where the travel lane ends and the road's shoulder begins. It is illegal to drive across the edge line, except when directed to do so by a police officer or other authorized official. An edge line which slants toward the center of the road shows that the road is narrower ahead.

Lines separating lanes of traffic moving in the same direction are white. Lines separating traffic moving in opposite directions are yellow. There may be two lines between lanes, and lines may be solid or broken. Read Chapter 6 for the rules on passing other vehicles.

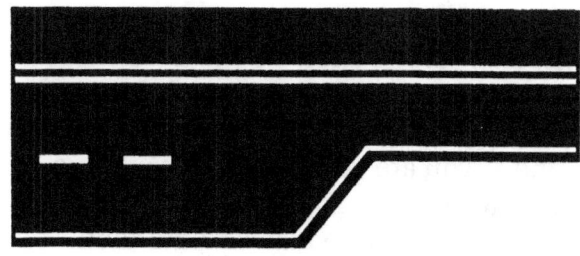

Here are what some lane line mean:

Single broken line: You may pass other vehicles or change lanes if you can do so safely and not interfere with traffic.

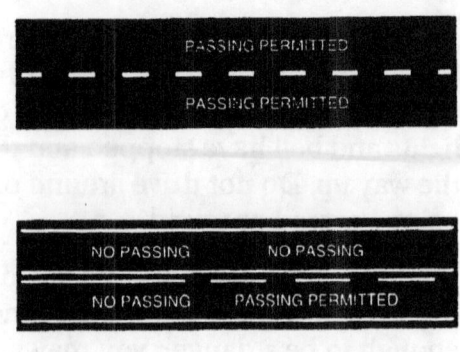

Solid line with broken line: If you're on the side with the solid line, you may not pass other vehicles or cross the line except to make a left turn into a driveway. If you're on the side with the broken line, you may pass if it is safe to do so and your driving will not interfere with traffic.

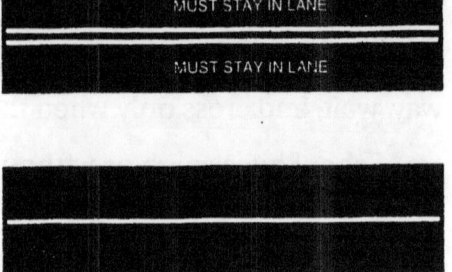

Double solid lines: You may not pass, or change lanes. You may not cross the lines except when turning left to enter or leave the highway (e.g., to or from a driveway or to perform a U-turn see Chapter 5).

Single solid line: You may pass other vehicles or change lanes, but you should do so only if obstructions in the road make it necessary or traffic conditions require it.

Stop and Crosswalk Lines: At an intersection controlled by a STOP sign, YIELD sign or traffic light, there may be a white stop line painted across the lane, and/or two parallel lines painted across the road, forming a crosswalk. When required to stop because of a sign or light, you must stop before reaching the stop line, if there is one, or the crosswalk. You need only stop at a stop line or crosswalk if required to do so by a light, sign or traffic officer, but be careful to look out for pedestrians at any crosswalk. (See "Pedestrians" in Chapter 11).

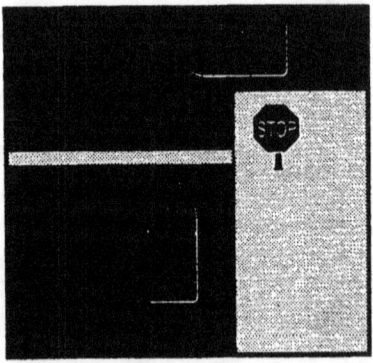
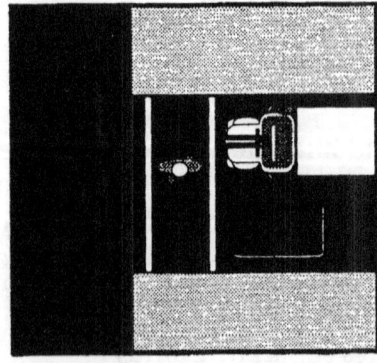

Arrows: Arrows show which lanes you must use. In this illustration, for example, you may turn right only from the right lane. If you are going straight, you must use the left lane. You should be in the proper lane before reaching the solid line which separates the lanes.

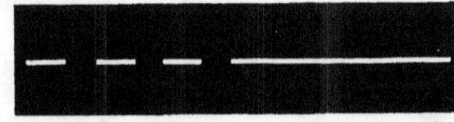

Diamond Symbol: This symbol is used to designate reserved lanes for buses, HOV's (High Occupancy Vehicles) such as carpools and van-pools, bicycles, or other special vehicles.  You may not enter and use these lanes unless your vehicle complies with the occupancy or other requirements of the accompanying regulatory signs for the times the special conditions are in effect. When used to designate reserved lanes on city streets, sections of the solid white line separating the diamond lanes from the regular lanes may be replaced by dashed white lines. In these locations, non-HOV's may enter the HOV lane if they make a right turn at the next intersection. Bus lanes and HOV lanes are used to promote the most efficient use of limited street and highway capacity by assuring that vehicles with the highest priority move the fastest.

TRAFFIC OFFICERS

Directions given by traffic officers take precedence over signs, signals or pavement markings. If a traffic officer signals you to stop at a green light, for example, you must stop. If an officer signals you to drive through a red light or stop sign, you must do so.

Among those authorized to direct traffic are police officers, peace officers such as on-duty auxiliary or fire police, highway work area flag persons, and school crossing guards.

QUESTIONS

Before going on to Chapter 5, make sure you can identify the signs in this chapter and know what they mean. Also, make sure you can answer these questions:

- A regulation sign is usually what shape?
- What is the usual color and shape of a warning sign?
- What color and shape is a destination sign?
- What must you do at a STOP sign?
- What color and shape is a railroad crossing warning sign?
- What would you do when facing each of the following: a flashing red light, flashing yellow light, steady yellow light, a red light with a green arrow?
- What does it mean if an edge line slants in toward the center of the road?
- What do each of these types of lines mean: single broken, single solid, double solid, solid and broken together?
- If an intersection has crosswalk lines but no STOP line, where would you stop for a red light at that intersection?

▶ What type of pavement marking is used to show you which lane you must use for a turn?

▶ Which of the following must you obey over the other three: steady red light, flashing red light, STOP sign, police officer?

CHAPTER 5 | Intersections and Turns

Most traffic crashes occur at intersections when a driver is making a turn. Many occur in large parking lots that are open to public use, such as at shopping centers. To avoid such crashes, you must understand the right-of-way rules and how to make proper turns.

RIGHT-OF-WAY

Traffic signs, signals, and pavement markings do not always resolve traffic conflicts. A green light, for example, does not resolve the conflict between a car turning left at an intersection while an oncoming car is going straight through. The right-of-way rules help resolve these kinds of conflicts. They tell drivers who goes first and who must wait in different situations.

Here are the right-of-way rules, with examples of how they apply on the road:

> *A driver approaching an intersection must yield the right-of-way to traffic already lawfully using the intersection.*

Example: You are nearing an intersection. The traffic light is green, and you want to drive straight through. Another vehicle is already in the intersection, turning left. You must let that vehicle complete its turn before you enter the intersection.

> *If drivers approaching from opposite directions reach an intersection at about the same time, a driver turning left must yield to approaching traffic going straight or turning right.*

Example: You want to turn left at an intersection ahead. A vehicle is approaching from the opposite direction, going straight ahead. You must wait for approaching traffic to go through before you turn. You may enter the intersection, however, to prepare for your left turn if the light is green and no other vehicle ahead of you is preparing for a left turn (see "Turns" later in this chapter). When you enter the intersection, stay to the right of the center line. Keep your wheels straight to avoid being pushed into oncoming traffic should a rear-end collision occur. When approaching traffic clears or stops for a red light, complete your turn.

You must also yield to approaching traffic when turning left into a driveway, alleyway, parking lot or other area, even if the turn is not controlled by signs or signals.

For any left turn, the law requires you to yield to any approaching traffic close enough to be a hazard. Deciding when traffic is too close takes experience and judgment. If you have any doubt, wait for traffic to pass before turning left.

> *At intersections not controlled by signs or signals, or where two or more drivers stop at STOP signs at the same time and they are at right angles to one another, the driver on the left must yield the right-of-way to the driver on the right.*

Example: You are stopped at a stop sign, and you are going to go straight through the intersection. A driver on the intersecting road has stopped at a stop sign on your right, and is also going to go straight. You must yield the right-of-way to the other driver.

> *A vehicle entering a roadway from a driveway, alley, private road, or any other place that is not a roadway, must stop and yield the right-of-way to traffic on the roadway, and to pedestrians.*

Example: You are driving out of a parking lot and turning right as you enter a street. A vehicle is approaching from your left. You must stop and wait for the vehicle to pass before turning onto the street. If you were turning left, you would have to yield to vehicles approaching from both directions. If a pedestrian were crossing the parking lot exit, you would have to wait for him or her to cross.

> *Drivers must yield to pedestrians legally using marked or unmarked crosswalks.*

Example: You are stopped at a red light. A pedestrian steps into the crosswalk, and then the light turns green. You must wait for the pedestrian to cross. You must also yield to pedestrians in crosswalks on your left or right before turning.

> *You may not enter an intersection if traffic is backed up on the other side and you cannot get all the way through the intersection. Wait until traffic ahead clears, so you do not block the intersection.*

> *A driver entering a traffic circle, sometimes called a rotary, must yield the right-of-way to drivers already in the circle.*

EMERGENCY VEHICLES

You must yield the right-of-way to fire, ambulance, police and other authorized emergency vehicles when they are responding to emergencies. They will display flashing red, or red and white, lights and sound a siren or air-horn. When you hear or see an emergency vehicle approaching your vehicle from any direction, including on your side of an expressway or limited access highway, safely pull over immediately to the right edge of the road and stop. Wait until the emergency vehicle passes before driving on. If you are in an intersection, drive out of it before you pull over.

You must pull over and stop for an emergency vehicle even if it is coming toward you in the opposite lane of a two-way roadway.

If you hear a siren or air-horn nearby but do not know exactly where the emergency vehicle is, you should pull over and stop until you are sure it is not approaching you.

An emergency vehicle using lights and a siren or air-horn may be unpredictable. The driver may legally exceed the speed limit, pass red lights and STOP or YIELD signs, go the wrong way on one-way streets and turn in directions not normally allowed. Although emergency vehicle drivers are required to exercise due care, be very cautious when an emergency vehicle approaches.

BLUE, GREEN AND AMBER LIGHTS

Personal vehicles driven by volunteer fire fighters responding to alarms are allowed to display blue lights, and those driven by volunteer ambulance or rescue squad members may display green lights. Amber lights on hazard vehicles such as snow plows and tow trucks warn other drivers of possible dangers. Flashing amber lights are also used on rural mail delivery vehicles and school buses to warn approaching traffic of their presence. The vehicles displaying blue, green, or amber lights are not authorized emergency vehicles. Their drivers must obey all traffic laws. While you are not required to yield the right-of-way, you should yield as a courtesy if you can do so safely.

TURNS

Always signal before you make a turn or change lanes. It is important that other highway users know your intentions. The law requires you to signal a turn or lane change with your directional lights or hand signals at

LEFT   RIGHT   STOP

least 100 feet (30 m) ahead. A good safety tip is to, whenever possible, signal your intention to turn before you actually begin braking to make the turn. The required hand signals are shown below:

Keep these other tips in mind when preparing to turn:

- Reduce your speed.
- Be alert for traffic on all sides. Take special care to check for motorcycles. Most crashes involving motorcycles and other vehicles are caused because the driver of the other vehicle has failed to see the motorcycle.
- Keep in mind that your rear wheels will travel inside the path of the front wheels, closer to the curb (right turn) or opposing traffic (left turn).
- Watch out for pedestrians, bicyclists and moped riders, especially on right turns. They are often difficult to see in traffic.

The following illustrations show the proper position of your vehicle for turns. These positions are based on requirements in the law, not just good advice.

RIGHT TURN:
As you prepare to turn, stay as far to the right as possible. Avoid making wide, sweeping turns. Unless signs direct you otherwise, turn into the right lane of the road you enter.

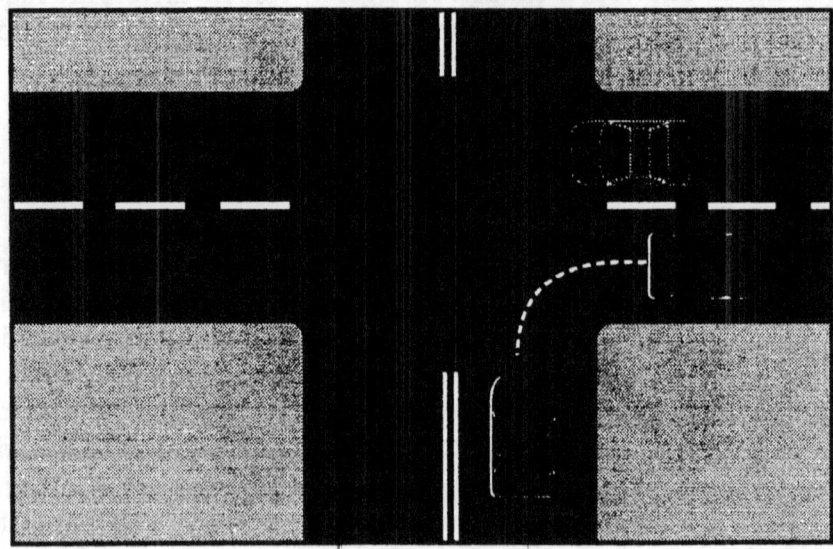

LEFT TURN FROM ONE-WAY ROAD INTO ONE-WAY ROAD:
Prepare to turn by getting into the left lane, or the left side of a single lane, as close as possible to the left curb or edge of the road. If the road you enter has two lanes, you must turn into its left lane.

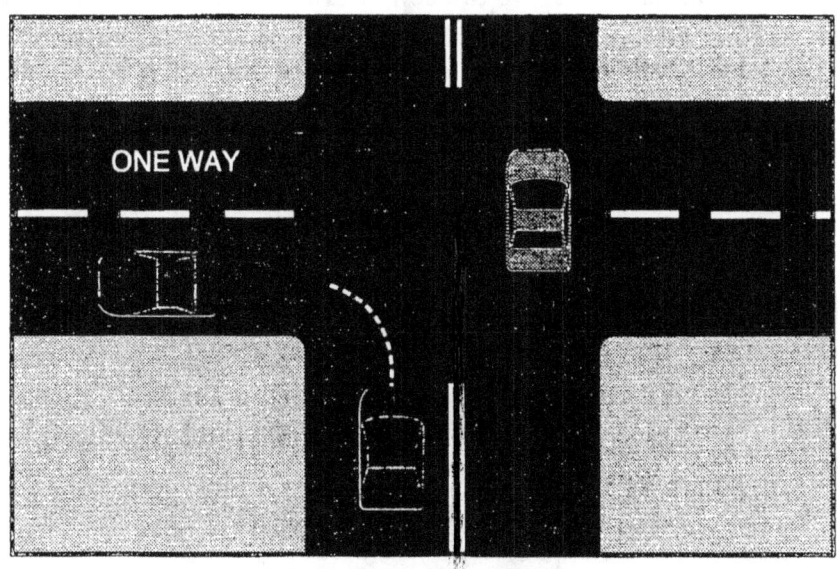

LEFT TURN FROM ONE-WAY ROAD INTO TWO-WAY ROAD:
Approach the turn in the left lane or from the left side of a single lane. As you cross the intersection, enter the two-way road to the right of its center line, but as close as possible to the center line. Be alert for traffic, especially motorcycles, approaching from the road to the left. Oncoming motorcycles are difficult to see, and it is difficult to judge their speed and distance away.

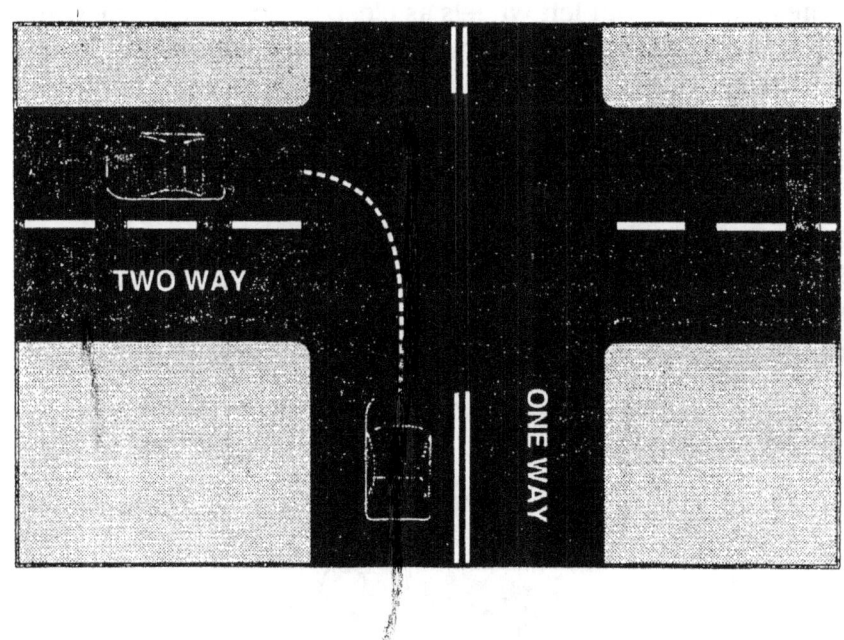

LEFT TURN FROM TWO-WAY ROAD INTO TWO-WAY ROAD:
Approach the turn with your left wheels as close as possible to the center line. Try to use the left side of the intersection to help ensure that you do not interfere with opposing traffic turning left. Stay to the right of the center line of the road you enter, but as close as possible to the center line. Be alert for traffic, especially motorcycles, approaching from the left and from the oncoming lane you are about to cross. Oncoming motorcycles are difficult to see, and it is difficult to judge their speed and distance away. Drivers often fail to see an oncoming motorcycle and collide with it while making a turn across a traffic lane.

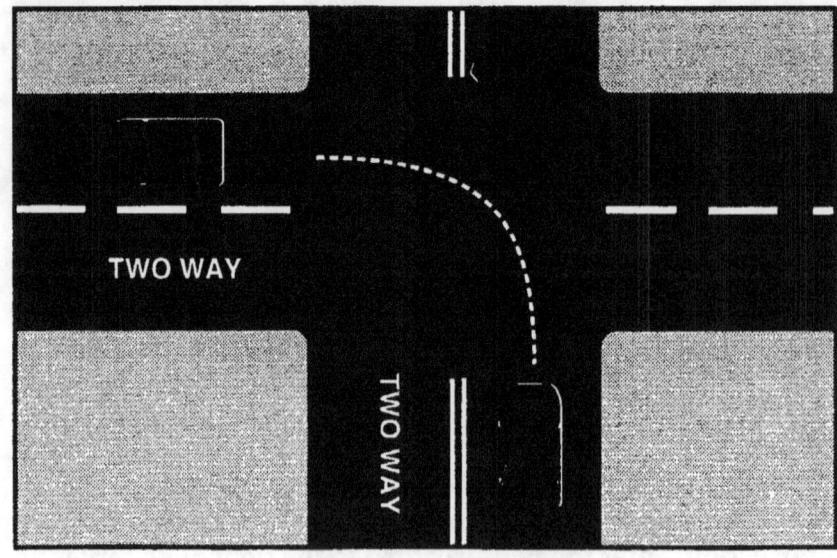

LEFT TURN FROM TWO-WAY ROAD INTO ONE-WAY ROAD:
Approach the turn with your left wheels as close as possible to the center line. Make the turn before reaching the center of the intersection, and turn into the left lane of the road you enter.

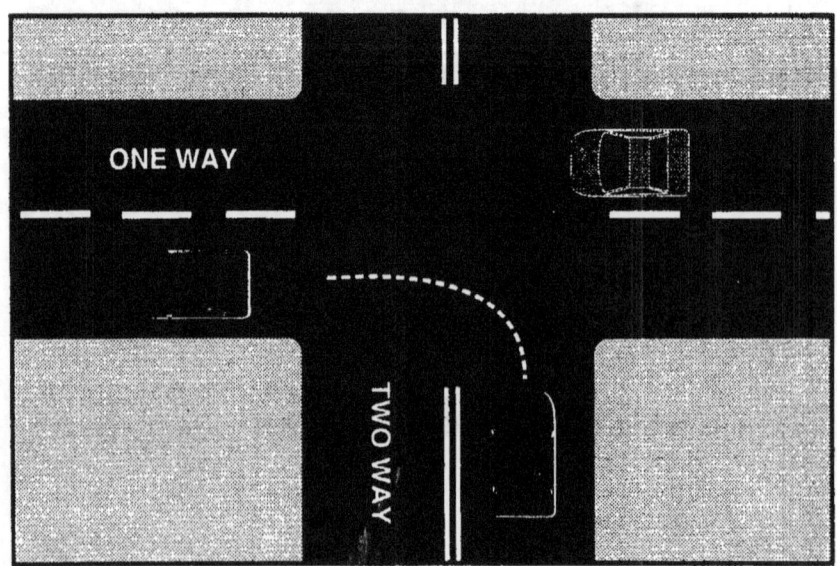

LEFT TURN FROM TWO-WAY ROAD INTO FOUR-LANE HIGHWAY:
Approach the turn with your left wheels as close as possible to the center line. Enter the left lane, to the right of the center line. When traffic permits, you may move out of the left lane.

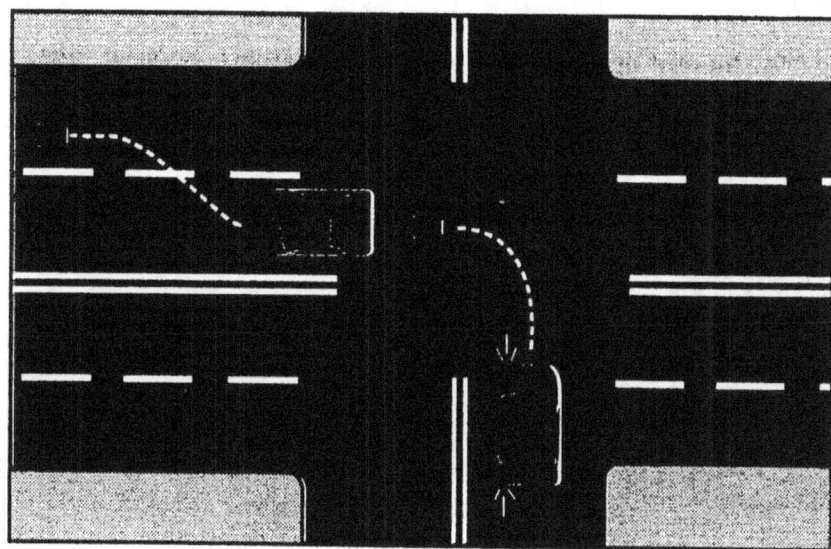

U-TURNS

A "U-turn" is any turn "executed so as to proceed in the opposite direction." Do not attempt a U-turn on a highway unless absolutely necessary. If you must turn around, use a parking lot, driveway or other area, and, if possible, re-enter the roadway going forward, not backing up.

You may make a U-turn only from the left portion of the lane closest to the centerline of the roadway, never from the right lane. Unless signs tell you otherwise, you may make a U-turn when you are given the go-ahead by a green arrow left-turn traffic signal, provided it is not prohibited and you yield to other traffic.

You may not make a U-turn near the crest of a hill, a curve or any other place where other drivers cannot see your vehicle from 500 feet (*150 m*) away in either direction. U-turns are also illegal in business districts of New York City and where NO U-TURN signs are posted. You may *never* make a U-turn on a limited access expressway, even if paths connect your side of the expressway with the other side.

Unless prohibited, a three-point turn may be used to turn around on a narrow, two-way street. You may be required to make one of these turns on your road test.

To make a three-point turn:

1. Signal with your right directional, then pull over to the right and stop. Signal with your left directional, then check carefully for approaching traffic.

2. Turn left, cross the road so you come to a stop while facing the left curb or edge of the road.

3. Check again for traffic. Turn your steering wheel as far to the right as possible, then back up to the right curb or edge of the road.

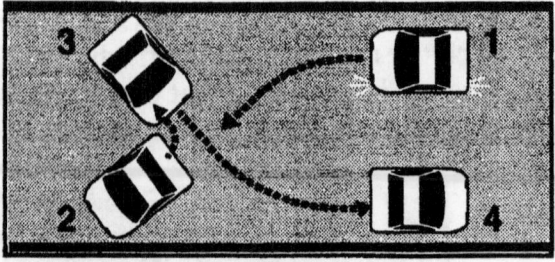

4. Stop, check again for other traffic, then pull away from the curb.

QUESTIONS

Before going on to Chapter 6, make sure you can answer these questions:

- What is the hand signal for a stop? A right turn?
- If two drivers enter an intersection from opposite directions at the same time, one going straight, the other turning left, which must yield the right-of-way?
- If you enter an intersection to make a left turn, but oncoming traffic prevents you from making the turn right away, what should you do?
- If you reach an uncontrolled intersection at the same time as a driver on your right, and both of you are going to go straight, who has the right-of-way?
- What must you do if you are entering a road from a driveway?
- You are facing a green light, but traffic on the other side of the intersection would keep you from going all the way through the intersection. May you enter the intersection?
- Does a vehicle about to enter a traffic circle or rotary have right-of-way over vehicles already in the circle?
- What should you do if you hear a siren nearby but cannot see where the emergency vehicle is?
- How far before a turn must you signal?
- When preparing for a right turn, should you stay as close to the center of the lane as possible?
- Where should you position your vehicle when preparing to make a left turn from a two-way roadway into a one-way roadway?

CHAPTER 6 — Passing

In general, the law requires that we drive on the right side of the road. When passing is allowed, we usually pass other vehicles on the left. Passing on the right is permitted only in limited circumstances, and should be done only when necessary and safe to do so.

When passing other vehicles or changing lanes to avoid hazards, do so with caution and only when necessary. You must *not* exceed the speed limit to pass another vehicle.

When passing a motorcycle, remember to give the motorcycle the same full lane width as other vehicles are allowed. <u>*Never*</u> move into the same lane space as a motorcycle, even if the lane is wide and the motorcyclist is riding to one side.

The law requires you to use directional or hand signals at least 100 feet (*30 m*) before making a lane change. You may <u>*never*</u> pass a vehicle which has stopped at a crosswalk to allow a pedestrian to cross.

PASSING ON THE LEFT

The left lane is usually used for passing other vehicles. However, you may **not** pass a vehicle on the left if:

- Your lane has a solid yellow center line.
- You cannot safely return to the right lane before reaching a solid yellow center line for the right lane.
- You cannot safely return to the right lane before any approaching vehicle comes within 200 feet (*60 m*) of you.
- You are approaching a curve or the crest of a hill on a two-way road and cannot see around or over it.
- You are within 100 feet (*30 m*) of a railroad crossing on a two-way roadway.

- You are within 100 feet (*30 m*) of a bridge, tunnel or viaduct on a two-way road and your view is obstructed.
- Passing will interfere with oncoming traffic.

If conditions are right for passing, check in your mirrors and signal your lane change. Before pulling into the left lane, glance briefly over your left shoulder, through the rear side window, to make sure no vehicle is passing you or close behind you in the left lane. Never rely on your mirrors alone when preparing to change lanes. Even properly adjusted mirrors will leave "blind spots" behind you on both sides. If a vehicle is in the blind spot, you may not see it in your mirrors. Always glance over your shoulder before changing lanes or passing.

When passing, move completely into the left lane. Before returning to the right lane, signal and look at your interior rearview mirror and make sure you can see the front bumper of the vehicle you just passed. Glance quickly over your right shoulder to double-check that you can see at least several feet of pavement between your vehicle and the one you passed. Then return to the right lane.

PASSING ON THE RIGHT

You should usually pass other vehicles on the left, but passing on the right is allowed in certain situations. You may pass a vehicle on the right only in the situations listed below, and only if you can do so safely. You may not drive on or across the shoulder or edge line of the road unless a sign permits it. You may pass on the right:

- When a vehicle ahead is making a left turn.
- When you are driving on a one-way road that is marked for two or more lanes or is wide enough for two or more lanes, and passing is not restricted by signs.

If you are going to pass on the right at an intersection, check traffic ahead carefully. Make sure an oncoming vehicle is not turning left into your path, and watch out at the right side of the road for pedestrians, bicyclists, in-line skaters and moped riders.

Before you pass on the right on multilane roads such as expressways, make sure you check your mirrors, use the proper signals for lane change, and look over your right shoulder for other vehicles. After passing, be sure to check over your left shoulder, and to signal, before returning to the left lane.

BEING PASSED

If another vehicle passes you on the left, slow down slightly and keep to the right. When the vehicle has safely passed and is well ahead of you, resume your normal speed.

If you find that many vehicles are passing you on the right, you should move into the right lane and allow them to pass you on the left.

SCHOOL BUSES

When a stopped school bus flashes its red light(s), traffic approaching from either direction, even in front of the school and in school parking lots, must stop before reaching the bus. You should stop at least 20 feet (6 m) away from the bus. You can identify this bus by a "SCHOOL BUS" sign, the red lights on top, and its unique yellow/orange color.

Before a school bus stops to load or unload passengers, the driver will usually flash yellow warning lights. When you see them, slow down and be prepared to stop.

Once stopped for a school bus, you may not drive again until the red lights stop flashing or when the bus driver or a traffic officer waves you on. <u>This law applies on all roadways in New York State. You must stop for a school bus even if it is on the opposite side of a divided highway.</u>

After stopping for a school bus, watch for children along the side of the road. Drive slowly until you have passed them.

Safety Tip: Most school bus-related deaths and injuries occur while children are crossing the street after leaving the bus, not in collisions involving school buses.

Keep in mind that vehicles transporting disabled persons may be equipped as school buses, and you must stop for them just as you would for other school buses.

The fine for passing a stopped school bus ranges from a minimum of $250 for a first violation to a maximum of $850 for three violations in three years. In addition, if you are convicted of three such violations in three years, your license will be revoked for a minimum of six months.

QUESTIONS

Before going on to Chapter 7, make sure you can answer these questions:

- In most situations, on which side should you pass another vehicle going in the same direction?
- What should you do before passing another vehicle?
- What should you see in your rearview mirror before attempting to return to the right lane after passing a vehicle on the left?
- In what situations may you pass a vehicle on the right?
- When may you pass a vehicle stopped at a crosswalk to allow a pedestrian to cross?

- What action should you take when another vehicle passes you on the left?
- What do flashing yellow lights on a school bus mean?
- What do flashing red lights on a school bus mean?

CHAPTER 7 Parking

Parallel parking takes practice and skill, and is part of every road test. You should also know where parking is illegal and what NO PARKING, NO STANDING and NO STOPPING signs mean.

HOW TO PARK

Many motorists consider parallel parking the most difficult part of driving. But practice will teach you how to back up properly and to judge distances and angles. Patience and self confidence will help you master the task.

The following instructions are basic and general. You must adjust parallel parking procedures to the particular situation. Plenty of practice is the only way to learn properly.

1. Select a space that is large enough for your vehicle on your side of the road. Check your mirrors before stopping, and signal to alert other drivers. Pull up alongside the vehicle in front of the space, leaving about two feet between the other vehicle and yours.

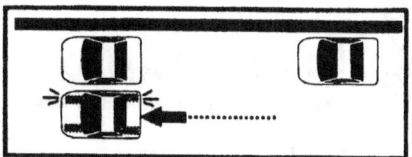

2. Look behind you over both shoulders to make sure you will not interfere with pedestrians or oncoming traffic. Back up slowly, and begin to turn your steering wheel all the way toward the near curb. Look through the rear window, not the rearview mirrors, as you back up. Check to the side and front occasionally to make sure you are clearing the vehicle ahead.

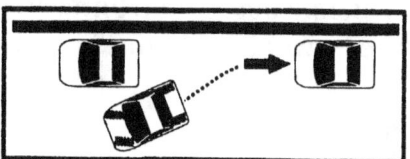

3. When your front wheels are opposite the rear bumper of the vehicle ahead, turn the steering wheel the other way while continuing to back up. Make sure you clear the vehicle ahead. Look back, and stop to avoid bumping the vehicle behind you.

4. Straighten your wheels, and pull forward. Allow room for the vehicles ahead and behind you to get out. In your final parking position, your wheels must be no more than one foot (*30 cm*) from the curb.

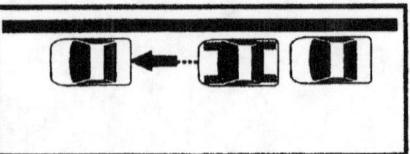

To get closer to the curb, alternately pull forward and back up, turning the steering wheel first toward the curb and then quickly straight again.

After parking, remember that you may not open the door on the road side if it will interfere with traffic.

PARKING ON A HILL

After you park on a hill, be sure to set your parking brake. Just in case the parking brake fails, turn the wheels so they will keep your vehicle from rolling into traffic.

If there is a curb, turn your steering wheel all the way away from it if you're facing uphill, or all the way toward it if you're facing downhill. If your vehicle starts to roll, the wheels should stop the vehicle at the curb and prevent it from rolling downhill. This method works best where the curb is relatively high. If there is no curb or a very low one, whether you are facing uphill or down, turn your wheels all the way toward the nearest side of the road. If your vehicle does start to roll, it will probably roll away from the street and traffic.

PULLING OUT

To pull out of a parking space, make sure your wheels are straight, back up to the vehicle behind you, and turn your wheels away from the curb.

Before pulling out, turn your head and check for traffic through the windows. Drive forward slowly, making sure you clear the vehicle ahead.

PARKING REGULATIONS

What people generally understand as "parking" is legally divided into three categories: parking, standing and stopping.

A **NO PARKING** sign means you may stop only *temporarily* to load or unload merchandise or passengers.

A **NO STANDING** sign means you may stop only *temporarily* to load or unload passengers.

A **NO STOPPING** sign means you may stop *only* in order to obey a traffic sign, signal or officer, or to avoid conflicts with other vehicles.

Besides posted parking, standing and stopping rules, there are statewide rules not always indicated by signs:

Parking, standing or stopping is not allowed:

- Within 15 feet (*5 m*) of a fire hydrant, unless a licensed driver remains in the vehicle to move it in an emergency.
- On the road side of a parked vehicle ("double parking").
- On a sidewalk or in a crosswalk.
- In an intersection, unless permitted by signs or parking meters.
- On railroad tracks.
- Alongside or opposite road excavations, construction or other obstructions if your vehicle would block traffic.
- Within 30 feet (*10 m*) of a pedestrian safety zone, unless another distance is marked.
- On a bridge or in a tunnel.

Parking or standing is not allowed:

- In front of a driveway.
- Within 20 feet (*6 m*) of a crosswalk at an intersection.
- Within 30 feet (*10 m*) of a traffic light, STOP sign or YIELD sign.
- Within 20 feet (*6 m*) of a fire station driveway, or within 75 feet (*23 m*) on the opposite side of the road.
- Along a curb that has been cut down, lowered or constructed for access to the sidewalk.

In addition, you may not park your vehicle within 50 feet (*15 m*) of a railroad crossing.

RESERVED PARKING FOR THE DISABLED

Parking reserved for people with disabilities is not merely a convenience, it is a legal requirement. These special parking spaces for motorists with disabilities ensures safe and equal access to goods and services, access which is taken for granted by most of us. You can help by parking in reserved spaces only if you have a permit or plates for people with disabilities, and only when the person who received the permit or plates is in the vehicle.

It is illegal for any vehicle to park, stop, or stand in a space reserved for the disabled it has license plates for the disabled issued by the DMV, a New York State Parking Permit for the Disabled (MV-664) issued by a locality, or a similar plate or permit issued by another state. In addition, the vehicle must actually be in use to transport the disabled person named in the registration or permit. This law applies to spaces reserved and posted by local ordinance on streets and highways, and those set aside by state law in shopping centers that have five or more stores and 20 or more off-street parking spaces available to the public.

It is a misdemeanor to make a false statement or give false information on an application for license plates. Making a false statement or providing misinformation to obtain a parking permit for a person with a disability is punishable by a fine from $250 to $1,000, plus a mandatory surcharge of $30, and potential civil penalties from $250 to $1,000. These penalties apply both to the applicant and to a doctor providing certification.

For more information about reserved parking for the disabled, and how to qualify and apply for a license plate or parking permit, see Parking for People With Disabilities (C-34). This publication is available from the DMV Internet Office, by request from a DMV Call Center, and at any motor vehicle office.

Reserved spaces should be marked with signs such as the one shown, and also may be designated with pavement markings. Also, do not park in the diagonally-striped spaces next to reserved parking areas. These spaces are needed to enable access by those with wheelchairs and specially-equipped vehicles.

The fines for on-street parking space violations are set by localities. Unless a locality sets higher penalties, the fine for a shopping center violation is $50 to $75 for a first offense and $75 to $150 for a second offense in the same locality. A mandatory surcharge of $30 will also be added to each penalty.

QUESTIONS

Before going on to Chapter 8, make sure you can answer these questions:
- After you have parallel parked, how close to the curb must your vehicle be?
- May you open a door on the road side of your vehicle if no traffic is coming?
- Before pulling out of a parking space, what should you do?
- What does a NO STOPPING sign mean?
- Can you stop to load or unload passengers at a NO STANDING or NO PARKING sign?
- May you park on a crosswalk in the middle of a block?

CHAPTER 8   Defensive Driving

Almost all drivers consider themselves good drivers. When you gain experience and confidence, you probably will think of yourself as a good driver, too. But even the best drivers make mistakes now and then. Equipment fails, weather conditions may be bad, and you may encounter drivers who ignore traffic laws or drive unpredictably. To avoid making mistakes yourself, or being involved in a traffic crash because of someone else's mistake, learn to drive defensively. The defensive driving rules are simple:

- Be prepared and look ahead.
- Maintain the proper speed.
- Signal before turning or changing lanes.
- Allow yourself space.
- Wear your seat belt.
- Do not drive if you are very tired, are on medication or have been drinking alcoholic beverages.
- Keep your vehicle in good operating condition.

BE PREPARED AND LOOK AHEAD

You should sit comfortably, but upright, and keep both hands on the steering wheel. Slumping in the driver's seat, or steering with one hand makes it harder to control your vehicle, and your "relaxed" position can lead to a dangerously relaxed attitude toward driving.

Traffic conditions change constantly. You cannot afford to let your attention wander from what is going on around you. Always scan the road ahead. Do not use the road or even the vehicle directly ahead as your only focal point. Look ahead so you can avoid, or lessen, potential problems.

Keep your eyes moving, notice what's happening at the sides of the road, and check behind you through your mirrors every few seconds.

Anticipate mistakes by other drivers and think about what you will do if a mistake does happen. For example, do not always assume that a driver approaching a STOP or YIELD sign on a side road is actually going to stop or yield. It is better to assume the other driver may not stop. Be ready to react.

It is important that the other drivers see you and understand what you intend to do. Sometimes, it is good to try to establish eye contact to make sure the other driver approaching an intersection has seen you. Watch for the rotation and angle of the wheels on a car approaching on a side road. The speed of rotation and angle of the front wheels give you clues to whether the driver is slowing to stop or planning to turn in a certain direction. If the rotation does not seem to be slowing as the driver approaches a required stop, you should pad your brake and prepare to stop, and lightly tap your horn to get the driver's attention. If the angle of the front wheels does not match the direction of the driver's turn signal, be prepared to react to an improper turn, or no turn. The earlier and deeper you look into upcoming cross streets, the more time and space you give yourself to react. *copywrite 1991 Lynn S. Fuchs*

AGGRESSIVE DRIVERS

Sometimes it is better to not make eye contact with another driver, especially where conflict can occur – the other driver may interpret eye contact as a "challenge." This often occurs when a driver is frustrated, impatient or easily irritated. Occasionally, even a person who ordinarily is calm and rational, and usually obeys the law, will operate a motor vehicle in an unsafe and hostile manner without regard for others. For some drivers, speeding can lead to following too closely, changing lanes frequently or abruptly without signaling, passing on the shoulder or unpaved portions of the roadway, or harassing motorists who just happen to be in front of them. Aggressive drivers also may run stop signs and red lights, pass stopped school buses, fail to keep right, drive while impaired by alcohol or drugs, and drive recklessly. A few threaten, or attempt to cause, physical damage to another driver.

When confronted by an aggressive driver:

- Avoid eye contact.
- Stay calm and relaxed.
- Make every attempt to get out of the way safely. Do not escalate the situation.
- Put your pride in the back seat. Do not challenge an aggressive driver by speeding up or attempting to hold your position in your travel lane.

- Wear a seat belt and encourage your passengers to do the same.
- Ignore harassing gestures and name calling, and do not return them.
- Report aggressive drivers to the appropriate law enforcement authorities by providing a vehicle description, location, license plate number, and direction of travel.
- If you are being followed by an aggressive or threatening driver, do not stop or get out of our vehicle. Drive directly to the nearest police station.
- If an aggressive driver is involved in a crash, stop a safe distance from the crash scene. When the police arrive, report the driving behavior you witnessed.

To avoid becoming an aggressive driver:

- Allow enough travel time to reach your destination on schedule.
- Alter your schedule to avoid driving during peak highway congestion periods.
- If you're running late, call ahead so you can relax.
- Do not drive when you are angry, upset or overly tired.
- Make your vehicle comfortable. Listen to relaxing music and avoid situations that raise your anxiety.
- When driving, relax and remain aware of your posture. Sit back in your seat, loosen your grip on the steering wheel and do not clench your teeth.
- Give others the benefit of the doubt; be polite, courteous and forgiving.
- You can control your own reactions to other drivers. If someone else drives aggressively, do not retaliate.

If you have the right-of-way, do not think of it as an *absolute right*. Be prepared to give up the right-of-way to avoid a crash or prevent confusion. Waiting a few seconds for another driver is far better than risking a crash. Knowing you were "in the right" will not make up for the expense or pain of a collision.

SPEED

You must obey the posted speed limit, or, if no limit is posted, drive no faster than 55 mph (*88 km/h*). Often, it is just common sense to keep your actual speed limit well below the posted limit. For example, the legal limit on an icy or foggy expressway might be 55 mph (*88 km/h*), or even 65 mph (*100 km/h*) on some highways, but the safe speed to drive would be much lower. Even if you were to drive at 50 mph (*80 km/h*) on that hazardous highway, a police officer could ticket you for driving at a speed "not reasonable and prudent" for existing conditions. As with right-of-way, speed limits are not absolutes. You must adjust your speed if conditions require it.

To keep traffic flowing smoothly, some highways also have minimum speed limits. Driving slower than the minimum speed can interrupt the traffic flow and create a dangerous situation. Even if there is no minimum speed limit, those driving much slower than the posted limit can be as dangerous as driving too fast.

Be aware that some cities have speed limits lower than 55 mph (*88 km/h*) that may not be posted. For example, the speed limit is 30 mph (*48 km/h*) in New York City unless another limit is posted.

ALLOWING YOURSELF SPACE

Four of every ten crashes involve rear-end collisions, usually because someone is following too closely (tailgating). Leave enough room between your vehicle and the one ahead so you can stop safely if the other vehicle stops suddenly.

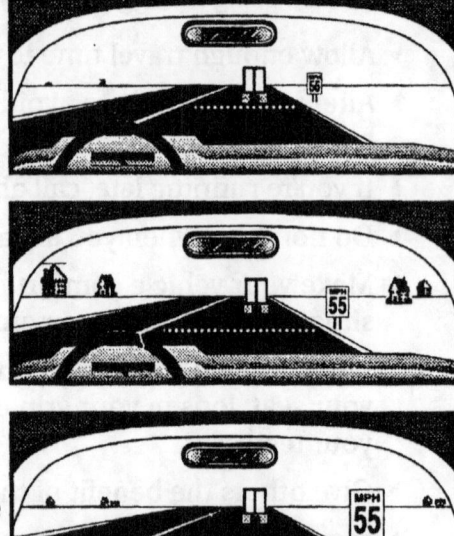

For a good "space cushion," use the two-second rule: Choose an object near or above the road ahead, such as a sign, tree or over-pass. As the vehicle ahead passes it, count aloud, slowly, "one thousand one, one thousand two." If you reach the same object before you finish counting, you are following too closely. Slow down and let the other vehicle get further ahead. In bad weather, increase the count to three or four seconds for extra space.

If the driver behind you is tailgating, move to another lane if possible, or slow down and pull off the road if necessary, to let the driver go by you. Be sure to signal when you drive off the road and when you return to it. Do not press your brakes to warn the offending driver – this could make a difficult situation become even more dangerous.

Brake early and gently when preparing to stop or turn. It gives drivers behind you plenty of warning that you are slowing down.

Be aware of space on either side of you, too, in case you have to change lanes quickly or pull over to avoid a hazard. If possible, leave yourself some "escape" room to your left and right.

SEAT BELTS, CHILD SAFETY SEATS, AND AIR BAGS

No matter how carefully you drive, there is always a chance you will be involved in a traffic crash. You cannot predict when it may happen. Your best protection in most vehicles is a lap belt and shoulder harness in combination with an air bag. Some vehicles also have air bags to protect against side-impact traffic crashes.

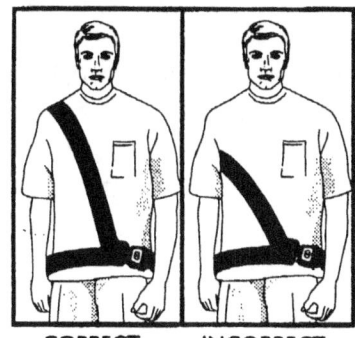
CORRECT   INCORRECT

A shoulder harness is worn across the shoulder and chest, not under the arm. Wearing the harness the wrong way could cause serious internal injuries in a crash.

If you are wearing a seat belt, your chances of being killed or seriously injured in a traffic crash are at least 50 percent better than if you are not wearing one. In addition, we all share the financial burden of deaths and injuries due to traffic crashes.

Seat belts save lives and reduce the severity of injuries. With the belt buckled around you, you become part of the vehicle, rather than a loose object that can be tossed around inside in a crash or thrown outside. If you stay inside the vehicle and also avoid hitting the vehicle interior, your chances are much better for surviving with no worse than minor injuries than if you are not wearing your seat belt.

All children under age 16 must also wear them, no matter where they ride in the vehicle. All children under age four must ride in federally-approved child safety seats. Many traffic safety experts recommend that children ride <u>only</u> in the vehicle's rear seat. **If your vehicle has side impact air bags, please refer to your owner's manual for additional safety tips.** Persons 16 and older are responsible for buckling themselves up, and can be fined if they do not. If a passenger under 16 is not properly protected, the driver can be fined. The maximum fine for each seat belt violation is $50. The fine for a violation involving a person under age 16 is at least $25, and can be up to $100.

New York is a "primary enforcement" state. A law enforcement officer can stop you and issue a traffic ticket just for failure to wear a seat belt or to make sure child passengers are properly buckled up or in safety seats. The law applies to out-of-state visitors as well as New York State residents.

New York's seat belt law applies to drivers and occupants of all vehicles except authorized emergency vehicles, taxies, liveries, buses (except for bus drivers), and 1964 and older model cars. Rural letter carriers are also exempt while delivering mail. Individuals who qualify for a medical exemption due to a physical disability which prevents seat belt use must carry a letter of exemption. This letter must be written on a physician's letterhead or prescription blank and signed by the physician. The DMV strongly recommends that medically exempted passengers ride in the back seat.

Whenever you drive, you should make sure everyone in your vehicle wears a seat belt. *In the event of a crash, a person without a belt becomes a projectile, and a danger to everyone else in the vehicle.* Make sure every child under age four in your vehicle is properly using an approved safety seat, and that the seat is properly installed.

As you practice the safe driving techniques in this manual, make buckling up part of your routine – a habit as automatic as turning the key in the ignition or turning on the radio.

Here are some facts to encourage you to buckle up:

- If you are thrown out of a vehicle in a crash, your chances of being killed are *25 times greater* than if you stay inside.

- Eight of ten crashes happen at speeds of *less than 40 mph (64 km/h)*, and people have been killed in crashes at speeds *as low as 12 mph (19.2 km/h)*. About 75 percent of crashes occur *within 25 miles (40 km)* of the driver's home. Wear your seat belt even on short trips or when traveling at low speeds.

- Do not worry about being trapped by your seat belt. *Less than one-half of one percent* of all traffic crashes involve a fire or a vehicle going underwater. Even in these rare incidents, a seat belt keeps you from being knocked unconscious or being too badly injured to escape. It only takes a second or two to unfasten the belt so you can get out of the vehicle.

- A seat belt can help you avoid a crash. It helps you stay in position behind the steering wheel and near the brake pedal if your vehicle goes out of control. With a belt on, you may be able to regain control. Without it, you may not even be able to stay in the driver's seat.

For added protection, adjust your vehicle's head rest, lock the doors and keep loose, heavy objects out of the passenger area. Put them in the trunk instead.

Air bags provide an extra degree of protection against injuries when used with seat belts. They are meant to work WITH seat belts, not to replace them. An air bag protects a front-seat occupant in a head-on crash by inflating upon impact and cushioning the occupant from colliding with the steering wheel, dashboard or windshield. The combination of a seat belt and an air bag offers maximum protection, partly because they help the driver maintain control of the vehicle and help avoid secondary collisions.

The air bag deploys rapidly from the steering wheel and/or dashboard. Most adults who are properly buckled up are safer in a vehicle with air bags, but the force of an air bag deploying may injure those who sit too close to it. You should sit with <u>at least 10 inches</u> between the center of your chest and the cover of your vehicle's air bag. Also, place your hands on the steering wheel at the 3 and 9 o'clock positions to keep them out of the way if the air bag deploys.

IMPORTANT: <u>NEVER</u> PUT AN INFANT IN A REAR-FACING CHILD SAFETY SEAT IN THE FRONT SEAT OF A VEHICLE THAT HAS A PASSENGER AIR BAG.

DROWSY AND FATIGUED DRIVING

Sleeping and driving do not mix. When you are behind the wheel of a car, being fatigued is dangerous. Drivers who are tired have slower reaction times, decreased awareness, and impaired judgment. As with drugs and alcohol, drowsiness can contribute to a traffic crash.

Symptoms of Fatigue – Researchers have found the following symptoms to be associated with drowsy driving:

- Your eyes close or go out of focus by themselves.
- You have trouble keeping your head up.
- You cannot stop yawning.
- You have wandering disconnected thoughts.
- You do not remember driving the last few miles.
- You drift between lanes, tailgate, or miss traffic signs.
- You keep jerking the car back into the lane.
- You have drifted off the road and hit the rumble strips which produce a loud noise and vibrations.

Who is Most At Risk? All Drivers who are:

- Sleep-deprived or fatigued.
- Driving long distances without rest breaks.
- Driving through the night, the early afternoon, or at other times when you are normally asleep.
- Taking medication that increases sleepiness or drinking alcohol
- Driving alone.
- Driving on long, rural, boring roads.
- Frequent travelers, e.g., business travelers and long-distance commuters.
- **Young People** – Sleep related crashes are most common in young people, who tend to stay up late, sleep too little, and drive at night.
- **Shift Workers** – Studies suggest individuals with non-traditional work schedules have a greater risk of being involved in a fatigue-related driving traffic crash.
- **People With Undiagnosed Sleep Disorders** – The presence of a sleep disorder also increases the risk of crashes. If you find you are regularly tired during the day or experience any of these symptoms on a regular basis, you may have a sleep disorder and should seek medical help.

Effective Countermeasures

Prevention – Before you embark on a trip, you should:

- Get a good night's sleep.
- Plan to drive long trips with a companion.
- Schedule regular stops, every 100 miles or 2 hours.
- Avoid alcohol and medications (over-the-counter and prescribed) that may impair performance. Check with your doctor or pharmacist about any medication you are taking. Alcohol interacts with fatigue; increasing its effects.

Actions for the Drowsy Driver – Once driving, you should:

- Recognize that you are in danger of falling asleep and cannot predict when sleep may occur.
- Not count on the radio, open window or other "tricks" to keep you awake.
- Respond to symptoms of fatigue by finding a safe place to stop for a break.
- Pull off into a safe area from traffic and take a brief nap (15 to 45 minutes).
- Drink coffee or another source of caffeine to promote short-term alertness if needed. (It takes about 30 minutes for caffeine to enter the bloodstream.)

You are not at your best if you are ill or very tired. Do not drive for at least 15 minutes after waking from sleep.

NOTE: See Chapter 9 for more information about the dangers of driving under the influence of alcohol and other drugs.

VEHICLE CONDITION

Vehicles must be inspected at least once a year, but that does not mean it is the only time you should have safety equipment checked. Follow your owner's manual for routine maintenance and have any problems that arise corrected by a qualified mechanic as soon as possible. Do not wait until mechanical problems result in breakdowns or traffic crashes.

Pay special attention to the maintenance and repair of the brakes, steering mechanism, lights, tires and horn. Rely on your owner's manual and a knowledgeable mechanic as your guides to a safe, smooth-running vehicle.

Here are some common problems and some quick equipment checks you can do yourself:

- **BRAKES** - Brakes that pull to one side may be wet, or may need to be adjusted or repaired. If wet, you can dry them by riding lightly on the pedal. If this does not help, have your brakes checked by a mechanic. If you notice any change in the performance of your brakes, have them checked right away.
- **STEERING** - There should not be too much "play" in the steering wheel. If you have power steering, check the fluid level periodically. A whining noise when you make a sharp turn can be a sign of trouble.
- **LIGHTS** - Keep your lights clean and clear of dirt, snow and ice. Broken lenses can cause dangerous glare for other drivers, so have them replaced as soon as possible. Make sure your headlights are adjusted properly to give you the best view of the road and to avoid blinding approaching drivers.

- **TIRES** - The law requires that your vehicle's tires have at least 2/32nds of an inch (.16 cm) of tread. You can check tread depth with a penny. Place it upside down in the tread. If the top of Lincoln's head shows, the tires are too worn and should be replaced. It is also illegal to drive with tires that have cuts down to the cords, knots bumps or bulges. Consult your owner's manual or a tire store about proper tire pressure, and check their pressure often with a reliable gauge.
- **GLASS** - Keep your windows clean and clear all the way around. Replace wiper blades that streak, keep your defroster and rear window defogger in good working condition, and make sure you have enough windshield washing fluid.
- **HORN** - Your vehicle's horn may not seem to be an important safety equipment, but it could easily become your only way to warn other drivers or pedestrians of possible trouble. If the horn is not working, get it repaired as soon as possible. And remember, a horn is used as a warning to others. It should not be used unnecessarily or to express your anger at other drivers or pedestrians.

QUESTIONS

Before going on to Chapter 9, make sure you can answer these questions:

- Should you always look straight ahead when driving?
- If there is no posted speed limit, what is the fastest you may legally drive in New York State?
- Is it always safe to drive at the posted speed limit?
- What is the purpose of minimum speed limits?
- Who **must** wear seat belts? Who should wear them?
- How can you prevent fatigue on a long trip?

CHAPTER 9 Alcohol and Other Drugs

You have probably heard the facts before – driving while impaired or intoxicated is a serious traffic safety problem in the United States. In New York State, more than 20 percent of all highway deaths involve the use of alcohol or other drugs. But, the facts and statistics do not tell the whole story. Behind the numbers are thousands of lives cut short, permanent or disabling injuries, and families devastated because someone drove while under the influence of alcohol or other drugs.

After you drink alcohol or take other drugs, safe driving is simply not possible. Not every impaired or intoxicated driver causes a traffic crash, but each one is dangerous, risking his or her life and the lives of those sharing the road.

Young people, who have less experience with both alcohol and driving, are at greatest risk. Drivers under 21 years old represent about 5 percent of the driving population, but 15 percent of the drivers involved in alcohol or drug-related fatalities. This is one reason the license revocation penalties are more severe for young drivers under the influence of alcohol or other drugs.

Because driving "under the influence" is so dangerous, the penalties for alcohol or drug-related violations are very tough and enforcement by police is a priority. Your chances of being caught and convicted are very high, and New York State law does not allow you to plea bargain to an offense not related to alcohol or drugs.

WHAT ALCOHOL DOES

Alcohol slows your reflexes and reaction time, reduces your ability to see clearly, distorts your judgment of speed and distances, often reduces your inhibitions from taking chances, and makes you less alert. The important physical and mental skills you need to drive safely are weakened.

Because your vision is already restricted at night, driving after drinking is especially dangerous after dark. In addition to its other effects, alcohol reduces your ability to recover from headlight glare. When another vehicle approaches, you can be blinded by its headlights for a dangerously long period of time.

You do not have to look or feel drunk for these things to happen. The effects of alcohol can begin long before you become intoxicated or even legally impaired and begin with the first drink.

As alcohol limits your physical ability to drive, it also makes you less aware of what is happening to your safe driving abilities. It becomes difficult for you to judge your own condition. You may actually feel more confident about driving, when you should not be driving at all.

During each mile you drive, you literally make hundreds of decisions. You turn those decisions into actions that keep your vehicle under control and keep you from getting into traffic crashes. Alcohol makes it hard to make correct decisions and to take the safest actions.

For example: You have just stopped at a STOP sign. You see another vehicle approaching the intersection. You must quickly make a decision whether it is safe to go through the intersection. Under the influence of alcohol, you are more likely to make a wrong decision and "take a chance." Your slower reaction time, coupled with the poor decision, could mean real trouble. It could lead to a crash that should never have happened.

OTHER DRUGS

Many drugs other than alcohol, and many over-the-counter drugs, can affect your driving ability. They can have effects similar to alcohol or even worse. If you are taking medication, even a non-prescription allergy or cold remedy, check the label for warnings about its effects. If you're not sure, ask your doctor or pharmacist about driving after taking the medication.

Never drink alcohol while you are taking other drugs. It could be dangerous, often multiplying the effects of the alcohol and the other drug. For example, taking one drink when you are also using an allergy or cold remedy could affect you as much as several drinks.

It is a misdemeanor to drive while impaired by illegal drugs such as marijuana, cocaine, LSD, heroin and opium, and by some prescription drugs such as tranquilizers. Drugs can affect your reflexes, judgment, vision and alertness in ways similar to alcohol, and they may have other dangerous effects.

Combining alcohol with other drugs severely reduces your driving abilities and can cause serious health problems, including death.

ALCOHOL, DRUGS AND THE LAW

In New York State, you may be arrested for any of these offenses: driving while intoxicated (DWI), driving with a blood alcohol content of .10 percent or more (.10 BAC), driving while ability impaired by a drug (DWAI-drug), or driving while ability impaired by alcohol (DWAI).

Blood alcohol content (BAC) is the percentage of alcohol in your blood and is usually determined by a chemical test of breath, blood or urine. A BAC of more than .05 percent is legal evidence that you are impaired, and a BAC of .10 percent or higher is evidence of intoxication.

Many people think a chemical test evidence is required to prove you were intoxicated or impaired. However, a police officer's testimony about your appearance and behavior when arrested can provide enough evidence alone to convict you, even without a chemical test.

In New York State, an alcohol or drug-related driving arrest cannot be reduced to a different type of violation unless the district attorney determines there is not enough evidence to support the charge of impaired or intoxicated operation. Therefore, an alcohol or drug-related arrest is hardly ever so-called "plea bargained" to a charge such as speeding or reckless driving.

If you are found guilty of any alcohol or drug-related driving violation, the court must revoke or suspend your license at the time you are sentenced. In a rare situation, the court may allow you a 20-day continuation of driving privilege, but your license itself will be taken immediately.

The BAC standards and penalties for commercial drivers are even more strict than those indicated in this chapter. For complete information, see Section 1 of the *Commercial Driver's Manual* (CDL-10).

YOUR BAC

Your blood alcohol content (BAC) primarily depends on:

- How much alcohol you drink.
- How much time passes between drinks.
- Your weight.

Your BAC *does not* depend on what *kind* of alcoholic beverage you drink, how physically fit you are, or how well you can "hold your liquor."

Different types of drinks do *not* affect you differently. It is the amount of alcohol you consume, not whether it is in beer, wine or wine cooler, or liquor, that raises your BAC and lowers your driving ability. An ounce (*30 ml*) of 80 proof liquor, four ounces (*120 ml*) of 24 proof table wine, 12 ounces (*360 ml*) of beer, and 12 ounces (*360 ml*) of wine cooler each contains about the same amount of alcohol. None is "safer to drink" than the others.

For a male weighing 150 pounds, each one of these drinks would contain enough alcohol to increase his BAC by about .02 percent. On average, it takes the human body about one hour to dispose of that much alcohol. However, studies suggest that a woman's body may process and remove alcohol from the blood more slowly than a man's. This may result in a higher BAC over a longer period of time.

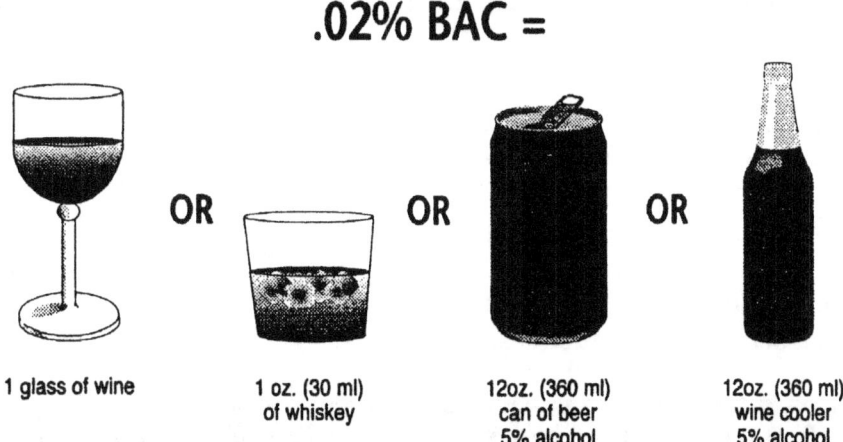

.02% BAC =

1 glass of wine OR 1 oz. (30 ml) of whiskey OR 12oz. (360 ml) can of beer 5% alcohol OR 12oz. (360 ml) wine cooler 5% alcohol

Compared to the 150-pound male described above, your own body weight can make some difference in the BAC and the effects of alcohol. But no one is immune to the effects of alcohol. **It is a simple fact: the more you drink in a given period of time, the higher your BAC will be, and the less safe your driving will be.**

It takes only a few drinks to raise your BAC to levels at which it is illegal to drive. And remember, the effects of alcohol on your driving ability actually begin at even lower BAC levels after just one drink.

Eating before or while you drink helps slow down alcohol absorption somewhat, but it cannot prevent you from becoming impaired or intoxicated if you have too many drinks.

Coffee, exercise and cold showers cannot reduce your BAC and the effects of alcohol. They might help you stay awake, but it cannot affect your BAC or make you sober. *The only way to effectively reduce your BAC is to spend time without drinking.* You must allow your body enough time to absorb and dispose of the alcohol.

CHEMICAL TESTS

Chemical tests, such as the "breathalyzer," measure a person's BAC. If you are arrested for an alcohol or drug-related violation, the police officer will almost surely request that you submit to a chemical test. Under New York's "Implied Consent" law, by driving a car in this state you are considered to have already given your consent to take such a test.

Chemical test refusal is a separate issue from whether or not you were guilty of an alcohol or drug-related violation. If you refuse to take the test after being arrested, your license will be suspended when you are arraigned in court on the alcohol or drug-related charge. Also, the fact that you refused a chemical test may be introduced in court when you are tried on the alcohol or drug-related charge. If a DMV hearing later confirms you did refuse the test, your license will be revoked even if you are found not guilty of the alcohol or drug-related violation. For information on license revocations and civil penalties for chemical test refusals, see Chapter 2.

THE CONSEQUENCES

The table below summarizes the fines, surcharges, license penalties and possible imprisonment you would face if convicted of an alcohol or drug-related violation. In addition to these penalties, impaired or intoxicated driving can carry other serious consequences.

PENALTIES FOR ALCOHOL/DRUG-RELATED VIOLATIONS

Violation	Mandatory Fine[1]	Maximum Jail Term	Mandatory Action[2] Against License
Driving While Intoxicated (DWI)[3]	$500-$1,000	1 year	Revoked at least 6 months
Driving While Ability Impaired by Drug (DWAI-Drug)	$500-$1,000	1-year	Suspended 6 months
DWI, .10 BAC or DWAI-Drug within 10 years of any previous violation; Class E felony	$1,000-$5,000	4 years	Revoked at least 1 year
Third DWI violation in 10 years; Class D felony	$2,000 - $10,000	up to 7 years	Revoked at least 1 year
Driving While Ability Impaired by Alcohol (DWAI)	$300-$500	15 days	Suspended 90 days
DWAI committed within 5 years of any previous violation[4]	$500-$750	30 days	Revoked at least 6 months
Third DWAI Violation in 10 years[4]	$750-$1500	180 days	Revoked at least 6 months
Zero Tolerance (Drivers Under 21, with BAC .02 to .07)	$125 minimum, plus $100 Suspension Termination Fee		Suspended 6 months
Zero Tolerance, second offense	$125 minimum, plus $100 Re-application fee		Revoked 1 year or until age 21, whichever is longer

[1] Additional surcharges of $90 for misdemeanors and $155 for felonies apply.

[2] License penalties for drivers holding a Commercial Driver License (CDL) are covered in Chapter 2.

[3] Penalties also apply to driving with .10 percent alcohol in blood, or while impaired by a drug.

[4] Penalties listed apply if DWAI violation follows any alcohol or drug-related violations.

Zero Tolerance for Drivers Under 21

The legal purchase and possession age for alcoholic beverages in New York State is 21. Under the state's Zero Tolerance law, it is a violation for a person under age 21 to drive with *any* measurable BAC (.02 to .07). After a finding of violation is determined at hearing, the driver's license will be suspended for six months. The driver will then have to pay a $100 suspension termination fee and a $125 civil penalty to be re-licensed. For a second Zero Tolerance violation, the driver's license will be revoked for at least one year or until the driver reaches age 21, whichever is longer.

The Ignition Interlock Program

Under some circumstances, a court can order a driver to purchase and install an ignition interlock device as a condition of probation following conviction for an alcohol-related offense. The device connects to a motor vehicle ignition system and measures the alcohol content of the operator's breath. It prevents the vehicle from being started until the motorist provides an appropriate sample breath. In some counties, during the remaining period of probation, the motorist may be eligible to hold a post-revocation conditional license. This conditional license will be revoked if the motorist fails to comply with the terms of probation or for conviction of any traffic offense other than illegal parking, stopping or standing.

A FEW IMPORTANT REMINDERS

- If you kill or seriously injure another person because of an alcohol or drug-related violation, you can be convicted of vehicular manslaughter or assault, carrying a fine of up to $5,000 and a jail term of up to seven years.
- If you are convicted of two DWI violations, both resulting in physical injury traffic crashes, your license will be revoked permanently.
- If you drive while your license is suspended or revoked, you face a mandatory fine of up to $1000, and a mandatory jail term or probation. If impaired or intoxicated at the time of arrest, the maximum mandatory fine is $5,000, and the vehicle may be seized and forfeited.
- Liability insurance may not cover the cost of injuries and damage from a traffic crash. You could be sued for thousands of dollars. You'd also find it difficult and expensive to buy liability insurance for several years.
- In addition to fines and surcharges, you could also face very expensive legal fees.
- You could have a criminal record, making it more difficult to get a job or advance your career.

The worst consequence, however, is death or injury to yourself or someone else. It may be hard for you to imagine that you could be involved in a fatal or injury traffic crash while driving impaired or intoxicated – but it happens to thousands of drivers every year who also thought it could never happen to them.

Alcohol and drugs give you a false sense of confidence. You are not likely to worry about the consequences while you already are impaired or intoxicated. The time to consider them, and how to avoid them, is *before* you are under the influence.

AVOIDING TROUBLE

The only sure way to avoid the consequences of drunken and drugged driving is not to use alcohol or drugs before you drive, and when you are driving. There are several ways to do this:

- If you regularly go to social events with the same group of friends, rotate drivers. Each friend takes a turn being the "designated driver" who does not drink alcohol.
- Arrange to stay overnight or ride home with a friend who does not drink. Make plans ahead of time, before you start drinking.
- Before you begin drinking, give your car keys to a friend who does not drink and who will not let you drive after drinking.
- Call a cab or use public transportation.

With a little thought and planning ahead of time, you can stay out of trouble. You can take other precautions:

- If you drink, choose beverages with lower alcohol content, such as low-alcohol beers and wines.
- Drink slowly. Alternate between drinks with alcohol and drinks without any alcohol.
- Do not make alcohol the centerpiece of your social event. Conversation, games and recreation are the real reasons we get together with friends.
- Eat a good meal before you drink, and have snacks while you drink.
- If you feel you've had too much alcohol to drink, stop drinking several hours before you intend to leave and allow time for your body to lower your BAC.
- Listen to your friends. Accept their help. If they warn you about not driving, take their concern seriously. Do not laugh it off or become angry.

QUESTIONS

Before going on to Chapter 10, make sure you can answer these questions:

- How does drunken driving rank as a highway safety problem?
- What are the effects of alcohol on the skills you need to drive?

- Which of these drugs could affect your driving ability: marijuana, a cold remedy, a tranquilizer?
- If you are taking a non-prescription drug, what should you do before driving?
- What is a likely effect of taking another drug while drinking alcoholic beverages?
- On what three factors does your blood alcohol content (BAC) depend?
- Which of these contains more alcohol than the other two: one ounce (*30 ml*) of 80 proof liquor, four ounces (*120 ml*) 24 proof wine, 12 ounces (*360 ml*) of beer, 12 ounces (*360 ml*) of wine-cooler?
- On average, how long does it take your body to dispose of the alcohol contained in 12 ounces of beer?
- What is the only effective way to reduce your BAC?
- What happens to your driver's license if you refuse a chemical test?
- Other than fines, action against your license and a possible jail term, what are some of the consequences of driving under the influence of alcohol or other drugs?

CHAPTER 10 Special Driving Situations

Even under the best conditions, driving demands your full attention and your best judgment. When special situations or hazards arise, attention and judgment become even more important. To be a competent and safe driver, you must learn how to drive on expressways, at night, in poor weather and when an emergency occurs.

EXPRESSWAY DRIVING

"Expressway" means any divided highway where traffic is going in one direction on two or more lanes. You usually enter or exit the expressway by using ramps (controlled-access). The speed limit is usually 55 mph (*88 km/h*), but may be posted at 65 mph (*100 km/h*) in some rural areas. Examples are the New York State Thruway, major interstate routes, and parkways.

Before traveling an expressway, identify your entrance and exit points on a road map. Know where to get on and off the expressway, and be prepared to get into the proper lanes for your entrance and exit. If you miss an exit, however, **never** back up to get back on the expressway. Get off at the next exit, and look for signs that tell you how to get back on the expressway going the other way. There will usually be an exit for your destination from that side of the expressway.

Unless there is a STOP or YIELD sign or traffic light on the entrance ramp, use the ramp to accelerate to expressway speed and blend with traffic. Signal, then look over your shoulder for approaching traffic already on the expressway. If necessary, slow down to safely merge into traffic.

If the entrance lane is too short to allow acceleration to expressway speed, the safest way to enter is to stop and wait for a large gap in traffic. Then enter the expressway and accelerate quickly. To avoid conflicts with other entrance lane traffic, stop only if necessary and merge into expressway traffic as soon as possible.

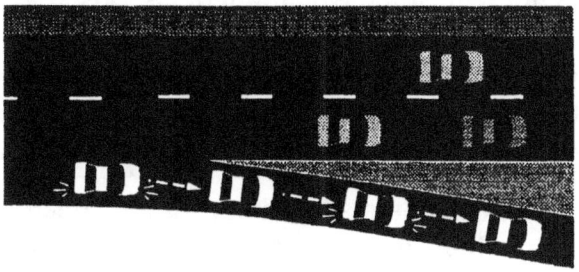

As you drive on the expressway, be sure to signal all lane changes and check over your shoulder to be sure you will not cut off any vehicles behind you. Make sure your directional signal goes off after you change lanes.

Stay alert for traffic entering ahead. If possible, move out of the right lane as you approach entrances to allow more room for merging traffic.

To avoid a last-minute lane change, check destination and exit signs, and get into the proper lane for your exit well ahead of time. Be sure to signal your exit at least 100 feet (*30 m*) before you reach the exit ramp. Once you are on the exit ramp, slow down. There is often a lower speed posted for the ramp.

After you leave an expressway, look for speed limit signs and check your speedometer to be sure you're driving within the posted limit. You are probably no longer on a 55 mph (*88 km/h*) road.

Expressway driving usually combines high speeds with heavy traffic, and you must be alert. The higher speed and traffic volume require you to think faster and handle your vehicle more efficiently than in most other driving situations. On long trips, plan frequent rest stops. On a bright day, sunglasses can reduce glare and eye fatigue.

NIGHT DRIVING

About 90 percent of your driving decisions are based on what you see. At night, you must use extra caution to make up for reduced visibility. You should also be aware that the ability to see well at night generally declines with age.

Night driving is more dangerous because the distance you can see ahead or to the side is reduced. You should drive slower than you would in daylight, especially in unfamiliar areas or on narrow, winding roads. Your headlights cover about 350 feet ahead. It is important that you drive at a speed that allows you to react and stop safely within that distance. This is called "driving within the range" of your headlights.

The law requires you to use your headlights from one-half hour after sunset to one-half hour before sunrise, when visibility is less than 1,000 feet (*300 m*) and whenever you are using your windshield wipers to clear rain, snow, sleet, etc. Turn your headlights on at dawn and dusk and in fog, too. Even when headlights do not help you see in low light periods, they make it much easier for other drivers and pedestrians to see your vehicle. Do not use parking lights or daytime running lights as a substitute, headlights do a better job. If an approaching driver flashes headlights at you during a period of low visibility, it probably means your vehicle was hard to see, and you should turn on your headlights.

Be considerate in using your high beams. Your headlights must be on low beam when you are within 500 feet (*150 m*) of an approaching vehicle, or within 200 feet (*60 m*) of a vehicle ahead of you, even if the vehicle ahead is in a different lane. You should also dim your lights for pedestrians approaching you.

If an approaching driver does not dim his or her lights, flash yours to high beam for a second, then back to low beam. To help avoid the glare of approaching high beams, shift your eyes to the right. Use the road edge as a guide until the approaching vehicle passes by.

To reduce glare from the lights of following vehicles, switch your interior rear view mirror to the "night" position.

Light from inside your vehicle or from street lights makes it harder for you to see the road ahead. Keep the interior dome light off and dim the dashboard lights. Adjust your sun visor to reduce glare from overhead lights.

You cannot see well at night with dirty headlights or windows. A dirty windshield greatly increases glare from approaching headlights. Make sure your lights and glass are clean for night driving.

DRIVING IN RAIN, FOG, OR SNOW

When it starts to rain, dust and oil form a slick, greasy film on the road. Wet leaves can also be slippery and hazardous. So be aware that roads may be very slippery, even in a light rain. Increase your following distance (see Chapter 8). Be extra careful on curves, turns and expressway ramps.

In heavy rain, your tires may actually begin to ride on the water, rather than the pavement. This "hydroplaning" results in a loss of traction and control. It usually occurs at higher speeds, so drive slower in heavy rain. If you feel your vehicle losing traction, slow down even more. Good tires with deep tread help prevent hydroplaning.

Rain also makes it more difficult to see through the windshield. The law requires you to turn on your vehicle's headlights whenever the weather conditions would ordinarily require the use of windshield wipers to clear rain, snow, sleet, etc. If your windshield wipers cause streaks or smears, the blades must be replaced.

In fog, keep your headlights on low beam. High beams reflect off the fog and make it even harder to see. Signal your turns well in advance, and brake early as you approach a stop to give other drivers plenty of warning.

WINTER DRIVING

Winter is the most difficult driving season. Not only do you have snow and ice to deal with, but there are fewer hours of daylight as well.

Before winter weather arrives, make sure your vehicle is in good condition. Make sure your vehicle has good snow tires. Put them on the vehicle early, before the first snowfall. Never combine radial and non-radial tires on the same vehicle. On front-wheel drive cars, it is best to put snow tires or "all-season" tires on all four wheels, not just the front. Tires with metal studs may be used in New York State only from October 16 through April 30.

During ice or snowstorms, especially when a traveler's advisory is issued, do not drive unless it is absolutely necessary. If you must drive, first clear the ice and snow from your vehicle, including the headlights and taillights, the windshield wipers and *all* of the windows. Be sure the windshield washer reservoir is adequately filled with a freeze-resistant cleaning solution.

Drive slowly. Even if your vehicle has good traction in ice and snow, other drivers will be traveling cautiously. Do not disrupt the flow of traffic by driving faster than everyone else.

In a rear-wheel drive vehicle, you can usually feel a loss of traction or the beginning of a skid. With a front-wheel drive vehicle, there may be no warning. Though front-wheel drive and four-wheel drive vehicles generally *do* handle better in ice and snow, they *do not* have flawless traction; skids can occur unexpectedly. Do not let the better feel and handling of a vehicle with front-wheel drive or four-wheel drive cause you to drive faster than you should.

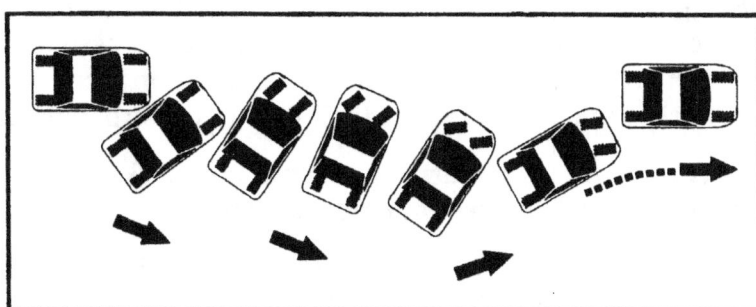

Despite popular misconception, the best approach to recovering from a skid is the same for both front and rear-wheel drive vehicles. If your *rear wheels* start to skid:

- Turn the steering wheel in the direction you want the front wheels to go. If your rear wheels are sliding left, steer left. If they're sliding right, steer right.
- If your rear wheels start sliding the other way as you recover, ease the steering wheel toward that side. You might have to steer left and right a few times to get your vehicle completely under control.

- If your vehicle has an anti-lock braking system (ABS), keep your foot with even pressure on the brake pedal. If your vehicle does not have ABS, pump the pedal gently, pumping more rapidly only as your car slows down. Braking hard with non-anti-lock brakes will make the skid worse.

If your *front wheels* skid:

- Take your foot off the gas and shift to neutral or push in the clutch, but do not try to immediately steer.
- As the wheels skid sideways, they will slow the vehicle and traction will return. As it does, steer in the direction you want to go. Then put the transmission in "drive" or release the clutch, and accelerate gently.

To avoid skids on snow and ice, brake early, carefully and gently. "Squeeze" your brakes in slow, steady strokes. Allow the wheels to keep rolling. If they begin to lock up, ease off the brake pedal. As your vehicle slows, you also may want to shift into a lower gear.

When sleet, freezing rain or snow start to fall, remember that bridges, ramps, and overpasses are likely to freeze first. Also be aware that slippery spots may still remain after road crews have cleared the highways.

AVOIDING COLLISIONS WITH DEER

Two-thirds of all deer/vehicle collisions happen during the months of October, November and December. This is also breeding season, when deer are most actively traveling about. Daily deer activity peaks at dawn and dusk, which often is peak motor-vehicle commuter traveling times. Deer travel in groups – if you see one, expect more. Highway areas where there have been numerous deer/vehicle collisions often are already marked with deer crossing signs. The New York State Department of Environmental Conservation recommends these precautions motorists can take to reduce their chances of striking a deer:

- Use extreme caution when driving at dawn and dusk; this is when driver visibility is poor and the deer are most active.
- The risk of deer/vehicle collisions is greatest when deer movements peak due to the onset of the breeding season during the months of October, November and December
- Slow down when approaching deer that are standing near roadsides. Deer may "bolt" or change direction at the last minute.
- If you see a deer cross the road, slow down and use extreme caution. Deer travel in groups, expect other deer to follow.
- Use flashers or a headlight signal to warn other drivers when deer are spotted on or near the road.
- Use caution and be alert when driving on roadways marked with deer crossing signs. These signs are placed in areas that have had a large number of deer/vehicle collisions.

DRIVING EMERGENCIES

The single most important rule in any emergency is *do not panic.* You have a better chance of handling the emergency safely if you do not let fear take over. In most emergencies, you will have a second or two to think before you act.

Here is what to do in various emergency situations:

TIRE BLOWOUT - A thumping sound may be a warning that a blowout is about to occur. If you hear it, get safely off the road and check your tires. If a tire blows out, hold the steering wheel firmly, and ease your foot off the gas pedal. If your vehicle skids, handle it as you would on ice or snow. Do not use your brake until your vehicle is under control. Get off the road as soon as it safe to do so.

LOSS OF A WHEEL - Handle this as you would a blow out. A thump or clunk in the wheel may be a warning sound. Pull off the roadway and stop. Then check your vehicle or have it checked.

STEERING FAILURE - If your vehicle suddenly stops responding to the steering wheel, ease your foot off the gas pedal, turn on your vehicle's four-way flashers and keep your foot off the brake pedal for as long as it is safe and practical. The vehicle's natural balance should allow it to continue going straight, but a sudden change in speed could spin it out of control. As the vehicle slows down, you may be able to brake very gently to bring it to a stop.

BRAKE FAILURE - If your brake pedal suddenly sinks to the floor, try pumping it to build up pressure. If that does not help, use your emergency or parking brake – but use it gently. Shifting to a lower gear will also help your vehicle slow down.

HEADLIGHT FAILURE - If your headlights suddenly go out, try your vehicle's four-way flashers, parking lights and directional signals. These may still work and should give you enough light to get safely off the road. If your headlights begin to dim, drive to a nearby service station, or pull off the road and go for help.

STUCK GAS PEDAL - Hook your toe under the pedal and see if you can free it. If not, shift into neutral and use the brake to slow your vehicle and get off the road. Do not turn off the ignition if your vehicle has power steering or a steering wheel that has a locking column because, if you do, you will lose power steering or not be able to steer at all.

RUNNING OFF THE PAVEMENT - If your wheels drift off the pavement onto the shoulder of the road, do not yank the steering wheel back. Ease your foot off the gas pedal, and brake gently. When your vehicle has slowed down, check for traffic behind you, then steer gently back onto the pavement.

VEHICLE APPROACHING HEAD-ON IN YOUR LANE - Slow down, pull over to the right and sound your horn to alert the other driver. Do not swing over to the left lane. If you do, the other driver may suddenly recover and pull back into that lane, too, causing a head-on collision.

STALLING ON RAILROAD TRACKS - If a train is approaching, unfasten your seat belt, get out of the vehicle and get as far away as you can from the tracks. Run toward the general direction the train is coming from. If you run "down the track," in the same direction the train is heading, you may be hit with debris when the train strikes your vehicle. <u>Only if you are absolutely sure no trains are coming</u>, open your window to listen for an approaching train and try to start the engine. If that fails, shift your vehicle into neutral and push it off the tracks.

GOING INTO WATER - A vehicle will usually float for a while, and you should have time to get out before it starts sinking. Unfasten your seat belt and escape through a window. Opening a door would cause water to rush in, and the car could overturn on top of you.

If the vehicle sinks before you can get out, climb into the rear seat. An air pocket may form there as the weight of the engine pulls the vehicle down nose first. When the vehicle settles, take a breath and escape through a window. As you rise, air pressure will build in your lungs. Let it out in small breaths through your nose or lips as you surface. Do not hold you breath tightly or try to blow air out; just allow the air to escape naturally.

FIRE - If you see smoke come from under your vehicle's hood, pull off the road and park your vehicle. Turn off the ignition. Get away from the car and call the fire department. Trying to fight the fire yourself is dangerous.

BLOCKED VISION - If your vehicle's hood flies open suddenly, or your vision through the windshield becomes blocked by some other object or wipers that have failed, you should roll down the side window so you can see. Turn on your vehicle's four-way flashers and carefully pull your vehicle off the road and park it.

QUESTIONS

Before going on to Chapter 11, make sure you can answer questions:

- What should you do if you miss an expressway exit?
- What are expressway entrance ramps used for?
- What should you do if an entrance ramp is very short?
- When should you signal that you are exiting an expressway?
- What should you check for after leaving an expressway?
- Why is expressway driving different from ordinary driving?
- What is the main reason night driving is more difficult than daytime driving?
- Driving within the range of your headlights means you should be able to stop your vehicle within about how many feet?
- What should you do if headlights on approaching vehicles make it hard for you to see?
- Is it best to keep your headlights on high beam or low beam in fog?

- Which way should you turn your steering wheel to get out of a skid?
- How should you use your brake pedal on a slippery road?
- What is the most important rule to remember in any driving emergency?
- What should you do if one of your tires blows out?
- What is the first thing you should do if your brakes fail?
- What should you do if your wheels drift off the pavement?

CHAPTER 11 — Sharing the Road

You must learn to safely share the road with large vehicles, motorcycles, mopeds, pedestrians, bicyclists, in-line skaters, roller skaters, slow moving vehicles and horseback riders. These other highway users face special problems, and they pose special problems for car and truck drivers. You should know how to safely deal with these problems and understand the special rules that apply to other highway users.

PEDESTRIANS

Pedestrians are the highway users most at risk in traffic. As a driver, you must use extra caution to avoid colliding with pedestrians. Regardless of the rules of the road or right-of-way, the law specifically requires you to exercise great care to avoid striking pedestrians.

Children are often the least predictable pedestrians and the most difficult to see. Take extra care to look out for children, especially near schools, bus stops, playgrounds, parks and frozen desert vehicles such as ice cream trucks.

When backing your vehicle, remember to look through your rear window for pedestrians. Do not rely only on rearview mirrors. Before backing into, or out of, a driveway when children are near, get out of the vehicle and check behind it.

Pedestrians are supposed to walk on the side of the road facing traffic, so they should be on your right. Be especially watchful for pedestrians when you make a right turn.

Remember also that pedestrians legally crossing at intersections *always* have the right-of-way. Do not pull in front of or behind them or to "hurry them along" – wait until they are out of the intersection. Elderly and disabled pedestrians may require extra time to complete their crossings.

There is a special right-of-way law for blind pedestrians crossing the road with a guide dog or a white or metallic cane. You must always give them the right-of-way, even if the traffic signals or other right-of-way rules are not in their favor.

Remember to keep your eyes moving as you drive. Glance to either side every few seconds. This defensive driving rule will help you spot pedestrians near or approaching the roadway.

The law gives pedestrians some responsibilities too. They must:

- Obey traffic and pedestrian signals and traffic officers.
- Use sidewalks when available, or walk facing traffic, as far to the left as possible.
- Never stand in the road to hitchhike or conduct business with passing motorists.

BICYCLISTS AND IN-LINE SKATERS

Bicyclists and in-line skaters have the right to share the road and travel in the same direction as motor vehicles. Like pedestrians, bicyclists and in-line skaters are often difficult to notice in traffic, and they have little protection from a traffic crash. When driving a motor vehicle, be sure to check your vehicle's "blind spots" before you parallel park, or open a driver's side door, or leave a curb. Don't rely only on your rearview mirrors – turn your head to look for bicyclists and in-line skaters that may be alongside or approaching.

When driving, approach bicyclists and in-line skaters with extreme caution. Give them room and slow down as you pass them. Air pressure from a quickly passing vehicle can throw them off balance.

Be aware that the bicyclist or in-line skater near or in front of you may react to road hazards just as a motorcyclist would and suddenly change speed, direction, or lane position.

The rules of the road and right-of-way apply to, and protect, bicyclists and in-line skaters. You must yield the right-of-way to them just as you would to another vehicle. Bicyclists in-line skaters must obey the rules of the road, just as vehicle drivers do.

Bicyclists and in-line skaters must:

- Wear an approved helmet if age one through 13 years old.
- Obey any local laws or regulations concerning helmet use for adults.
- Ride in a bicycle lane, if a usable one is available. Where there is none, the bicyclist must ride near the right curb or edge of the road, or on a usable right shoulder of the road, to avoid undue interference with other traffic. The rule of staying to the right does not apply when a

bicyclist or in-line skater is preparing for a left turn or must move left to avoid hazards.
- Come to a full stop before entering a roadway from a driveway, alley or over a curb.
- Never travel with more than two abreast in a single lane.
- Never ride on a sidewalk if local laws prohibit it.

Bicyclists also must:

- Signal turns, lane changes and stops using the hand signals shown. A bicyclist may signal a right turn by extending the right arm straight out to the right, instead of using the standard signal for car drivers. Never carry an infant under a year old as a passenger. It is against the law. The law also requires child passengers one through four years old wear approved bicycle safety helmets and ride in securely attached bicycle safety seats.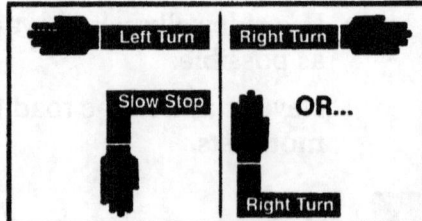
- Never carry a passenger unless the bicycle has a passenger seat.
- Keep at least one hand on the handlebars at all times, and not carry anything which interferes with proper control of the bicycle.
- Report to DMV within 10 days of the incident, any bicycle crash that results in death or serious injury. Bicycle accident report forms are available at any motor vehicle office.

A bicycle driven on public highways must be equipped with adequate brakes and a horn or bell that can be heard at least 100 feet (*30 m*) away. A bicycle used at night must have a headlight visible from at least 500 feet (*150 m*) ahead and a red taillight visible from at least 300 feet (*90 m*) behind. One of these lights must also be visible from at least 200 feet (*60 m*) away on each side. A bicycle sold by a dealer must have wide-angle, spoke-mounted reflectors or reflective tires, a wide-angle rear reflector and pedal reflectors.

For more information on bicycle and in-line skating regulations and safety, see the publication Sharing the Road Safely (C-77), available at any motor vehicle office and by request from a DMV Call Center.

MOTORCYCLISTS

Motorcycles travel as fast as automobiles, and motorcyclists must obey the same traffic laws. But motorcyclists also share problems faced by pedestrians, bicyclists, and in-line skaters: lower visibility, less stability, and less protection.

To improve their visibility, motorcyclists are required to keep their vehicle's headlights and taillights on at all times. For protection, motorcyclists are required to wear approved helmets, as defined by USDOT federal motor vehicle safety standards (FMVSS218), and goggles or a face shield in conformance with regulations issued by the Vehicle Equipment Safety Commission (VESC-8).

It is often hard to judge how far away a motorcycle is or how fast it is approaching. Many motorcycle crashes that involve other vehicles occur when the driver of the other vehicle misjudges the motorcyclist's speed or distance, or fails to see the motorcycle at all, and then stops or turns left in front of the motorcyclist.

On most motorcycles, the directional signal does not go off automatically after a turn. Before stopping or turning in front of a motorcyclist signaling a turn, be sure the motorcyclist is actually going to turn.

A motorcyclist has the right to the full use of a lane, and motorcyclists are allowed to ride two abreast in a single lane. An experienced motorcyclist will often change position within a lane to get a clearer view of traffic, avoid hazards and be more visible to drivers. You may not pass or drive alongside a motorcycle in the same lane, and a motorcyclist may not share a lane with you.

Take care when passing a motorcyclist. Like bicycles, motorcycles can be affected by the air pressure of passing vehicles.

Because motorcyclists must take extra precautions when they come upon special highway surfaces, you should be aware of what a motorcyclist may do in certain situations:

- The motorcyclist may quickly change speed or lane position to avoid loose gravel, debris, seams or grooves in the pavement, sewer or access covers, or small animals.
- When approaching a railroad crossing, a motorcyclist may slow down and rise off the seat to cushion the rough crossing and change direction to cross the tracks at a right angle.
- On bridges with metal grates (often marked STEEL DECK BRIDGE), the motorcyclist may move to the center of the lane to compensate for the uneven surface. Stay well behind a motorcyclist in this situation.

MOPED OPERATORS

Limited use motorcycles, often called mopeds, are low speed, two-wheeled vehicles intended for limited use on public highways. There are three different classes of mopeds based on maximum performance speed. The chart below outlines the requirements for moped operation.

Class B and C mopeds may be driven only in the right lane of traffic, as far to the right as possible. Class A mopeds are allowed to drive in any lane, and any portion of a lane. Mopeds are not permitted on expressways or other controlled access highways unless posted signs permit it.

When approaching a moped, use the same precautions and care you would when approaching a bicyclist.

GUIDE TO LIMITED USE MOTORCYCLE (MOPEDS) OPERATION

Class	A	B	C
Top speed range mph (km/h) (Over 48 to 64)	Over 30 to 40 (over 32 to 48)	Over 20 to 30 (32 or less)	20 or less
Type of license or learner permit required[4]	M	ANY CLASS[4]	ANY CLASS[4]
Registration required	YES (A Plate)	YES (B Plate)	YES (C Plate)
Headlight to be on when operating	YES	YES	YES
Helmet & eye protection required when operating[5]	YES	YES	Recommended
Where operation is permitted	Any Traffic Lane Only[1] & Shoulder	Right Hand Lane Only[1] & Shoulder	Right Hand Lane
Mandatory insurance required	YES	YES	Recommended[2]
Safety responsibility[3] applies	YES	YES	YES
Annual inspection required	YES	Recommended	Recommended
Title required	NO	NO	NO

[1] Except when making a left hand turn.

[2] If a Class C limited use motorcycle is used in a rental business, insurance is mandatory.

[3] Safety responsibility is the requirement to pay for or post security for damage or personal injury you may cause in a traffic crash.

[4] Usual learner permit and junior license restrictions apply.

[5] Motorcyclists must wear approved motorcycle helmets, as defined by USDOT federal motor vehicle safety standards (FMVSS 218). To improve the motorcyclist's visibility, the DMV recommends that helmets have at least four square inches of reflective material on both sides. Motorcyclists must also wear approved eye protection, even if the motorcycle is equipped with a windshield. Prescription or made-to-order safety glasses may be used if the user can present written certification that they meet DMV standards. The eye protection must be manufactured in conformity with the regulations issued by the Vehicle Equipment Safety Commission (VESC-8).

LARGE VEHICLES

In more than 60 percent of all fatal crashes involving cars and big trucks, police report that the car driver, rather than the truck driver, contributed to the cause of the traffic crash.

Because these trucks are much bigger and heavier than cars, the driver of the car, not the truck, is killed in a fatal car-truck traffic crash four out of five times. However, many of these crashes could be avoided if motorists know about truck (and bus) limitations and how to steer clear of unsafe situations involving large vehicles.

Remember: Large trucks, recreational vehicles, and buses are not simply big cars. The bigger they are:

- The bigger their blind spots,
- The longer it takes them to stop,
- The more room they need to maneuver,
- The longer it takes an auto to pass them.

Blind Spots

Unlike cars, large vehicles have deep blind spots directly behind them. They also have much larger blind spots on both sides than cars do. Tractors with long hoods may also have a blind spot of up to 20 feet directly in front of the vehicle. You should stay out of these "no zones."

Side Blind Spots

Large vehicles have much larger blind spots on both sides than cars do. If you drive in these blind spots for any length of time, you cannot be seen by the vehicle's driver. Even if the vehicle's driver knows you are there, remaining alongside a large vehicle may hamper the driver's ability to evade a dangerous situation.

Rear Blind Spots

If you stay in the rear blind spot of a large vehicle, you increase the possibility of a traffic crash. The other driver cannot see your auto, and your view of the traffic will be cut off.

Stopping Distance

Large vehicles – especially tractor trailers – take considerably longer to stop than a car traveling at the same speed. The difference comes primarily from brake lag, which is unique to trucks. Air brakes which transmit braking power from the tractor to the trailer are subject to a lag that can add many feet to stopping distance. A good strategy is to leave plenty of space between your car and the truck. If you are driving in front of a truck, indicate your intention to turn or change lanes early. Avoid sudden moves.

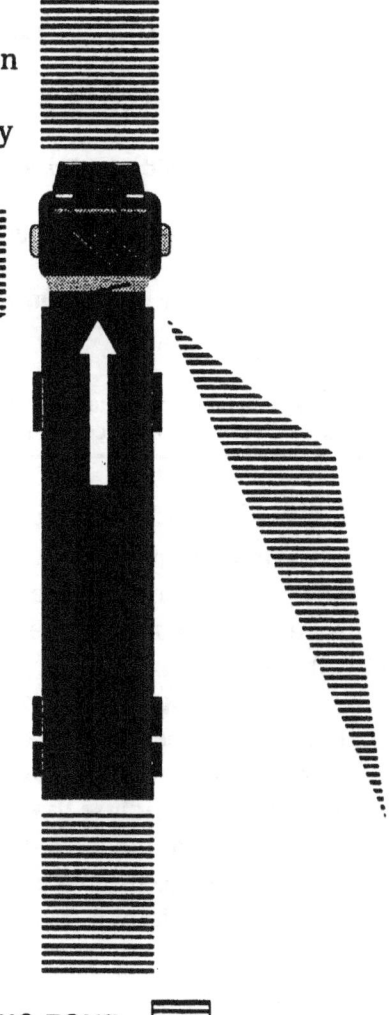

NO-ZONE =

Maneuverability

Large vehicles are not designed to be as maneuverable as cars. They take longer to stop and to accelerate, and because of their size, they often need to swing wide to make their turns.

You can reduce the likelihood of a collision with a large vehicle if you:

- Do not cut abruptly in front of the large vehicle; if exiting, take a few extra seconds to slow down and exit behind it, and if passing, do not pull in front of the vehicle unless you can see the whole front of the vehicle in your rear view mirror.
- Pay close attention to the large vehicle's turn signals. Because trucks make wide right turns, they need to swing to the left before turning right-make sure you know which way the vehicle is turning by observing turn signals.
- Do not linger beside a large vehicle, because you may not be visible to the driver in the wide area the truck needs for maneuvering a turn.

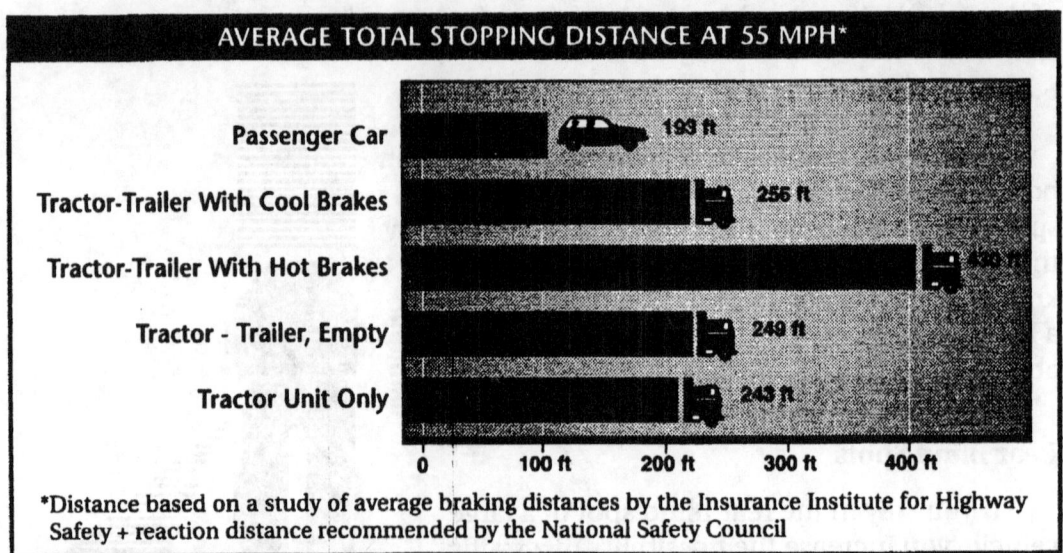

AVERAGE TOTAL STOPPING DISTANCE AT 55 MPH*

- Passenger Car: 193 ft
- Tractor-Trailer With Cool Brakes: 256 ft
- Tractor-Trailer With Hot Brakes: 430 ft
- Tractor - Trailer, Empty: 249 ft
- Tractor Unit Only: 243 ft

*Distance based on a study of average braking distances by the Insurance Institute for Highway Safety + reaction distance recommended by the National Safety Council

Passing

Passing a large vehicle, especially a tractor-trailer or other combination vehicle, takes a longer time and requires more space than passing a car. On a two-way road, leave yourself more time and space when passing a large vehicle. Make sure you can see the whole front of the vehicle before returning to its lane after passing. Remember that on an upgrade or steep hill, a large vehicle usually loses speed. Look far ahead when driving. In case you will need to pass a large vehicle ahead of you, be prepared by knowing in advance when you are approaching an incline that may cause the other vehicle to slow down. Also, as your own vehicle begins a downgrade, remember that the speed of the other vehicle is likely to increase significantly as it also travels downhill. This would require your vehicle to take more time to pass.

Backing up

Never pass close behind a large vehicle that is backing up. Often a truck driver has no choice but to temporarily block a road to back into a loading area. Be patient!

It is far better to wait until the large vehicle has completed its backing maneuver than to try to pass. If you try to pass in this situation, it is likely that you will enter one of the vehicle's blind spots, thus making you invisible to the driver and increasing the chance of a traffic crash.

Approaching A Truck

Do not underestimate the size and speed of an approaching tractor-trailer or other large vehicle. Its larger size will often make it appear to be traveling at a slower speed than it really is. Also, from a distance it may not appear to be as large as it really is. Even so, the other vehicle will often reach you sooner than you expect! When driving on an undivided highway, it is often better to move as far to the right as possible, as soon as possible, to make sure your vehicle will not be sideswiped by an approaching tractor-trailer or other large vehicle.

Stopping Behind A Truck

Always leave space when you stop behind a truck or bus at a traffic light or stop sign, especially when facing uphill. The truck or bus could stall or roll backward slightly when starting. If you leave enough room between your vehicle and the vehicle ahead, you may be able to pull out from behind and go around it.

SLOW MOVING VEHICLES

The "slow moving vehicle" emblem, a fluorescent or reflective orange triangle, must be displayed on the rear of vehicles drawn by animals, and most farm vehicles and construction equipment. The United States Postal Service also requires these orange safety-triangles to be displayed on all rural mail delivery vehicles. Use caution when approaching a slow moving vehicle and be sure it is safe before you pass.

HORSEBACK RIDERS

Horseback riders are subject to, and protected by, the rules of the road. They also must ride single file near the right curb or road edge, or on a usable right shoulder, lane or path.

The law requires you to exercise due care when approaching a horse being ridden or led along a road. You must drive at a reasonable speed, and at a reasonable distance away from the horse. It is illegal to sound your horn when approaching or passing a horse.

QUESTIONS

Before going on to Chapter 12, make sure you can answer these questions:

- How do the blind spots surrounding a large commercial vehicle differ from the blind spots surrounding a car?
- How does the stopping distance of a large vehicle with air brakes compare with the stopping distance of a car?
- After passing a large vehicle, what should you be sure of before returning to the lane in which the large vehicle is traveling?
- What is the best strategy to follow when approaching a large vehicle that is backing up into a loading area?
- When children are nearby, what should you do before backing out of a driveway?
- How can you identify a blind pedestrian to whom you must yield the right-of-way?
- Where must a pedestrian walk when there are no sidewalks?
- How should you approach a bicyclist?
- Must a bicyclist obey traffic laws and signs?
- Where there is no bicycle lane, on what portion of the road must a bicyclist ride?
- What extra equipment must a bicycle have when used at night?
- May motorcyclists ride three abreast in a single lane?
- What does a slow moving vehicle emblem look like?

CHAPTER 12 If You Are in a Traffic Crash

There are more than 300,000 traffic crashes in New York State each year. If you obey the law and follow the advice in this manual, you have a good chance of avoiding crashes. Still, even the most careful drivers are involved in crashes caused by unexpected events or the mistakes of other drivers. If you are involved in a traffic crash, you must be ready to react responsibly at the scene and obey the law in reporting the incident.

You may choose to carry a basic emergency kit in your vehicle, containing flares and first aid supplies. Emergency road-kits often are available in automotive or department stores.

AT THE SCENE

If you are involved in a crash you must stop, regardless of the extent of damage. It is a traffic violation to leave the scene of an incident, such as a traffic crash involving property damage. It is a criminal violation to leave the scene of an incident involving a fatality or personal injury. Even if the crash involves only property damage, you must exchange information with other drivers involved. Give your name, address, the motorist identification (ID) number from your license, and vehicle registration and insurance information, including the insurance policy number and effective date, to the other drivers and police on the scene. If a parked vehicle or property other than a vehicle is damaged, or if a domestic animal is injured, you must try to locate the owner or notify the police.

If any person is injured or killed, the police must be notified, immediately, and you should make sure an ambulance or rescue squad has been called.

If possible, move your vehicle off the road. Protect the scene with reflectors or flares, but be alert for leaking fuel. Be sure to protect yourself and others from oncoming traffic.

EMERGENCY FIRST AID

Do not stop at a crash scene unless you are involved or emergency help has not yet arrived. Otherwise, keep your attention on driving and the directions given by traffic officers.

Follow these basic first-aid tips if help is not immediately available:

- Do not move an injured person unless it is absolutely necessary because of fire or another life threatening danger. If you must move an injured person, keep the back and neck as straight as possible by putting your arms under the back, and gently support the neck with your upper arms. Take hold of clothing with your hands, and pull the victim headfirst away from danger.
- If there are wires down, do not go near them. If wires are touching the vehicle or lying near it, warn occupants to stay inside until help arrives.
- Check to see if the injured person is breathing. If the person is not breathing and you are trained in cardiopulmonary resuscitation (CPR), begin administering CPR or mouth-to-mouth breathing as shown below.

CPR (Cardiopulmonary Resuscitation)

If necessary, carefully position the victim on his or her back, then open the airway as shown. Listen for breathing, look for the chest to rise and fall and feel for flow of air. If the victim is not breathing, begin rescue breathing.

To rescue-breath, seal your lips over the victim's mouth, pinch the nose closed and give two full breaths, watching for the chest to rise. Remove your mouth to allow air to escape. If the chest does not rise, carefully reposition the victim's head to open the airway. Check to see if the victim is breathing. If he or she is not breathing, give one breath every five seconds, pausing every few minutes to see if the victim is breathing without assistance. If the victim is breathing, stop rescue-breathing.

Illustrations courtesy of American Medical Association. Used by permission.

REPORTS TO DMV

If you are involved in a traffic crash involving a fatality or personal injury, you must report it to DMV. You must also report any traffic incident or crash involving $1000 or more in damage to any one person's property. The form Report of Motor Vehicle Accident (MV-104) is available at any motor vehicle office, from most insurance agents, by request from a DMV Call Center, and from the DMV Internet Office.

Reporting a crash or incident to your insurance company *does not* fulfill your legal obligation. You must file a report with DMV within 10 days of the event. Your license may be suspended if you don't.

If the driver is injured and unable to complete the report, a passenger or the vehicle owner may do so.